HARDPRESS.NET
HOME OF HARD-TO-FIND BOOKS

Barchester Towers
by Anthony Trollope

COLLECTION

OF

BRITISH AUTHORS.

VOL. CCCCXCI.

BARCHESTER TOWERS BY ANTHONY TROLLOPE.

IN TWO VOLUMES.

VOL. I.

TAUCHNITZ EDITION.

By the same Author,

BARCHESTER TOWERS.

BY

ANTHONY TROLLOPE,

AUTHOR OF "THE WARDEN," "THE BERTRAMS," ETC. ETC.

COPYRIGHT EDITION.

IN TWO VOLUMES.

VOL. I.

LEIPZIG

BERNHARD TAUCHNITZ

1859.

The Right of Translation is reserved.

CONTENTS

OF VOLUME I.

BARCHESTER TOWERS.

CHAPTER I.

WHO WILL BE THE NEW BISHOP?

In the latter days of July in the year 185—, a most important question was for ten days hourly asked in the cathedral city of Barchester, and answered every hour in various ways—Who was to be the new Bishop?

The death of old Dr. Grantly, who had for many years filled that chair with meek authority, took place exactly as the ministry of Lord—was going to give place to that of Lord—. The illness of the good old man was long and lingering, and it became at last a matter of intense interest to those concerned whether the new appointment should be made by a conservative or liberal government.

It was pretty well understood that the out-going premier had made his selection, and that if the question rested with him, the mitre would descend on the head of Archdeacon Grantly, the old bishop's son. The archdeacon had long managed the affairs of the diocese; and for some months previous to the demise of his father, rumour had confidently assigned to him the reversion of his father's honours.

Bishop Grantly died as he had lived, peaceably, slowly, without pain and without excitement. The breath ebbed from him almost imperceptibly, and for a month before his death, it was a question whether he were alive or dead.

A trying time was this for the archdeacon, for whom was designed the reversion of his father's see by those who then had the giving away of episcopal thrones. I would not be understood to say that the prime minister had in so many words promised the bishopric to Dr. Grantly. He was too discreet a man for that. There is a proverb with reference to the killing of cats, and those who know anything either of high or low government places, will be well aware that a promise may be made without positive words, and that an expectant may be put into the highest state of encouragement, though the great man on whose breath he hangs may have done no more than whisper that "Mr. So-and-so is certainly a rising man."

Such a whisper had been made, and was known by those who heard it to signify that the cures of the diocese of Barchester should not be taken out of the hands of the archdeacon. The then prime minister was all in all at Oxford, and had lately passed a night at the house of the master of Lazarus. Now the master of Lazarus—which is, by the bye, in many respects the most comfortable, as well as the richest college at Oxford,—was the archdeacon's most intimate friend and most trusted counsellor. On the occasion of the prime minister's visit, Dr. Grantly was of course present, and the meeting was very gracious. On the following morning Dr. Gwynne, the master, told the archdeacon that in his opinion the thing was settled.

At this time the bishop was quite on his last legs; but the ministry also were tottering. Dr. Grantly returned from Oxford happy and elated, to resume his place in the palace, and to continue to perform for the father the last duties of a son; which, to give him his due, he performed with more tender care than was to be expected from his usual somewhat worldly manners.

A month since the physicians had named four weeks as the outside period during which breath could be supported within the body of the dying man. At the end of the month the physicians wondered, and named another fortnight. The old man lived on wine alone, but at the end of the fortnight he still lived; and the tidings of the fall of the ministry became more frequent. Sir Lamda Mewnew and Sir Omicron Pie, the two great London doctors, now came down for the fifth time, and declared, shaking their learned heads, that another week of life was impossible; and as they sat down to lunch in the episcopal dining-room, whispered to the archdeacon their own private knowledge that the ministry must fall within five days. The son returned to his father's room, and after administering with his own hands the sustaining modicum of madeira, sat down by the bedside to calculate his chances.

The ministry were to be out within five days: his father was to be dead within—No, he rejected that view of the subject. The ministry were to be out, and the diocese might probably be vacant at the same period. There was much doubt as to the names of the men who were to succeed to power, and a week must elapse before a Cabinet was formed. Would not vacancies be filled by the out-going men during this week? Dr. Grantly had a kind of idea that such would be the case, but did not know; and then he wondered at his own ignorance on such a question.

He tried to keep his mind away from the subject, but he could not. The race was so very close, and the stakes were so very high. He then looked at the dying man's impassive, placid face. There was no sign there of death or disease; it was something thinner than of yore, somewhat grayer, and the deep lines of age more marked; but, as far as he could judge, life might yet hang there for weeks to come. Sir Lamda Mewnew and Sir Omicron Pie had thrice been wrong, and might yet be wrong thrice again. The old bishop slept during twenty of the twenty-four hours, but during the short periods of his waking moments, he knew both his son and his dear old friend, Mr. Harding, the archdeacon's father-in-law, and would thank them tenderly for their care and love. Now he lay sleeping like a baby, resting easily on his back, his mouth just open, and his few gray hairs straggling from beneath his cap; his breath was perfectly noiseless, and his thin, wan hand, which lay above the coverlid, never moved. Nothing could be easier than the old man's passage from this world to the next.

But by no means easy were the emotions of him who sat there watching. He knew it must be now or never. He was already over fifty, and there was little chance that his friends who were now leaving office would soon return to it. No probable British prime minister but he who was now in, he who was so soon to be out, would think of making a bishop of Dr. Grantly. Thus he thought long and sadly, in deep silence, and then gazed at that still living face, and then at last dared to ask himself whether he really longed for his father's death.

The effort was a salutary one, and the question was answered in a moment. The proud, wishful, worldly man, sank on his knees by the bedside, and taking the bishop's hand within his own, prayed eagerly that his sins might be forgiven him.

His face was still buried in the clothes when the door of the bed-room opened noiselessly, and Mr. Harding entered with a velvet step. Mr. Harding's attendance at that bedside had been nearly as constant as that of the archdeacon, and his ingress and egress was as much a matter of course as that of his son-in-law. He was standing close beside the archdeacon before he was perceived, and would also have knelt in prayer had he not feared that his doing so might have caused some sudden start, and have disturbed the dying man. Dr. Grantly, however, instantly perceived him, and rose from his knees. As he did so Mr. Harding took both his hands, and pressed them warmly. There was more fellowship between them at that moment than there had ever been before, and it so happened that after circumstances greatly preserved the feeling. As they stood there pressing each other's hands, the tears rolled freely down their cheeks.

"God bless you, my dears"—said the bishop with feeble voice as he woke—"God bless you—may God bless you both, my dear children:" and so he died.

There was no loud rattle in the throat, no dreadful

struggle, no palpable sign of death; but the lower jaw fell a little from its place, and the eyes, which had been so constantly closed in sleep, now remained fixed and open. Neither Mr. Harding nor Dr. Grantly knew that life was gone, though both suspected it.

"I believe it's all over," said Mr. Harding, still pressing the other's hands. "I think—nay, I hope it is."

"I will ring the bell," said the other, speaking all but in a whisper. "Mrs. Phillips should be here."

Mrs. Phillips, the nurse, was soon in the room, and immediately, with practised hand, closed those staring eyes.

"It's all over, Mrs. Phillips?" asked Mr. Harding.

"My lord's no more," said Mrs. Phillips, turning round and curtseying low with solemn face; "his lordship's gone more like a sleeping babby than any that I ever saw."

"It's a great relief, archdeacon," said Mr. Harding, "a great relief—dear, good, excellent old man. Oh that our last moments may be as innocent and as peaceful as his!"

"Surely," said Mrs. Phillips. "The Lord be praised for all his mercies; but, for a meek, mild, gentle-spoken Christian, his lordship was——" and Mrs. Phillips, with unaffected but easy grief, put up her white apron to her flowing eyes.

"You cannot but rejoice that it is over," said Mr. Harding, still consoling his friend. The archdeacon's mind, however, had already travelled from the death chamber to the closet of the prime minister. He had brought himself to pray for his father's life, but now that that life was done, minutes were too precious to be lost. It was now useless to dally with the fact of the bishop's death—useless to lose perhaps everything for the pretence of a foolish sentiment.

But how was he to act while his father-in-law stood there holding his hand? how, without appearing unfeeling, was he to forget his father in the bishop—to overlook what he had lost, and think only of what he might possibly gain?

"No; I suppose not," said he, at last, in answer to Mr. Harding. "We have all expected it so long."

Mr. Harding took him by the arm and led him from the room. "We will see him again to-morrow morning," said he; "we had better leave the room now to the women." And so they went down stairs.

It was already evening and nearly dark. It was most important that the prime minister should know that night that the diocese was vacant. Everything might depend on it; and so, in answer to Mr. Harding's further consolation, the archdeacon suggested that a telegraph message should be immediately sent off to London. Mr. Harding who had really been somewhat surprised to find Dr. Grantly, as he thought so much affected, was rather taken aback; but he made no objection. He knew that the archdeacon had some hope of succeeding to his father's place, though he by no means knew how highly raised that hope had been.

"Yes," said Dr. Grantly, collecting himself and shaking off his weakness, "we must send a message at once; we don't know what might be the consequence of delay. Will you do it?"

"I! oh yes; certainly: I'll do anything, only I don't know exactly what it is you want."

Dr. Grantly sat down before a writing table, and taking pen and ink, wrote on a slip of paper as follows:—

"By Electric Telegraph.
"For the Earl of——, Downing Street, or elsewhere.
" 'The Bishop of Barchester is dead.'
"Message sent by the Rev. Septimus Harding."

"There," said he, "just take that to the telegraph office at the railway station, and give it in as it is; they'll probably make you copy it on to one of their own slips; that's all you'll have to do: then you'll have to pay them half-a-crown;" and the archdeacon put his hand in his pocket and pulled out the necessary sum.

Mr. Harding felt very much like an errand-boy, and also felt that he was called on to perform his duties as such at rather an unseemly time; but he said nothing, and took the slip of paper and the proffered coin.

"But you've put my name into it, archdeacon."

"Yes," said the other, "there should be the name of some clergyman you know, and what name so proper as that of so old a friend as yourself? The Earl won't look at the name, you may be sure of that; but my dear Mr. Harding, pray don't lose any time."

Mr. Harding got as far as the library door on his way to the station, when he suddenly remembered the news with which he was fraught when he entered the poor bishop's bed-room. He had found the moment so inopportune for any mundane tidings, that he had repressed the words which were on his tongue, and immediately afterwards all recollection of the circumstance was for the time banished by the scene which had occurred.

"But, archdeacon," said he, turning back, "I forgot to tell you—The ministry are out."

"Out!" ejaculated the archdeacon, in a tone which too plainly showed his anxiety and dismay, although under the circumstances of the moment he endeavoured to control himself: "Out! who told you so?"

Mr. Harding explained that news to this effect had come down by electric telegraph, and that the tidings had been left at the palace door by Mr. Chadwick.

The archdeacon sat silent for awhile meditating, and Mr. Harding stood looking at him. "Never mind," said the archdeacon at last; "send the message all the same. The news must be sent to some one, and there is at present no one else in a position to receive it. Do it at once, my dear friend; you know I would not trouble you, were I in a state to do it myself. A few minutes' time is of the greatest importance."

Mr. Harding went out and sent the message, and it may be as well that we should follow it to its destination. Within thirty minutes of its leaving Barchester it reached the Earl of——in his inner library. What elaborate letters, what eloquent appeals, what indignant remonstrances, he might there have to frame, at such a moment, may be conceived, but not described! How he was preparing his thunder for successful rivals, standing like a British peer with his back to the sea-coal fire, and his hands in his breeches pockets,—how his fine eye was lit up with anger, and his forehead gleamed with patriotism,—how he stamped his foot as he thought of his heavy associates,—how he all but swore as he remembered how much too clever one of them had been,—my creative readers may

imagine. But was he so engaged? No: history and
truth compel me to deny it. He was sitting easily in
a lounging chair, conning over a Newmarket list, and
by his elbow on the table was lying open an uncut
French novel on which he was engaged.

He opened the cover in which the message was
enclosed, and having read it, he took his pen and
wrote on the back of it—

> "For the Earl of——,
> "With the Earl of——'s compliments,"

and sent it off again on its journey.

Thus terminated our unfortunate friend's chance of
possessing the glories of a bishopric.

The names of many divines were given in the
papers as that of the bishop elect. "The British Grandmother" declared that Dr. Gwynne was to be the man,
in compliment to the late ministry. This was a heavy
blow to Dr. Grantly, but he was not doomed to see
himself superseded by his friend. "The Anglican
Devotee" put forward confidently the claims of a
great London preacher of austere doctrines; and "The
Eastern Hemisphere," an evening paper supposed to
possess much official knowledge, declared in favour of
an eminent naturalist, a gentleman most completely
versed in the knowledge of rocks and minerals, but
supposed by many to hold on religious subjects no
special doctrines whatever. "The Jupiter," that daily
paper, which, as we all know, is the only true source
of infallibly correct information on all subjects, for a
while was silent, but at last spoke out. The merits of
all these candidates were discussed and somewhat
irreverently disposed of, and then "The Jupiter" declared that Dr. Proudie was to be the man.

Dr. Proudie was the man. Just a month after the demise of the late bishop, Dr. Proudie kissed the Queen's hand as his successor elect.

We must beg to be allowed to draw a curtain over the sorrows of the archdeacon as he sat, sombre and sad at heart, in the study of his parsonage at Plumstead Episcopi. On the day subsequent to the despatch of the message he heard that the Earl of——had consented to undertake the formation of a ministry, and from that moment he knew that his chance was over. Many will think that he was wicked to grieve for the loss of episcopal power, wicked to have coveted it, nay, wicked even to have thought about it, in the way and at the moments he had done so.

With such censures I cannot profess that I completely agree. The *nolo episcopari*, though still in use, is so directly at variance with the tendency of all human wishes, that it cannot be thought to express the true aspirations of rising priests in the Church of England. A lawyer does not sin in seeking to be a judge, or in compassing his wishes by all honest means. A young diplomate entertains a fair ambition when he looks forward to be the lord of a first-rate embassy; and a poor novelist when he attempts to rival Dickens or rise above Fitzjeames, commits no fault, though he may be foolish. Sydney Smith truly said that in these recreant days we cannot expect to find the majesty of St. Paul beneath the cassock of a curate. If we look to our clergymen to be more than men, we shall probably teach ourselves to think that they are less, and can hardly hope to raise the character of the pastor by denying to him the right to entertain the aspirations of a man.

Our archdeacon was worldly—who among us is not so? He was ambitious—who among us is ashamed to own that "last infirmity of noble minds!" He was avaricious, my readers will say. No—it was for no love of lucre that he wished to be bishop of Barchester. He was his father's only child, and his father had left him great wealth. His preferment brought him in nearly three thousand a year. The bishopric, as cut down by the Ecclesiastical Commission was only five. He would be a richer man as archdeacon than he could be as bishop. But he certainly did desire to play first fiddle; he did desire to sit in full lawn sleeves among the peers of the realm; and he did desire, if the truth must out, to be called "My Lord" by his reverend brethren.

His hopes, however, were they innocent or sinful, were not fated to be realised; and Dr. Proudie was consecrated Bishop of Barchester.

CHAPTER II.

HIRAM'S HOSPITAL ACCORDING TO ACT OF PARLIAMENT.

IT is hardly necessary that I should here give to the public any lengthened biography of Mr. Harding, up to the period of the commencement of this tale. The public cannot have forgotten how ill that sensitive gentleman bore the attack that was made on him in the columns of the Jupiter, with reference to the income which he received as warden of Hiram's Hospital, in the city of Barchester. Nor can it yet be forgotten that a law-suit was instituted against him on the matter of that charity by Mr. John Bold, who afterwards married his, Mr. Harding's, younger and then only unmarried daughter.   Under pressure of these attacks, Mr. Harding had resigned his wardenship, though strongly recommended to abstain from doing so, both by his friends and by his lawyers.   He did, however, resign it, and betook himself manfully to the duties of the small parish of St. Cuthbert's, in the city, of which he was vicar, continuing also to perform those of precentor of the cathedral, a situation of small emolument which had hitherto been supposed to be joined, as a matter of course, to the wardenship of the Hospital above spoken of.

When he left the hospital from which he had been so ruthlessly driven, and settled himself down in his own modest manner in the High Street of Barchester, he had not expected that others would make more fuss about it than he was inclined to do himself; and the extent of his hope was, that the movement might have been made in time to prevent any further paragraphs in the Jupiter.   His affairs, however, were not allowed to subside thus quietly, and people were quite as much inclined to talk about the disinterested sacrifice he had made, as they had before been to upbraid him for his cupidity.

The most remarkable thing that occurred, was the receipt of an autograph letter from the Archbishop of Canterbury, in which the primate very warmly praised his conduct, and begged to know what his intentions were for the future.   Mr. Harding replied that he intended to be rector of St. Cuthbert's, in Barchester: and so that matter dropped.   Then the newspapers took up his case, the Jupiter among the rest, and wafted his name in eulogistic strains through every reading-room in the nation.   It was discovered also,

that he was the author of that great musical work,
Harding's Church music,—and a new edition was
spoken of, though, I believe, never printed.   It is,
however, certain that the work was introduced into
the Royal Chapel at St. James's, and that a long
criticism appeared in the Musical Scrutator, declaring
that in no previous work of the kind had so much
research been joined with such exalted musical ability,
and asserting that the name of Harding would henceforward be known wherever the Arts were cultivated,
or Religion valued.

This was high praise, and I will not deny that
Mr. Harding was gratified by such flattery; for if Mr.
Harding was vain on any subject, it was on that of
music.   But here the matter rested.   The second edition, if printed, was never purchased; the copies which
had been introduced into the Royal Chapel disappeared
again, and were laid by in peace, with a load of
similar literature.   Mr. Towers, of the Jupiter, and his
brethren, occupied themselves with other names, and
the undying fame promised to our friend was clearly
intended to be posthumous.

Mr. Harding had spent much of his time with his
friend the bishop, much with his daughter Mrs. Bold,
now, alas, a widow; and had almost daily visited the
wretched remnant of his former subjects, the few surviving bedesmen now left at Hiram's Hospital.   Six of
them were still living.   The number, according to old
Hiram's will, should always have been twelve.   But
after the abdication of their warden, the bishop had
appointed no successor to him, no new occupants of the
charity had been nominated, and it appeared as though
the hospital at Barchester would fall into abeyance,

unless the powers that be should take some steps to-wards putting it once more into working order.

During the past five years, the powers that be had not overlooked Barchester Hospital, and sundry political doctors had taken the matter in hand. Shortly after Mr. Harding's resignation, the Jupiter had very clearly shown what ought to be done. In about half a column it had distributed the income, rebuilt the building, put an end to all bickerings, regenerated kindly feeling, provided for Mr. Harding, and placed the whole thing on a footing which could not but be satisfactory to the city and Bishop of Barchester, and to the nation at large. The wisdom of this scheme was testified by the number of letters which "Common Sense," "Veritas," and "One that loves fair play" sent to the Jupiter, all expressing admiration, and amplifying on the details given. It is singular enough that no adverse letter appeared at all, and, therefore, none of course was written.

But Cassandra was not believed, and even the wisdom of the Jupiter sometimes falls on deaf ears. Though other plans did not put themselves forward in the columns of the Jupiter, reformers of church charities were not slack to make known in various places their different nostrums for setting Hiram's Hospital on its feet again. A learned bishop took occasion, in the Upper House, to allude to the matter, intimating that he had communicated on the subject with his right reverend brother of Barchester. The radical member for Staleybridge had suggested that the funds should be alienated for the education of the agricultural poor of the country, and he amused the house by some anec-dotes touching the superstition and habits of the agri-

culturists in question. A political pamphleteer had
produced a few dozen pages, which he called "Who
are John Hiram's heirs?" intending to give an infallible rule for the governance of all such establishments; and, at last, a member of the government promised that in the next session a short bill should be
introduced for regulating the affairs of Barchester, and
other kindred concerns.

The next session came, and, contrary to custom,
the bill came also. Men's minds were then intent on
other things. The first threatenings of a huge war
hung heavily over the nation, and the question as to
Hiram's heirs did not appear to interest very many
people either in or out of the house. The bill, however, was read and re-read, and in some undistinguished
manner passed through its eleven stages without appeal
or dissent. What would John Hiram have said in the
matter, could he have predicted that some forty-five
gentlemen would take on themselves to make a law
altering the whole purport of his will, without in the
least knowing at the moment of their making it, what
it was that they were doing? It is however to be hoped
that the under-secretary for the Home Office knew,
for to him had the matter been confided.

The bill, however, did pass, and at the time at
which this history is supposed to commence, it had
been ordained that there should be, as heretofore,
twelve old men in Barchester Hospital, each with 1 s.
4 d. a day; that there should also be twelve old women
to be located in a house to be built, each with 1 s. 2 d.
a day; that there should be a matron, with a house
and 70 l. a year; a steward with 150 l. a year; and
latterly, a warden with 450 l. a year, who should have

the spiritual guidance of both establishments, and the temporal guidance of that appertaining to the male sex. The bishop, dean, and warden were, as formerly, to appoint in turn the recipients of the charity, and the bishop was to appoint the officers. There was nothing said as to the wardenship being held by the precentor of the cathedral, nor a word as to Mr. Harding's right to the situation.

It was not, however, till some months after the death of the old bishop, and almost immediately consequent on the installation of his successor, that notice was given that the reform was about to be carried out. The new law and the new bishop were among the earliest works of a new ministry, or rather of a ministry who, having for a while given place to their opponents, had then returned to power; and the death of Dr. Grantly occurred, as we have seen, exactly at the period of the change.

Poor Eleanor Bold! How well does that widow's cap become her, and the solemn gravity with which she devotes herself to her new duties. Poor Eleanor!

Poor Eleanor! I cannot say that with me John Bold was ever a favourite. I never thought him worthy of the wife he had won. But in her estimation he was most worthy. Hers was one of those feminine hearts which cling to a husband, not with idolatry, for worship can admit of no defect in its idol, but with the perfect tenacity of ivy. As the parasite plant will follow even the defects of the trunk which it embraces, so did Eleanor cling to and love the very faults of her husband. She had once declared that whatever her father did should in her eyes be right. She then transferred her allegiance, and became ever ready to defend the worst failings of her lord and master.

And John Bold was a man to be loved by a woman; he was himself affectionate, he was confiding and manly; and that arrogance of thought, unsustained by first-rate abilities, that attempt at being better than his neighbours which jarred so painfully on the feelings of his acquaintance, did not injure him in the estimation of his wife.

Could she even have admitted that he had a fault, his early death would have blotted out the memory of it. She wept as for the loss of the most perfect treasure with which mortal woman had ever been endowed; for weeks after he was gone the idea of future happiness in this world was hateful to her; consolation, as it is called, was insupportable, and tears and sleep were her only relief.

But God tempers the wind to the shorn lamb. She knew that she had within her the living source of other cares. She knew that there was to be created for her another subject of weal or woe, of unutterable joy or despairing sorrow, as God, in his mercy might vouchsafe to her. At first this did but augment her grief! To be the mother of a poor infant, orphaned before it was born, brought forth to the sorrows of an ever desolate hearth, nurtured amidst tears and wailing, and then turned adrift into the world without the aid of a father's care! There was at first no joy in this.

By degrees, however, her heart became anxious for another object, and, before its birth, the stranger was expected with all the eagerness of a longing mother. Just eight months after the father's death a second John Bold was born, and if the worship of one creature can be innocent in another, let us hope that the adoration offered over the cradle of the fatherless infant may not be imputed as a sin.

It will not be worth our while to define the character of the child, or to point out in how far the faults of the father were redeemed within that little breast by the virtues of the mother. The baby, as a baby, was all that was delightful, and I cannot foresee that it will be necessary for us to inquire into the facts of his after life. Our present business at Barchester will not occupy us above a year or two at the furthest, and I will leave it to some other pen to produce, if necessary, the biography of John Bold the Younger.

But, as a baby, this baby was all that could be desired. This fact no one attempted to deny. "Is he not delightful?" she would say to her father, looking up into his face from her knees, her lustrous eyes overflowing with soft tears, her young face encircled by her close widow's cap and her hands on each side of the cradle in which her treasure was sleeping. The grandfather would gladly admit that the treasure was delightful, and the uncle archdeacon himself would agree, and Mrs. Grantly, Eleanor's sister, would re-echo the word with true sisterly energy; and Mary Bold—— but Mary Bold was a second worshipper at the same shrine.

The baby was really delightful; he took his food with a will, struck out his toes merrily whenever his legs were uncovered, and did not have fits. These are supposed to be the strongest points of baby perfection, and in all these our baby excelled.

And thus the widow's deep grief was softened, and a sweet balm was poured into the wound which she had thought nothing but death could heal. How much kinder is God to us than we are willing to be to ourselves! At the loss of every dear face, at the last going of every well beloved one, we all doom ourselves to an eternity of sorrow, and look to waste ourselves away in an ever-running fountain of tears. How seldom does such grief endure! how blessed is the goodness which forbids it to do so! "Let me ever remember my living friends, but forget them as soon as dead," was the prayer of a wise man who understood the mercy of God. Few perhaps would have the courage to express such a wish, and yet to do so would only be to ask for that release from sorrow, which a kind Creator almost always extends to us.

I would not, however, have it imagined that Mrs. Bold forgot her husband. She daily thought of him with all conjugal love, and enshrined his memory in the innermost centre of her heart. But yet she was happy in her baby. It was so sweet to press the living toy to her breast, and feel that a human being existed who did owe, and was to owe everything to her; whose daily food was drawn from herself; whose little wants could all be satisfied by her; whose little heart would first love her and her only; whose infant tongue would make its first effort in calling her by the sweetest name a woman can hear. And so Eleanor's bosom became tranquil, and she set about her new duties eagerly and gratefully.

As regards the concerns of the world, John Bold had left his widow in prosperous circumstances. He had bequeathed to her all that he possessed, and that comprised an income much exceeding what she or her friends thought necessary for her. It amounted to nearly a thousand a year; and when she reflected on its extent, her dearest hope was to hand it over, not only unimpaired but increased, to her husband's son, to her own darling, to the little man who now lay sleeping on her knee, happily ignorant of the cares which were to be accumulated in his behalf.

When John Bold died she earnestly implored her father to come and live with her, but this Mr. Harding declined, though for some weeks he remained with her as a visitor. He could not be prevailed upon to forego the possession of some small home of his own, and so remained in the lodgings he had first selected over a chemist's shop in the High Street of Barchester.

CHAPTER III.

DR. AND MRS. PROUDIE.

THIS narrative is supposed to commence immediately after the installation of Dr. Proudie. I will not describe the ceremony, as I do not precisely understand its nature. I am ignorant whether a bishop be chaired like a member of parliament, or carried in a gilt coach like a lord mayor, or sworn in like a justice of peace, or introduced like a peer to the upper house, or led between two brethren like a knight of the garter; but I do know that every thing was properly done, and that nothing fit or becoming to a young bishop was omitted on the occasion.

Dr. Proudie was not the man to allow anything to be omitted that might be becoming to his new dignity. He understood well the value of forms, and knew that the due observance of rank could not be maintained unless the exterior trappings belonging to it were held

in proper esteem. He was a man born to move in
high circles; at least so he thought himself, and circumstances had certainly sustained him in this view.
He was the nephew of an Irish baron by his mother's
side, and his wife was the niece of a Scotch earl. He
had for years held some clerical office appertaining to
courtly matters, which had enabled him to live in
London, and to entrust his parish to his curate. He
had been preacher to the royal beefeaters, curator of
theological manuscripts in the Ecclesiastical Courts,
chaplain to the Queen's yeomanry guard, and almoner
to his Royal Highness the Prince of Rappe-Blanken-
berg.

His residence in the metropolis, rendered necessary
by the duties thus entrusted to him, his high connec-
tions, and the peculiar talents and nature of the man,
recommended him to persons in power; and Dr. Proudie
became known as a useful and rising clergyman.

Some few years since, even within the memory of
many who are not yet willing to call themselves old,
a liberal clergyman was a person not frequently to be
met. Sydney Smith was such, and was looked on as
little better than an infidel; a few others also might be
named, but they were "raræ aves," and were regarded
with doubt and distrust by their brethren. No man
was so surely a tory as a country rector—nowhere
were the powers that be so cherished as at Oxford.

When, however, Dr. Whately was made an archbishop, and Dr. Hampden some years afterwards regius
professor, many wise divines saw that a change was
taking place in men's minds, and that more liberal
ideas would henceforward be suitable to the priests as
well as to the laity. Clergymen began to be heard of

who had ceased to anathematise papists on the one
hand, or vilify dissenters on the other. It appeared
clear that high church principles, as they are called,
were no longer to be surest claims to promotion with
at any rate one section of statesmen, and Dr. Proudie
was one among those who early in life adapted himself to the views held by the whigs on most theological
and religious subjects. He bore with the idolatry of
Rome, tolerated even the infidelity of Socinianism, and
was hand and glove with the Presbyterian Synods of
Scotland and Ulster.

Such a man at such a time was found to be useful,
and Dr. Proudie's name began to appear in the newspapers. He was made one of a commission who went
over to Ireland to arrange matters preparative to the
working of the national board; he became honorary
secretary to another commission nominated to inquire
into the revenues of cathedral chapters; and had had
something to do with both the regium donum and the
Maynooth grant.

It must not on this account be taken as proved
that Dr. Proudie was a man of great mental powers,
or even of much capacity for business, for such qualities
had not been required in him. In the arrangement
of those church reforms with which he was connected,
the ideas and original conception of the work to be
done were generally furnished by the liberal statesmen
of the day, and the labour of the details was borne by
officials of a lower rank. It was, however, thought expedient that the name of some clergyman should appear in such matters, and as Dr. Proudie had become
known as a tolerating divine, great use of this sort
was made of his name. If he did not do much active

good, he never did any harm; he was amenable to
those who were really in authority, and at the sittings
of the various boards to which he belonged maintained
a kind of dignity which had its value.

He was certainly possessed of sufficient tact to
answer the purpose for which he was required without
making himself troublesome; but it must not therefore
be surmised that he doubted his own power, or failed
to believe that he could himself take a high part in
high affairs when his own turn came. He was biding
his time, and patiently looking forward to the days
when he himself would sit authoritative at some board,
and talk and direct, and rule the roast, while lesser
stars sat round and obeyed, as he had so well accustomed himself to do.

His reward and his time had now come. He was
selected for the vacant bishopric, and on the next
vacancy which might occur in any diocese would take
his place in the House of Lords, prepared to give not
a silent vote in all matters concerning the weal of the
church establishment. Toleration was to be the basis
on which he was to fight his battles, and in the honest
courage of his heart he thought no evil would come
to him in encountering even such foes as his brethren
of Exeter and Oxford.

Dr. Proudie was an ambitious man, and before he
was well consecrated Bishop of Barchester, he had begun to look up to archiepiscopal splendour, and the
glories of Lambeth, or at any rate of Bishopsthorpe.
He was comparatively young, and had, as he fondly
flattered himself, been selected as possessing such gifts,
natural and acquired, as must be sure to recommend
him to a yet higher notice, now that a higher sphere

was opened to him. Dr. Proudie was, therefore, quite prepared to take a conspicuous part in all theological affairs appertaining to these realms; and having such views, by no means intended to bury himself at Barchester as his predecessor had done. No: London should still be his ground: a comfortable mansion in a provincial city might be well enough for the dead months of the year. Indeed Dr. Proudie had always felt it necessary to his position to retire from London when other great and fashionable people did so; but London should still be his fixed residence, and it was in London that he resolved to exercise that hospitality so peculiarly recommended to all bishops by St. Paul. How otherwise could he keep himself before the world? how else give to the government, in matters theological, the full benefit of his weight and talents?

This resolution was no doubt a salutary one as regarded the world at large, but was not likely to make him popular either with the clergy or people of Barchester. Dr. Grantly had always lived there; and in truth it was hard for a bishop to be popular after Dr. Grantly. His income had averaged 9000*l.* a year; his successor was to be rigidly limited to 5000*l.* He had but one child on whom to spend his money; Dr. Proudie had seven or eight. He had been a man of few personal expenses, and they had been confined to the tastes of a moderate gentleman; but Dr. Proudie had to maintain a position in fashionable society, and had that to do with comparatively small means. Dr. Grantly had certainly kept his carriage, as became a bishop; but his carriage, horses, and coachman, though they did very well for Barchester, would have been almost ridiculous at Westminster. Mrs. Proudie determined that her husband's equipage should not shame her, and things on which Mrs. Proudie resolved, were generally accomplished.

From all this it was likely to result that Dr. Proudie would not spend much money at Barchester; whereas his predecessor had dealt with the tradesmen of the city in a manner very much to their satisfaction. The Grantlys, father and son, had spent their money like gentlemen; but it soon became whispered in Barchester that Dr. Proudie was not unacquainted with those prudent devices by which the utmost show of wealth is produced from limited means.

In person Dr. Proudie is a good looking man; spruce and dapper, and very tidy. He is somewhat below middle height, being about five feet four; but he makes up for the inches which he wants by the dignity with which he carries those which he has. It is no fault of his own if he has not a commanding eye, for he studies hard to assume it. His features are well formed, though perhaps the sharpness of his nose may give to his face in the eyes of some people an air of insignificance. If so, it is greatly redeemed by his mouth and chin, of which he is justly proud.

Dr. Proudie may well be said to have been a fortunate man, for he was not born to wealth, and he is now bishop of Barchester; but nevertheless he has his cares. He has a large family, of whom the three eldest are daughters, now all grown up and fit for fashionable life; and he has a wife. It is not my intention to breathe a word against the character of Mrs. Proudie, but still I cannot think that with all her virtues she adds much to her husband's happiness. The truth is that in matters domestic she rules supreme

over her titular lord, and rules with a rod of iron.
Nor is this all. Things domestic Dr. Proudie might
have abandoned to her, if not voluntarily, yet willingly.
But Mrs. Proudie is not satisfied with such home dominion, and stretches her power over all his movements,
and will not even abstain from things spiritual. In
fact, the bishop is henpecked.

The archdeacon's wife, in her happy home at Plumstead, knows how to assume the full privileges of her
rank, and express her own mind in becoming tone and
place. But Mrs. Grantly's sway, if sway she has, is easy
and beneficent. She never shames her husband; before
the world she is a pattern of obedience; her voice is
never loud, nor her looks sharp: doubtless she values
power, and has not unsuccessfully striven to acquire it;
but she knows what should be the limits of a woman's
rule.

Not so Mrs. Proudie. This lady is habitually
authoritative to all, but to her poor husband she is
despotic. Successful as has been his career in the eyes
of the world, it would seem that in the eyes of his
wife he is never right. All hope of defending himself
has long passed from him; indeed he rarely even attempts self-justification; and is aware that submission
produces the nearest approach to peace which his own
house can ever attain.

Mrs. Proudie has not been able to sit at the boards
and committees to which her husband has been called
by the state; nor, as he often reflects, can she make
her voice heard in the House of Lords. It may be
that she will refuse to him permission to attend to this
branch of a bishop's duties; it may be that she will
insist on his close attendance to his own closet. He

has never whispered a word on the subject to living
ears, but he has already made his fixed resolve. Should
such an attempt be made he will rebel. Dogs have
turned against their masters, and even Neapolitans
against their rulers, when oppression has been too
severe. And Dr. Proudie feels within himself that if
the cord be drawn too tight, he also can muster courage
and resist.

The state of vassalage in which our bishop has
been kept by his wife has not tended to exalt his character in the eyes of his daughters, who assume in ad-
dressing their father too much of that authority which
is not properly belonging, at any rate, to them. They
are, on the whole, fine engaging young ladies. They
are tall and robust like their mother, whose high
cheek-bones, and——, we may say auburn hair, they
all inherit. They think somewhat too much of their
grand uncles, who have not hitherto returned the compliment by thinking much of them. But now that their
father is a bishop, it is probable that family ties will
be drawn closer. Considering their connection with the
church, they entertain but few prejudices against the
pleasures of the world; and have certainly not dis-
tressed their parents, as too many English girls have
lately done, by any enthusiastic wish to devote themselves to the seclusion of a protestant nunnery. Dr.
Proudie's sons are still at school.

One other marked peculiarity in the character of
the bishop's wife must be mentioned. Though not
averse to the society and manners of the world, she
is in her own way a religious woman; and the form
in which this tendency shows itself in her is by a
strict observance of Sabbatarian rule. Dissipation and

low dresses during the week are, under her control, atoned for by three services, an evening sermon read by herself, and a perfect abstinence from any cheering employment on the Sunday. Unfortunately for those under her roof to whom the dissipation and low dresses are not extended, her servants namely and her husband, the compensating strictness of the Sabbath includes all. Woe betide the recreant housemaid who is found to have been listening to the honey of a sweetheart in the Regent's park, instead of the soul-stirring evening discourse of Mr. Slope. Not only is she sent adrift, but she is so sent with a character which leaves her little hope of a decent place. Woe betide the sixfoot hero who escorts Mrs. Proudie to her pew in red plush breeches, if he slips away to the neighbouring beer-shop, instead of falling into the back seat appropriated to his use. Mrs. Proudie has the eyes of Argus for such offenders. Occasional drunkenness in the week may be overlooked, for six feet on low wages are hardly to be procured if the morals are always kept at a high pitch; but not even for grandeur or economy will Mrs. Proudie forgive a desecration of the Sabbath.

In such matters Mrs. Proudie allows herself to be often guided by that eloquent preacher, the Rev. Mr. Slope, and as Dr. Proudie is guided by his wife, it necessarily follows that the eminent man we have named has obtained a good deal of control over Dr. Proudie in matters concerning religion. Mr. Slope's only preferment has hitherto been that of reader and preacher in a London district church: and on the consecration of his friend the new bishop, he readily gave this up to undertake the onerous but congenial duties of domestic chaplain to his lordship.

3*

Mr. Slope, however, on his first introduction must not be brought before the public at the tail of a chapter.

CHAPTER IV.

THE BISHOP'S CHAPLAIN.

Of the Rev. Mr. Slope's parentage I am not able to say much. I have heard it asserted that he is lineally descended from that eminent physician who assisted at the birth of Mr. T. Shandy, and that in early years he added an "e" to his name, for the sake of euphony, as other great men have done before him. If this be so, I presume he was christened Obadiah, for that is his name, in commemoration of the conflict in which his ancestor so distinguished himself. All my researches on the subject have, however, failed in enabling me to fix the date on which the family changed its religion.

He had been a sizar at Cambridge, and had there conducted himself at any rate successfully, for in due process of time he was an M.A., having university pupils under his care. From thence he was transferred to London, and became preacher at a new district church built on the confines of Baker Street. He was in this position when congenial ideas on religious subjects recommended him to Mrs. Proudie, and the intercourse had become close and confidential.

Having been thus familiarly thrown among the Misses Proudie, it was no more than natural that some softer feeling than friendship should be engendered. There have been some passages of love between him and the eldest hope, Olivia; but they have hitherto resulted in no favourable arrangement. In truth, Mr. Slope having made a declaration of affection, afterwards withdrew it on finding that the doctor had no immediate worldly funds with which to endow his child; and it may easily be conceived that Miss Proudie, after such an announcement on his part, was not readily disposed to receive any further show of affection. On the appointment of Dr. Proudie to the bishopric of Barchester, Mr. Slope's views were in truth somewhat altered. Bishops, even though they be poor, can provide for clerical children, and Mr. Slope began to regret that he had not been more disinterested. He no sooner heard the tidings of the doctor's elevation, than he recommenced his siege, not violently, indeed, but respectfully, and at a distance. Olivia Proudie, however, was a girl of spirit: she had the blood of two peers in her veins, and, better still, she had another lover on her books; so Mr. Slope sighed in vain; and the pair soon found it convenient to establish a mutual bond of inveterate hatred.

It may be thought singular that Mrs. Proudie's friendship for the young clergyman should remain firm after such an affair; but, to tell the truth, she had known nothing of it. Though very fond of Mr. Slope herself, she had never conceived the idea that either of her daughters would become so, and remembering their high birth and social advantages, expected for them matches of a different sort. Neither the gentleman nor the lady found it necessary to enlighten her. Olivia's two sisters had each known of the affair, so had all the servants, so had all the people living in the adjoining houses on either side; but Mrs. Proudie had been kept in the dark,

Mr. Slope soon comforted himself with the reflection, that as he had been selected as chaplain to the bishop, it would probably be in his power to get the good things in the bishop's gift, without troubling himself with the bishop's daughter; and he found himself able to endure the pangs of rejected love. As he sat himself down in the railway carriage, confronting the bishop and Mrs. Proudie, as they started on their first journey to Barchester, he began to form in his own mind a plan of his future life. He knew well his patron's strong points, but he knew the weak ones as well. He understood correctly enough to what attempts the new bishop's high spirit would soar, and he rightly guessed that public life would better suit the great man's taste, than the small details of diocesan duty.

He, therefore, he, Mr. Slope, would in effect be bishop of Barchester. Such was his resolve; and to give Mr. Slope his due, he had both courage and spirit to bear him out in his resolution. He knew that he should have a hard battle to fight, for the power and patronage of the see would be equally coveted by another great mind—Mrs. Proudie would also choose to be bishop of Barchester. Mr. Slope, however, flattered himself that he could out-manœuvre the lady. She must live much in London, while he would always be on the spot. She would necessarily remain ignorant of much, while he would know everything belonging to the diocese. At first, doubtless, he must flatter and cajole, perhaps yield, in some things; but he did not doubt of ultimate triumph. If all other means failed, he could join the bishop against his wife, inspire courage into the unhappy man, lay an axe to the root of the woman's power, and emancipate the husband.

Such were his thoughts as he sat looking at the sleeping pair in the railway carriage, and Mr. Slope is not the man to trouble himself with such thoughts for nothing. He is possessed of more than average abilities, and is of good courage. Though he can stoop to fawn, and stoop low indeed, if need be, he has still within him the power to assume the tyrant; and with the power he has certainly the wish. His acquirements are not of the highest order, but such as they are they are completely under control, and he knows the use of them. He is gifted with a certain kind of pulpit eloquence, not likely indeed to be persuasive with men, but powerful with the softer sex. In his sermons he deals greatly in denunciations, excites the minds of his weaker hearers with a not unpleasant terror, and leaves an impression on their minds that all mankind are in a perilous state, and all womankind too, except those who attend regularly to the evening lectures in Baker Street. His looks and tones are extremely severe, so much so that one cannot but fancy that he regards the greater part of the world as being infinitely too bad for his care. As he walks through the streets, his very face denotes his horror of the world's wickedness; and there is always an anathema lurking in the corner of his eye.

In doctrine, he, like his patron, is tolerant of dissent, if so strict a mind can be called tolerant of anything. With Wesleyan-Methodists he has something in common, but his soul trembles in agony at the iniquities of the Puseyites. His aversion is carried to things outward as well as inward. His gall rises at a new church with a high pitched roof; a full-breasted black silk waistcoat is with him a symbol of Satan; and a profane jest-book would not, in his view, more

foully desecrate the church seat of a Christian, than a
book of prayer printed with red letters, and ornamented
with a cross on the back. Most active clergymen have
their hobby, and Sunday observances are his. Sunday,
however, is a word which never pollutes his mouth—
it is always "the Sabbath." The "desecration of the
Sabbath," as he delights to call it, is to him meat and
drink:—he thrives upon that as policemen do on the
general evil habits of the community. It is the loved
subject of all his evening discourses, the source of all
his eloquence, the secret of all his power over the
female heart. To him the revelation of God appears
only in that one law given for Jewish observance. To
him the mercies of our Saviour speak in vain, to him
in vain has been preached that sermon which fell from
divine lips on the mountain—"Blessed are the meek,
for they shall inherit the earth"—"Blessed are the
merciful, for they shall obtain mercy." To him the
New Testament is comparatively of little moment, for
from it can be drawn no fresh authority for that
dominion which he loves to exercise over at least a
seventh part of man's allotted time here below.

Mr. Slope is tall, and not ill made. His feet and
hands are large, as has ever been the case with all his
family, but he has a broad chest and wide shoulders to
carry off these excrescences, and on the whole his figure
is good. His countenance, however, is not specially
prepossessing. His hair is lank, and of a dull pale
reddish hue. It is always formed into three straight
lumpy masses, each brushed with admirable precision,
and cemented with much grease; two of them adhere
closely to the sides of his face, and the other lies at
right angles above them. He wears no whiskers, and

is always punctiliously shaven. His face is nearly of the same colour as his hair, though perhaps a little redder: it is not unlike beef,—beef, however, one would say, of a bad quality. His forehead is capacious and high, but square and heavy, and unpleasantly shining. His mouth is large, though his lips are thin and bloodless; and his big, prominent, pale brown eyes inspire anything but confidence. His nose, however, is his redeeming feature: it is pronounced straight and well-formed; though I myself should have liked it better did it not possess a somewhat spongy, porous appearance, as though it had been cleverly formed out of a red coloured cork.

I never could endure to shake hands with Mr. Slope. A cold, clammy perspiration always exudes from him, the small drops are ever to be seen standing on his brow, and his friendly grasp is unpleasant.

Such is Mr. Slope—such is the man who has suddenly fallen into the midst of Barchester Close, and is destined there to assume the station which has heretofore been filled by the son of the late bishop. Think, oh, my meditative reader, what an associate we have here for those comfortable prebendaries, those gentlemanlike clerical doctors, those happy well-used well-fed minor canons, who have grown into existence at Barchester under the kindly wings of Bishop Grantly!

But not as a mere associate for these does Mr. Slope travel down to Barchester with the bishop and his wife. He intends to be, if not their master, at least the chief among them. He intends to lead, and to have followers; he intends to hold the purse strings of the diocese, and draw round him an obedient herd of his poor and hungry brethren.

And here we can hardly fail to draw a comparison between the archdeacon and our new private chaplain; and despite the manifold faults of the former, one can hardly fail to make it much to his advantage.

Both men are eager, much too eager, to support and increase the power of their order. Both are anxious that the world should be priest-governed, though they have probably never confessed so much, even to themselves. Both begrudge any other kind of dominion held by man over man. Dr. Grantly, if he admits the Queen's supremacy in things spiritual, only admits it as being due to the *quasi* priesthood conveyed in the consecrating qualities of her coronation; and he regards things temporal as being by their nature subject to those which are spiritual. Mr. Slope's ideas of sacerdotal rule are of quite a different class. He cares nothing, one way or the other, for the Queen's supremacy; these to his ears are empty words, meaning nothing. Forms he regards but little, and such titular expressions as supremacy, consecration, ordination, and the like, convey of themselves no significance to him. Let him be supreme who can. The temporal king, judge, or gaoler, can work but on the body. The spiritual master, if he have the necessary gifts, and can duly use them, has a wider field of empire. He works upon the soul. If he can make himself be believed, he can be all powerful over those who listen. If he be careful to meddle with none who are too strong in intellect, or too weak in flesh, he may indeed be supreme. And such was the ambition of Mr. Slope.

Dr. Grantly interfered very little with the worldly doings of those who were in any way subject to him. I do not mean to say that he omitted to notice misconduct among his clergy, immorality in his parish, or omissions in his family; but he was not anxious to do so where the necessity could be avoided. He was not troubled with a propensity to be curious, and as long as those around him were tainted with no heretical leaning towards dissent, as long as they fully and freely admitted the efficacy of Mother Church, he was willing that that mother should be merciful and affectionate, prone to indulgence, and unwilling to chastise. He himself enjoyed the good things of this world, and liked to let it be known that he did so. He cordially despised any brother rector who thought harm of dinner-parties, or dreaded the dangers of a moderate claret-jug; consequently dinner-parties and claret-jugs were common in the diocese. He liked to give laws and to be obeyed in them implicitly, but he endeavoured that his ordinances should be within the compass of the man, and not unpalatable to the gentleman. He had ruled among his clerical neighbours now for sundry years, and as he had maintained his power without becoming unpopular, it may be presumed that he had exercised some wisdom.

Of Mr. Slope's conduct much cannot be said, as his grand career is yet to commence; but it may be premised that his tastes will be very different from those of the archdeacon. He conceives it to be his duty to know all the private doings and desires of the flock entrusted to his care. From the poorer classes he exacts an unconditional obedience to set rules of conduct, and if disobeyed he has recourse, like his great ancestor, to the fulminations of an Ernulfus; "Thou shalt be damned in thy going in and in thy coming out—in thy eating and thy drinking," &c. &c. &c.

With the rich, experience has already taught him that
a different line of action is necessary. Men in the
upper walks of life do not mind being cursed, and the
women, presuming that it be done in delicate phrase,
rather like it. But he has not, therefore, given up so
important a portion of believing Christians. With the
men, indeed, he is generally at variance; they are
hardened sinners, on whom the voice of the priestly
charmer too often falls in vain; but with the ladies, old
and young, firm and frail, devout and dissipated, he is,
as he conceives, all powerful. He can reprove faults
with so much flattery, and utter censure in so caressing
a manner, that the female heart, if it glow with a spark
of low church susceptibility, cannot withstand him. In
many houses he is thus an admired guest: the husbands,
for their wives' sake, are fain to admit him; and when
once admitted it is not easy to shake him off. He has,
however, a pawing, greasy way with him, which does
not endear him to those who do not value him for their
souls' sake, and he is not a man to make himself at
once popular in a large circle such as is now likely to
surround him at Barchester.

CHAPTER V.
A MORNING VISIT.

It was known that Dr. Proudie would immediately
have to reappoint to the wardenship of the hospital
under the act of Parliament to which allusion has been
made; but no one imagined that any choice was left to
him—no one for a moment thought that he could
appoint any other than Mr. Harding. Mr. Harding
himself, when he heard how the matter had been

settled, without troubling himself much on the subject, considered it as certain that he would go back to his pleasant house and garden.   And though there would be much that was melancholy, nay, almost heart-rending, in such a return, he still was glad that it was to be so.   His daughter might probably be persuaded to return there with him.   She had, indeed, all but promised to do so, though she still entertained an idea that that greatest of mortals, that important atom of humanity, that little god upon earth, Johnny Bold her baby, ought to have a house of his own over his head.

Such being the state of Mr. Harding's mind in the matter, he did not feel any peculiar personal interest in the appointment of Dr. Proudie to the bishopric. He, as well as others at Barchester, regretted that a man should be sent among them who, they were aware, was not of their way of thinking; but Mr. Harding himself was not a bigoted man on points of church doctrine, and he was quite prepared to welcome Dr. Proudie to Barchester in a graceful and becoming manner. He had nothing to seek and nothing to fear; he felt that it behoved him to be on good terms with his bishop, and he did not anticipate any obstacle that would prevent it.

In such a frame of mind he proceeded to pay his respects at the palace the second day after the arrival of the bishop and his chaplain. But he did not go alone. Dr. Grantly proposed to accompany him, and Mr. Harding was not sorry to have a companion, who would remove from his shoulders the burden of the conversation in such an interview. In the affair of the consecration Dr. Grantly had been introduced to the

bishop, and Mr. Harding had also been there. He had,
however, kept himself in the background, and he
was now to be presented to the great man for the first
time.

The archdeacon's feelings were of a much stronger
nature. He was not exactly the man to overlook his
own slighted claims, or to forgive the preference shown
to another. Dr. Proudie was playing Venus to his Juno,
and he was prepared to wage an internecine war
against the owner of the wished-for apple, and all his
satellites, private chaplains, and others.

Nevertheless, it behoved him also to conduct himself towards the intruder as an old archdeacon should
conduct himself to an in-coming bishop; and though
he was well aware of all Dr. Proudie's abominable
opinions as regarded dissenters, church reform, the
hebdomadal council, and such like; though he disliked
the man, and hated the doctrines, still he was prepared to show respect to the station of the bishop. So
he and Mr. Harding called together at the palace.

His lordship was at home, and the two visitors
were shown through the accustomed hall into the well-
known room, where the good old bishop used to sit.
The furniture had been bought at a valuation, and
every chair and table, every bookshelf against the wall,
and every square in the carpet, was as well known to
each of them as their own bedrooms. Nevertheless
they at once felt that they were strangers there. The
furniture was for the most part the same, yet the place
had been metamorphosed. A new sofa had been introduced, a horrid chintz affair, most unprelatical and
almost irreligious: such a sofa as never yet stood in
the study of any decent high church clergyman of the

Church of England. The old curtains had also been given away. They had, to be sure, become dingy, and that which had been originally a rich and goodly ruby had degenerated into a reddish brown. Mr. Harding, however, thought the old reddish brown much preferable to the gaudy buff-coloured trumpery moreen which Mrs. Proudie had deemed good enough for her husband's own room in the provincial city of Barchester.

Our friends found Dr. Proudie sitting on the old bishop's chair, looking very nice in his new apron; they found too, Mr. Slope standing on the hearth-rug, persuasive and eager, just as the archdeacon used to stand; but on the sofa they also found Mrs. Proudie, an innovation for which a precedent might in vain be sought in all the annals of the Barchester bishopric!

There she was, however, and they could only make the best of her. The introductions were gone through in much form. The archdeacon shook hands with the bishop, and named Mr. Harding, who received such an amount of greeting as was due from a bishop to a precentor. His lordship then presented them to his lady wife; the archdeacon first, with archidiaconal honours, and then the precentor with diminished parade. After this Mr. Slope presented himself. The bishop, it is true, did mention his name, and so did Mrs. Proudie too, in a louder tone; but Mr. Slope took upon himself the chief burden of his own introduction. He had great pleasure in making himself acquainted with Dr. Grantly; he had heard much of the archdeacon's good works in that part of the diocese in which his duties as archdeacon had been exercised (thus purposely ignoring the archdeacon's hitherto unlimited dominion over the diocese at large). He was aware that his lordship depended greatly on the assistance which Dr. Grantly would be able to give him in that portion of his diocese. He then thrust out his hand, and grasping that of his new foe, bedewed it unmercifully. Dr. Grantly in return bowed, looked stiff, contracted his eyebrows, and wiped his hand with his pocket-handkerchief. Nothing abashed, Mr. Slope then noticed the precentor, and descended to the grade of the lower clergy. He gave him a squeeze of the hand, damp indeed, but affectionate, and was very glad to make the acquaintance of Mr.———; oh yes, Mr. Harding; he had not exactly caught the name—"Precentor in the cathedral," surmised Mr. Slope. Mr. Harding confessed that such was the humble sphere of his work. "Some parish duty as well," suggested Mr. Slope. Mr. Harding acknowledged the diminutive incumbency of St. Cuthbert's. Mr. Slope then left him alone, having condescended sufficiently, and joined the conversation among the higher powers.

There were four persons there, each of whom considered himself the most important personage in the diocese; himself, indeed, or herself, as Mrs. Proudie was one of them; and with such a difference of opinion it was not probable that they would get on pleasantly together. The bishop himself actually wore the visible apron, and trusted mainly to that—to that and his title, both being facts which could not be overlooked. The archdeacon knew his subject, and really understood the business of bishoping, which the others did not; and this was his strong ground. Mrs. Proudie had her sex to back her, and her habit of command,

and was nothing daunted by the high tone of Dr. Grantly's face and figure. Mr. Slope had only himself and his own courage and tact to depend on, but he nevertheless was perfectly self-assured, and did not doubt but that he should soon get the better of weak men who trusted so much to externals, as both bishop and archdeacon appeared to do.

"Do you reside in Barchester, Dr. Grantly?" asked the lady with her sweetest smile.

Dr. Grantly explained that he lived in his own parish of Plumstead Episcopi, a few miles out of the city. Whereupon the lady hoped that the distance was not too great for country visiting, as she would be so glad to make the acquaintance of Mrs. Grantly. She would take the earliest opportunity, after the arrival of her horses at Barchester; their horses were at present in London; their horses were not immediately coming down, as the bishop would be obliged, in a few days, to return to town. Dr. Grantly was no doubt aware that the bishop was at present much called upon by the "University Improvement Committee:" indeed, the Committee could not well proceed without him, as their final report had now to be drawn up. The bishop had also to prepare a scheme for the "Manufacturing Towns Morning and Evening Sunday School Society," of which he was a patron, or president, or director and therefore the horses would not come down to Barchester at present; but whenever the horses did come down, she would take the earliest opportunity of calling at Plumstead Episcopi, providing the distance was not too great for country visiting.

The archdeacon made his fifth bow: he had made one at each mention of the horses; and promised that

Mrs. Grantly would do herself the honour of calling at the palace on an early day. Mrs. Proudie declared that she would be delighted: she hadn't liked to ask, not being quite sure whether Mrs. Grantly had horses; besides, the distance might have been, &c. &c.

Dr. Grantly again bowed, but said nothing. He could have bought every individual possession of the whole family of the Proudies, and have restored them as a gift, without much feeling the loss; and had kept a separate pair of horses for the exclusive use of his wife since the day of his marriage; whereas Mrs. Proudie had been hitherto jobbed about the streets of London at so much a month during the season; and at other times had managed to walk, or hire a smart fly from the livery stables.

"Are the arrangements with reference to the Sabbath-day schools generally pretty good in your archdeaconry?" asked Mr. Slope.

"Sabbath-day schools!" repeated the archdeacon with an affectation of surprise. "Upon my word, I can't tell; it depends mainly on the parson's wife and daughters. There is none at Plumstead."

This was almost a fib on the part of the Archdeacon, for Mrs. Grantly has a very nice school. To be sure it is not a Sunday school exclusively, and is not so designated; but that exemplary lady always attends there an hour before church, and hears the children say their catechism, and sees that they are clean and tidy for church, with their hands washed, and their shoes tied; and Grisel and Florinda, her daughters, carry thither a basket of large buns, baked on the Saturday afternoon, and distribute them to all the children not especially under disgrace, which buns are carried home after church with considerable content, and eaten hot at tea, being then split and toasted. The children of Plumstead would indeed open their eyes if they heard their venerated pastor declare that there was no Sunday school in his parish.

Mr. Slope merely opened his eyes wider, and slightly shrugged his shoulders. He was not, however, prepared to give up his darling project.

"I fear there is a great deal of Sabbath travelling here," said he. "On looking at the 'Bradshaw,' I see that there are three trains in and three out every Sabbath. Could nothing be done to induce the company to withdraw them? Don't you think, Dr. Grantly, that a little energy might diminish the evil?"

"Not being a director, I really can't say. But if you can withdraw the passengers, the company I dare say, will withdraw the trains," said the doctor. "It's merely a question of dividends."

"But surely, Dr. Grantly," said the lady, "surely we should look at it differently. You and I, for instance, in our position: surely we should do all that we can to control so grievous a sin. Don't you think so, Mr. Harding?" and she turned to the precentor, who was sitting mute and unhappy.

Mr. Harding thought that all porters and stokers, guards, breaksmen, and pointsmen ought to have an opportunity of going to church, and he hoped that they all had.

"But surely, surely," continued Mrs. Proudie, "surely that is not enough. Surely that will not secure such an observance of the Sabbath as we are taught to conceive is not only expedient but indispensable; surely——"

4*

Come what come might, Dr. Grantly was not to be
forced into a dissertation on a point of doctrine with
Mrs. Proudie, nor yet with Mr. Slope; so without much
ceremony he turned his back upon the sofa, and began
to hope that Dr. Proudie had found that the palace
repairs had been such as to meet his wishes.

"Yes, yes," said his lordship; upon the whole he
thought so — upon the whole, he didn't know that
there was much ground for complaint; the architect,
perhaps, might have——but his double, Mr. Slope, who
had sidled over to the bishop's chair, would not allow
his lordship to finish his ambiguous speech.

"There is one point I would like to mention, Mr.
Archdeacon. His lordship asked me to step through
the premises, and I see that the stalls in the second
stable are not perfect."

"Why—there's standing there for a dozen horses,"
said the archdeacon.

"Perhaps so," said the other; "indeed, I've no
doubt of it; but visitors, you know, often require so
much accommodation. There are so many of the
bishop's relatives who always bring their own horses."

• Dr. Grantly promised that due provision for the
relatives' horses should be made, as far at least as the
original stable building would allow. He would himself communicate with the architect.

"And the coach-house, Dr. Grantly," continued Mr.
Slope; "there is really hardly room for a second carriage in the large coach-house, and the smaller one,
of course, holds only one."

"And the gas," chimed in the lady, "there is no
gas through the house, none whatever, but in the
kitchen and passages. Surely the palace should have

been fitted through with pipes for gas, and hot water too. There is no hot water laid on anywhere above the ground-floor; surely there should be the means of getting hot water in the bed-rooms without having it brought in jugs from the kitchen."

The bishop had a decided opinion that there should be pipes for hot water. Hot water was very essential for the comfort of the palace. It was, indeed, a requisite in any decent gentleman's house.

Mr. Slope had remarked that the coping on the garden wall was in many places imperfect.

Mrs. Proudie had discovered a large hole, evidently the work of rats, in the servants' hall.

The bishop expressed an utter detestation of rats. There was nothing, he believed, in this world, that he so much hated as a rat.

Mr. Slope had, moreover, observed that the locks of the out-houses were very imperfect: he might specify the coal-cellar, and the wood-house.

Mrs. Proudie had also seen that those on the doors of the servants' bedrooms were in an equally bad condition; indeed the locks all through the house were old-fashioned and unserviceable.

The bishop thought that a great deal depended on a good lock, and quite as much on the key. He had observed that the fault very often lay with the key, especially if the wards were in any way twisted.

Mr. Slope was going on with his catalogue of grievances, when he was somewhat loudly interrupted by the archdeacon, who succeeded in explaining that the diocesan architect, or rather his foreman, was the person to be addressed on such subjects; and that he, Dr. Grantly, had inquired as to the comfort of the palace, merely as a point of compliment. He was sorry, however, that so many things had been found amiss: and then he rose from his chair to escape.

Mrs. Proudie, though she had contrived to lend her assistance in recapitulating the palatial dilapidations, had not on that account given up her hold of Mr. Harding, nor ceased from her cross-examinations as to the iniquity of Sabbatical amusements. Over and over again had she thrown out her "Surely, surely," at Mr. Harding's devoted head,.and ill had that gentleman been able to parry the attack.

He had never before found himself subjected to such a nuisance. Ladies hitherto, when they had consulted him on religious subjects, had listened to what he might choose to say with some deference, and had differed, if they differed, in silence. But Mrs. Proudie interrogated him, and then lectured. "Neither thou, nor thy son, nor thy daughter, nor thy man servant, nor thy maid servant," said she, impressively, and more than once, as though Mr. Harding had forgotten the words. She shook her finger at him as she quoted the favourite law, as though menacing him with punishment; and then called upon him categorically to state whether he did not think that travelling on the Sabbath was an abomination and a desecration.

Mr. Harding had never been so hard pressed in his life. He felt that he ought to rebuke the lady for presuming so to talk to a gentleman and a clergyman many years her senior; but he recoiled from the idea of scolding the bishop's wife, in the bishop's presence, on his first visit to the palace; moreover, to tell the truth, he was somewhat afraid of her. She, seeing him sit silent and absorbed, by no means refrained from the attack.

"I hope, Mr. Harding," said she, shaking her head slowly and solemnly, "I hope you will not leave me to think that you approve of Sabbath travelling," and she looked a look of unutterable meaning into his eyes.

There was no standing this, for Mr. Slope was now looking at him, and so was the bishop, and so was the archdeacon, who had completed his adieux on that side of the room. Mr. Harding therefore got up also, and putting out his hand to Mrs. Proudie said: "If you will come to St. Cuthbert's some Sunday, I will preach you a sermon on that subject."

And so the archdeacon and the precentor took their departure, bowing low to the lady, shaking hands with the lord, and escaping from Mr. Slope in the best manner each could. Mr. Harding was again maltreated; but Dr. Grantly swore deeply in the bottom of his heart, that no earthly consideration should ever again induce him to touch the paw of that impure and filthy animal.

And now, had I the pen of a mighty poet, would I sing in epic verse the noble wrath of the archdeacon. The palace steps descend to a broad gravel sweep, from whence a small gate opens out into the street, very near the covered gateway leading into the close. The road from the palace door turns to the left, through the spacious gardens, and terminates on the London-road, half a mile from the cathedral.

Till they had both passed this small gate and entered the close, neither of them spoke a word; but the precentor clearly saw from his companion's face that a tornado was to be expected, nor was he himself inclined to stop it. Though by nature far less irritable than the archdeacon, even he was angry: he even— that mild and courteous man—was inclined to express himself in anything but courteous terms.

CHAPTER VI.

WAR.

"Good heavens!" exclaimed the archdeacon, as he placed his foot on the gravel walk of the close, and raising his hat with one hand, passed the other somewhat violently over his now grizzled locks; smoke issued forth from the uplifted beaver as it were a cloud of wrath, and the safety-valve of his anger opened, and emitted a visible steam, preventing positive explosion and probable apoplexy. "Good heavens!"—and the archdeacon looked up to the gray pinnacles of the cathedral tower, making a mute appeal to that still living witness which had looked down on the doings of so many bishops of Barchester.

"I don't think I shall ever like that Mr. Slope," said Mr. Harding.

"Like him!" roared the archdeacon, standing still for a moment to give more force to his voice; "like him!" All the ravens of the close cawed their assent. The old bells of the tower, in chiming the hour, echoed the words; and the swallows flying out from their nests mutely expressed a similar opinion. Like Mr. Slope! Why no, it was not very probable that any Barchester-bred living thing should like Mr. Slope!

"Nor Mrs. Proudie either," said Mr. Harding.

The archdeacon hereupon forgot himself. I will not follow his example, nor shock my readers by transcribing the term in which he expressed his feeling as to the lady who had been named. The ravens and the last lingering notes of the clock bells were less scrupulous, and repeated in corresponding echoes the very improper exclamation. The archdeacon again raised his hat, and another salutary escape of steam was effected.

There was a pause, during which the precentor tried to realise the fact that the wife of a bishop of Barchester had been thus designated, in the close of the cathedral, by the lips of its own archdeacon: but he could not do it.

"The bishop seems to be a quiet man enough," suggested Mr. Harding, having acknowledged to himself his own failure.

"Idiot!" exclaimed the doctor, who for the nonce was not capable of more than such spasmodic attempts at utterance.

"Well he did not seem very bright," said Mr. Harding, "and yet he has always had the reputation of a clever man. I suppose he's cautious and not inclined to express himself very freely."

The new bishop of Barchester was already so contemptible a creature in Dr. Grantly's eyes, that he could not condescend to discuss his character. He was a puppet to be played by others; a mere wax doll, done up in an apron and a shovel hat, to be stuck on a throne or elsewhere, and pulled about by wires as others chose. Dr. Grantly did not choose to let himself down low enough to talk about Dr. Proudie; but he saw that he would have to talk about the other members of his household, the coadjutor bishops, who had brought his lordship down, as it were, in a box, and were about to handle the wires as they willed. This in itself was a terrible vexation to the archdeacon. Could he have ignored the chaplain, and have fought the bishop, there would have been, at any rate, nothing degrading in such a contest. Let the Queen make whom she would bishop of Barchester; a man, or even an ape, when once a bishop, would be a respectable adversary, if he would but fight, himself. But what was such a person as Dr. Grantly to do, when such another person as Mr. Slope was put forward as his antagonist?

If he, our archdeacon, refused the combat, Mr. Slope would walk triumphant over the field, and have the diocese of Barchester under his heel.

If, on the other hand, the archdeacon accepted as his enemy the man whom the new puppet bishop put before him as such, he would have to talk about Mr. Slope, and write about Mr. Slope, and in all matters treat with Mr. Slope, as a being standing, in some degree, on ground similar to his own. He would have to meet Mr. Slope: to——Bah! the idea was sickening. He could not bring himself to have to do with Mr. Slope.

"He is the most thoroughly bestial creature that ever I set my eyes upon," said the archdeacon.

"Who—the bishop?" asked the other, innocently.

"Bishop! no—I'm not talking about the bishop. How on earth such a creature got ordained!—they'll ordain anybody now, I know; but he's been in the church these ten years; and they used to be a little careful ten years ago."

"Oh! you mean Mr. Slope."

"Did you ever see any animal less like a gentleman?" asked Dr. Grantly.

"I can't say I felt myself much disposed to like him."

"Like him!" again shouted the doctor, and the assenting ravens again cawed an echo; "of course, you don't like him: it's not a question of liking. But what are we to do with him?"

"Do with him?" asked Mr. Harding.

"Yes—what are we to do with him? How are we to treat him? There he is, and there he'll stay. He has put his foot in that palace, and he will never take it out again till he's driven. How are we to get rid of him?"

"I don't suppose he can do us much harm."

"Not do harm!—Well, I think you'll find yourself of a different opinion before a month is gone. What would you say now, if he got himself put into the hospital? Would that be harm?"

Mr. Harding mused awhile, and then said he didn't think the new bishop would put Mr. Slope into the hospital.

"If he doesn't put him there, he'll put him somewhere else where he'll be as bad. I tell you that that man, to all intents and purposes, will be Bishop of Barchester;" and again Dr. Grantly raised his hat, and rubbed his hand thoughtfully and sadly over his head.

"Impudent scoundrel!" he continued after a while. "To dare to cross-examine me about the Sunday schools in the diocese, and Sunday travelling too: I never in my life met his equal for sheer impudence. Why, he must have thought we were two candidates for ordination!"

"I declare I thought Mrs. Proudie was the worst of the two," said Mr. Harding.

"When a woman is impertinent, one must only put up with it, and keep out of her way in future; but I am not inclined to put up with Mr. Slope. 'Sabbath travelling!'" and the doctor attempted to imitate the peculiar drawl of the man he so much disliked: "'Sabbath travelling!' Those are the sort of men who will ruin the Church of England, and make the profession of a clergyman disreputable. It is not the dissenters or the papists that we should fear, but the set of canting, low-bred hypocrites who are wriggling their way in among us; men who have no fixed principle, no standard ideas of religion or doctrine, but who take up some popular cry, as this fellow has done about 'Sabbath travelling.'"

Dr. Grantly did not again repeat the question aloud, but he did so constantly to himself, "What were they to do with Mr. Slope?" How was he openly, before the world, to show that he utterly disapproved of and abhorred such a man?

Hitherto Barchester had escaped the taint of any extreme rigour of church doctrine. The clergymen of the city and neighbourhood, though very well inclined to promote high-church principles, privileges, and prerogatives, had never committed themselves to tendencies, which are somewhat too loosely called Puseyite practices. They all preached in their black gowns, as their fathers had done before them; they wore ordinary black cloth waistcoats; they had no candles on their altars, either lighted or unlighted; they made no private genuflexions, and were contented to confine themselves to such ceremonial observances as had been in vogue for the last hundred years. The services were decently and demurely read in their parish churches, chanting was confined to the cathedral, and the science of intoning was unknown. One young man who had come direct from Oxford as a curate to Plumstead had, after the lapse of two or three Sundays, made a faint attempt, much to the bewilderment of the poorer part of the congregation. Dr. Grantly had not been present on the occasion; but Mrs. Grantly, who had her own opinion on the subject, immediately after the service expressed a hope that the young gentleman had not been taken ill, and offered to send him all kinds of condiments supposed to be good for a sore throat. After that there had been no more intoning at Plumstead Episcopi.

But now the archdeacon began to meditate on some strong measures of absolute opposition. Dr. Proudie and his crew were of the lowest possible order of Church of England clergymen, and therefore it behoved him, Dr. Grantly, to be of the very highest. Dr. Proudie would abolish all forms and ceremonies, and therefore Dr. Grantly felt the sudden necessity of multiplying them. Dr. Proudie would consent to deprive the church of all collective authority and rule, and therefore Dr. Grantly would stand up for the full power of convocation, and the renewal of all its ancient privileges.

It was true that he could not himself intone the service, but he could procure the co-operation of any number of gentleman-like curates well trained in the mystery of doing so. He would not willingly alter his own fashion of dress, but he could people Barchester with young clergymen dressed in the longest frocks, and in the highest-breasted silk waistcoats. He certainly was not prepared to cross himself, or to advocate the real presence; but, without going this length, there were various observances, by adopting which he could plainly show his antipathy to such men as Dr. Proudie and Mr. Slope.

All these things passed through his mind as he paced up and down the close with Mr. Harding. War, war, internecine war was in his heart. He felt that, as regarded himself and Mr. Slope, one of the two must be annihilated as far as the city of Barchester was concerned; and he did not intend to give way until there was not left to him an inch of ground on which he could stand. He still flattered himself that he could make Barchester too hot to hold Mr. Slope, and he had no weakness of spirit to prevent his bringing about such a consummation if it were in his power.

"I suppose Susan must call at the palace," said Mr. Harding.

"Yes, she shall call there; but it shall be once and once only. I dare say 'the horses' won't find it convenient to come out to Plumstead very soon, and when that once is done the matter may drop."

"I don't suppose Eleanor need call. I don't think Eleanor would get on at all well with Mrs. Proudie."

"Not the least necessity in life," replied the archdeacon, not without the reflection that a ceremony which was necessary for his wife, might not be at all binding on the widow of John Bold. "Not the slightest reason on earth why she should do so, if she doesn't like it. For myself, I don't think that any decent young woman should be subjected to the nuisance of being in the same room with that man."

And so the two clergymen parted, Mr. Harding

going to his daughter's house, and the archdeacon seeking the seclusion of his brougham.

The new inhabitants of the palace did not express any higher opinion of their visitors than their visitors had expressed of them. Though they did not use quite such strong language as Dr. Grantly had done, they felt as much personal aversion, and were quite as well aware as he was that there would be a battle to be fought, and that there was hardly room for Proudieism in Barchester as long as Grantlyism was predominant.

Indeed, it may be doubted whether Mr. Slope had not already within his breast a better prepared system of strategy, a more accurately-defined line of hostile conduct than the archdeacon. Dr. Grantly was going to fight because he found that he hated the man. Mr. Slope had predetermined to hate the man, because he foresaw the necessity of fighting him. When he had first reviewed the *carte du pays*, previous to his entry into Barchester, the idea had occurred to him of conciliating the archdeacon, of cajoling and flattering him into submission, and of obtaining the upper hand by cunning instead of courage. A little inquiry, however, sufficed to convince him that all his cunning would fail to win over such a man as Dr. Grantly to such a mode of action as that to be adopted by Mr. Slope; and then he determined to fall back upon his courage. He at once saw that open battle against Dr. Grantly and all Dr. Grantly's adherents was a necessity of his position, and he deliberately planned the most expedient methods of giving offence.

Soon after his arrival the bishop had intimated to the dean, that with the permission of the canon then in residence, his chaplain would preach in the cathedral on the next Sunday. The canon in residence happened to be the Hon. and Rev. Dr. Vesey Stanhope, who at this time was very busy on the shores of the Lake of Como, adding to that unique collection of butterflies for which he is so famous. Or, rather, he would have been in residence but for the butterflies and other such summer-day considerations; and the vicar-choral, who was to take his place in the pulpit, by no means objected to having his work done for him by Mr. Slope.

Mr. Slope accordingly preached, and if a preacher can have satisfaction in being listened to, Mr. Slope ought to have been gratified. I have reason to think that he was gratified, and that he left the pulpit with the conviction that he had done what he intended to do when he entered it.

On this occasion the new bishop took his seat for the first time in the throne allotted to him. New scarlet cushions and drapery had been prepared, with new gilt binding and new fringe. The old carved oak-wood of the throne, ascending with its numerous grotesque pinnacles half-way up to the roof of the choir, had been washed, and dusted, and rubbed, and it all looked very smart. Ah! how often sitting there, in happy early days, on those lowly benches in front of the altar, have I whiled away the tedium of a sermon in considering how best I might thread my way up amidst those wooden towers, and climb safely to the topmost pinnacle!

All Barchester went to hear Mr. Slope; either for that or to gaze at the new bishop. All the best bonnets of the city were there, and moreover all the best glossy clerical hats. Not a stall but had its fitting occupant; for though some of the prebendaries might be away in Italy or elsewhere, their places were filled by brethren, who flocked into Barchester on the occasion. The dean was there, a heavy old man, now too old, indeed, to attend frequently in his place; and so was the archdeacon. So also were the chancellor, the treasurer, the precentor, sundry canons and minor canons, and every lay member of the choir, prepared to sing the new bishop in with due melody and harmonious expression of sacred welcome.

The service was certainly very well performed. Such was always the case at Barchester, as the musical education of the choir had been good, and the voices had been carefully selected. The psalms were beautifully chanted; the Te Deum was magnificently sung; and the litany was given in a manner, which is still to be found at Barchester, but, if my taste be correct, is to be found nowhere else. The litany in Barchester cathedral has long been the special task to which Mr. Harding's skill and voice have been devoted. Crowded audiences generally make good performers, and though Mr. Harding was not aware of any extraordinary exertion on his part, yet probably he rather exceeded his usual mark. Others were doing their best, and it was natural that he should emulate his brethren. So the service went on, and at last Mr. Slope got into the pulpit.

He chose for his text a verse from the precepts addressed by St. Paul to Timothy, as to the conduct necessary in a spiritual pastor and guide, and it was immediately evident that the good clergy of Barchester were to have a lesson.

"Study to show thyself approved unto God, a work-man that needeth not to be ashamed, rightly dividing the word of truth." These were the words of his text, and with such a subject in such a place, it may be supposed that such a preacher would be listened to by such an audience. He was listened to with breathless attention, and not without considerable surprise. Whatever opinion of Mr. Slope might have been held in Barchester before he commenced his discourse, none of his hearers, when it was over, could mistake him either for a fool or a coward.

It would not be becoming were I to travestie a sermon, or even to repeat the language of it in the pages of a novel. In endeavouring to depict the characters of the persons of whom I write, I am to a certain extent forced to speak of sacred things. I trust, however, that I shall not be thought to scoff at the pulpit, though some may imagine that I do not feel all the reverence that is due to the cloth. I may question the infallibility of the teachers, but I hope that I shall not therefore be accused of doubt as to the thing to be taught.

Mr. Slope, in commencing his sermon, showed no slight tact in his ambiguous manner of hinting that, humble as he was himself, he stood there as the mouthpiece of the illustrious divine who sat opposite to him; and having premised so much, he gave forth a very accurate definition of the conduct which that prelate would rejoice to see in the clergymen now brought under his jurisdiction. It is only necessary to say, that the peculiar points insisted upon were exactly those which were most distasteful to the clergy of the diocese, and most averse to their practice and opinions;

and that all those peculiar habits and privileges which
have always been dear to high-church priests, to that
party which is now scandalously called the high-and-
dry church, were ridiculed, abused, and anathematised.
Now, the clergymen of the diocese of Barchester are
all of the high-and-dry church.

Having thus, according to his own opinion, explained
how a clergyman should show himself approved unto
God, as a workman that needeth not to be ashamed,
he went on to explain how the word of truth should
be divided; and here he took a rather narrow view of
the question, and fetched his arguments from afar. His
object was to express his abomination of all ceremo-
nious modes of utterance, to cry down any religious
feeling which might be excited, not by the sense, but
by the sound of words, and in fact to insult cathedral
practices. Had St. Paul spoken of rightly pronouncing
instead of rightly dividing the word of truth, this part
of his sermon would have been more to the purpose;
but the preacher's immediate object was to preach
Mr. Slope's doctrine, and not St. Paul's, and he contrived to give the necessary twist to the text with
some skill.

He could not exactly say, preaching from a cathedral pulpit, that chanting should be abandoned in cathedral services. By such an assertion, he would have
overshot his mark and rendered himself absurd, to the
delight of his hearers. He could, however, and did,
allude with heavy denunciations to the practice of intoning in parish churches, although the practice was
all but unknown in the diocese; and from thence he
came round to the undue preponderance, which he asserted, music had over meaning in the beautiful service

which they had just heard.   He was aware, he said,
that the practices of our ancestors could not be abandoned at a moment's notice; the feelings of the aged
would be outraged, and the minds of respectable men
would be shocked.   There were many, he was aware,
of not sufficient calibre of thought to perceive, of not
sufficient education to know, that a mode of service,
which was effective when outward ceremonies were of
more moment than inward feelings, had become all but
barbarous at a time when inward conviction was everything, when each word of the minister's lips should
fall intelligibly into the listener's heart.   Formerly the
religion of the multitude had been an affair of the
imagination: now, in these latter days, it had become
necessary that a Christian should have a reason for
his faith—should not only believe, but digest—not
only hear, but understand.   The words of our morning
service, how beautiful, how apposite, how intelligible
they were, when read with simple and distinct decorum! but how much of the meaning of the words was
lost when they were produced with all the meretricious
charms of melody! &c. &c.

Here was a sermon to be preached before Mr.
Archdeacon Grantly, Mr. Precentor Harding, and the
rest of them! before a whole dean and chapter assembled in their own cathedral! before men who had
grown old in the exercise of their peculiar services,
with a full conviction of their excellence for all intended purposes! This too from such a man, a clerical
parvenu, a man without a cure, a mere chaplain, an
intruder among them; a fellow raked up, so said Dr.
Grantly, from the gutters of Marylebone! They had
to sit through it! None of them, not even Dr. Grantly,

could close his ears, nor leave the house of God during the hours of service. They were under an obligation of listening, and that too, without any immediate power of reply.

There is, perhaps, no greater hardship at present inflicted on mankind in civilised and free countries, than the necessity of listening to sermons. No one but a preaching clergyman has, in these realms, the power of compelling an audience to sit silent, and be tormented. No one but a preaching clergyman can revel in platitudes, truisms, and untruisms, and yet receive, as his undisputed privilege, the same respectful demeanour as though words of impassioned eloquence, or persuasive logic, fell from his lips. Let a professor of law or physic find his place in a lecture-room, and there pour forth jejune words and useless empty phrases, and he will pour them forth to empty benches. Let a barrister attempt to talk without talking well, and he will talk but seldom. A judge's charge need be listened to per force by none but the jury, prisoner, and gaoler. A member of Parliament can be coughed down or counted out. Town-councillors can be tabooed. But no one can rid himself of the preaching clergyman. He is the bore of the age, the old man whom we Sindbads cannot shake off, the nightmare that disturbs our Sunday's rest, the incubus that overloads our religion and makes God's service distasteful. We are not forced into church! No: but we desire more than that. We desire not to be forced to stay away. We desire, nay, we are resolute, to enjoy the comfort of public worship; but we desire also that we may do so without an amount of tedium which ordinary human nature cannot endure with patience; that we may be able to leave the house of God, without that anxious longing for escape, which is the common consequence of common sermons.

With what complacency will a young parson deduce false conclusions from misunderstood texts, and then threaten us with all the penalties of Hades if we neglect to comply with the injunctions he has given us! Yes, my too self-confident juvenile friend, I do believe in those mysteries, which are so common in your mouth; I do believe in the unadulterated word which you hold there in your hand; but you must pardon me if, in some things, I doubt your interpretation. The bible is good, the prayer-book is good, nay, you yourself would be acceptable, if you would read to me some portion of those time-honoured discourses which our great divines have elaborated in the full maturity of their powers. But you must excuse me, my insufficient young lecturer, if I yawn over your imperfect sentences, your repeated phrases, your false pathos, your drawlings and denouncings, your humming and hawing, your oh-ing and ah-ing, your black gloves and your white handkerchief. To me, it all means nothing; and hours are too precious to be so wasted —— if one could only avoid it.

And here I must make a protest against the pretence, so often put forward by the working clergy, that they are overburdened by the multitude of sermons to be preached. We are all too fond of our own voices, and a preacher is encouraged in the vanity of making his heard by the privilege of a compelled audience. His sermon is the pleasant morsel of his life, his delicious moment of self-exaltation. "I have preached nine sermons this week," said a young friend to me the other day, with hand languidly raised to his brow, the picture of an overburdened martyr. "Nine this week, seven last week, four the week before. I have preached twenty-three sermons this month. It is really too much." "Too much, indeed," said I, shuddering; "too much for the strength of any one." "Yes," he answered meekly, "indeed it is; I am beginning to feel it painfully." "Would," said I, you could feel it—would that you could be made to feel it." But he never guessed that my heart was wrung for the poor listeners.

There was, at any rate, no tedium felt in listening to Mr. Slope on the occasion in question. His subject came too home to his audience to be dull; and, to tell the truth, Mr. Slope had the gift of using words forcibly. He was heard through his thirty minutes of eloquence with mute attention and open ears; but with angry eyes, which glared round from one enraged parson to another, with wide-spread nostrils from which already burst forth fumes of indignation, and with many shufflings of the feet and uneasy motions of the body, which betokened minds disturbed, and hearts not at peace with all the world.

At last the bishop, who, of all the congregation, had been most surprised, and whose hair almost stood on end with terror, gave the blessing in a manner not at all equal to that in which he had long been practising it in his own study, and the congregation was free to go their way.

CHAPTER VII.

THE DEAN AND CHAPTER TAKE COUNSEL.

ALL Barchester was in a tumult. Dr. Grantly could hardly get himself out of the cathedral porch before he exploded in his wrath. The old dean betook himself silently to his deanery, afraid to speak; and there sat, half stupefied, pondering many things in vain. Mr. Harding crept forth solitary and unhappy; and, slowly passing beneath the elms of the close, could scarcely bring himself to believe that the words which he had heard had proceeded from the pulpit of Barchester cathedral. Was he again to be disturbed? was his whole life to be shown up as a useless sham a second time? would he have to abdicate his precentorship, as he had his wardenship, and to give up chanting, as he had given up his twelve old bedesmen? And what if he did! Some other Jupiter, some other Mr. Slope, would come and turn him out of St. Cuthbert's. Surely he could not have been wrong all his life in chanting the litany as he had done! He began, however, to have his doubts. Doubting himself was Mr. Harding's weakness. It is not, however, the usual fault of his order.

Yes! all Barchester was in a tumult. It was not only the clergy who were affected. The laity also had listened to Mr. Slope's new doctrine, all with surprise, some with indignation, and some with a mixed feeling, in which dislike of the preacher was not so strongly blended. The old bishop and his chaplains, the dean and his canons and minor canons, the old choir, and especially Mr. Harding who was at the head of it, had all been popular in Barchester. They had spent their money and done good; the poor had not been ground down; the clergy in society had neither been overbearing nor austere; and the whole repute of the city was due to its ecclesiastical importance.   Yet there were those who had heard Mr. Slope with satisfaction.

It is so pleasant to receive a fillip of excitement when suffering from the dull routine of every-day life! The authems and Te Deums were in themselves delightful, but they had been heard so often! Mr. Slope was certainly not delightful, but he was new, and, moreover, clever.   They had long thought it slow, so said now many of the Barchesterians, to go on as they had done in their old humdrum way, giving ear to none of the religious changes which were moving the world without.   People in advance of the age now had new ideas, and it was quite time that Barchester should go in advance.   Mr. Slope might be right.   Sunday certainly had not been strictly kept in Barchester, except as regarded the cathedral services.   Indeed the two hours between services had long been appropriated to morning calls and hot luncheons.   Then Sunday schools! really more ought to have been done as to Sunday schools; Sabbath-day schools Mr. Slope had called them.   The late bishop had really not thought of Sunday schools as he should have done.   (These people probably did not reflect that catechisms and collects are quite as hard work to the young mind as book-keeping is to the elderly; and that quite as little feeling of worship enters into the one task as the other.) And then, as regarded that great question of musical services, there might be much to be said on Mr. Slope's side of the question.   It certainly was the fact, that people went to the cathedral to hear the music, &c. &c.

And so a party absolutely formed itself in Barchester on Mr. Slope's side of the question! This consisted, among the upper classes, chiefly of ladies. No man—that is, no gentleman—could possibly be attracted by Mr. Slope, or consent to sit at the feet of so abhorrent a Gamaliel. Ladies are sometimes less nice in their appreciation of physical disqualification; and, provided that a man speak to them well, they will listen, though he speak from a mouth never so deformed and hideous. Wilkes was most fortunate as a lover; and the damp, sandy-haired, saucer-eyed, red-fisted, Mr. Slope was powerful only over the female breast.

There were, however, one or two of the neighbouring clergy who thought it not quite safe to neglect the baskets in which for the nonce were stored the loaves and fishes of the diocese of Barchester. They, and they only, came to call on Mr. Slope after his performance in the cathedral pulpit. Among these Mr. Quiverful, the rector of Puddingdale, whose wife still continued to present him from year to year with fresh pledges of her love, and so to increase his cares and, it is to be hoped, his happiness equally. Who can wonder that a gentleman, with fourteen living children and a bare income of 400*l.* a year, should look after the loaves and fishes, even when they are under the thumb of a Mr. Slope?

Very soon after the Sunday on which the sermon was preached, the leading clergy of the neighbourhood held high debate together as to how Mr. Slope should be put down. In the first place he should never again preach from the pulpit of Barchester cathedral. This was Dr. Grantly's earliest dictum; and they all agreed,

providing only that they had the power to exclude him.
Dr. Grantly declared that the power rested with the
dean and chapter, observing that no clergyman out of
the chapter had a claim to preach there, saving only
the bishop himself. To this the dean assented, but
alleged that contests on such a subject would be unseemly; to which rejoined a meagre little doctor, one
of the cathedral prebendaries, that the contest must be
all on the side of Mr. Slope if every prebendary were
always there ready to take his own place in the pulpit.
Cunning little meagre doctor, whom it suits well to live
in his own cosy house within Barchester close, and
who is well content to have his little fling at Dr. Vesey
Stanhope and other absentees, whose Italian villas, or
enticing London homes, are more tempting than cathedral stalls and residences!

To this answered the burly chancellor, a man
rather silent indeed, but very sensible, that absent
prebendaries had their vicars, and that in such case
the vicar's right to the pulpit was the same as that of
the higher order. To which the dean assented, groan-
ing deeply at these truths. Thereupon, however, the
meagre doctor remarked that they would be in the
hands of their minor canons, one of whom might at
any hour betray his trust. Whereon was heard from
the burly chancellor an ejaculation sounding somewhat
like "Pooh, pooh. pooh!" but it might be that the
worthy man was but blowing out the heavy breath
from his windpipe. Why silence him at all? suggested
Mr. Harding. Let them not be ashamed to hear what
any man might have to preach to them, unless he
preached false doctrine; in which case, let the bishop
silence him. So spoke our friend; vainly; for human

ends must be attained by human means. But the dean saw a ray of hope out of those purblind old eyes of his. Yes, let them tell the bishop how distasteful to them was this Mr. Slope: a new bishop just come to his seat could not wish to insult his clergy while the gloss was yet fresh on his first apron.

Then up rose Dr. Grantly; and, having thus collected the scattered wisdom of his associates, spoke forth with words of deep authority. When I say up rose the archdeacon, I speak of the inner man, which then sprang up to more immediate action, for the doctor had, bodily, been standing all along with his back to the dean's empty fire-grate, and the tails of his frock coat supported over his two arms. His hands were in his breeches pockets.

"It is quite clear that this man must not be allowed to preach again in this cathedral. We all see that, except our dear friend here, the milk of whose nature runs so softly, that he would not have the heart to refuse the Pope the loan of his pulpit, if the Pope would come and ask it. We must not, however, allow the man to preach again here. It is not because his opinion on church matters may be different from ours —with that one would not quarrel. It is because he has purposely insulted us. When he went up into the pulpit last Sunday, his studied object was to give offence to men who had grown old in reverence of those things of which he dared to speak so slightingly. What! to come here a stranger, a young, unknown, and unfriended stranger, and tell us, in the name of the bishop his master, that we are ignorant of our duties, old-fashioned, and useless! I don't know whether most to admire his courage or his impudence! And one thing I will tell you: that sermon originated solely with the man himself. The bishop was no more a party to it than was the dean here. You all know how grieved I am to see a bishop in this diocese holding the latitudinarian ideas by which Dr. Proudie has made himself conspicuous. You all know how greatly I should distrust the opinion of such a man. But in this matter I hold him to be blameless. I believe Dr. Proudie has lived too long among gentlemen to be guilty, or to instigate another to be guilty, of so gross an outrage. No! that man uttered what was untrue when he hinted that he was speaking as the mouthpiece of the bishop. It suited his ambitious views at once to throw down the gauntlet to us—at once to defy us here in the quiet of our own religious duties—here within the walls of our own loved cathedral—here where we have for so many years exercised our ministry without schism and with good repute. Such an attack upon us, coming from such a quarter, is abominable."

"Abominable," groaned the dean. "Abominable," muttered the meagre doctor. "Abominable," re-echoed the chancellor, uttering the sound from the bottom of his deep chest. "I really think it was," said Mr. Harding.

"Most abominable and most unjustifiable," continued the archdeacon. "But, Mr. Dean, thank God, that pulpit is still our own: your own, I should say. That pulpit belongs solely to the dean and chapter of Barchester Cathedral, and, as yet, Mr. Slope is no part of that chapter. You, Mr. Dean, have suggested that we should appeal to the bishop to abstain from forcing this man on us; but what if the bishop allow himself

to be ruled by his chaplain? In my opinion, the matter
is in our own hands. Mr. Slope cannot preach there
without permission asked and obtained, and let that
permission be invariably refused. Let all participation
in the ministry of the cathedral service be refused to
him. Then, if the bishop choose to interfere, we shall
know what answer to make to the bishop. My friend
here has suggested that this man may again find his
way into the pulpit by undertaking the duty of some
of your minor canons; but I am sure that we may
fully trust to these gentlemen to support us, when it is
known that the dean objects to any such transfer."

"Of course you may," said the chancellor.

There was much more discussion among the learned
conclave, all of which, of course, ended in obedience
to the archdeacon's commands. They had too long
been accustomed to his rule to shake it off so soon;
and in this particular case they had none of them a
wish to abet the man whom he was so anxious to put
down.

Such a meeting as that we have just recorded is
not held in such a city as Barchester unknown and
untold of. Not only was the fact of the meeting talked
of in every respectable house, including the palace, but
the very speeches of the dean, the archdeacon, and
chancellor were repeated; not without many additions
and imaginary circumstances, according to the tastes
and opinions of the relaters.

All, however, agreed in saying that Mr. Slope was
to be debarred from opening his mouth in the cathedral of Barchester; many believed that the vergers
were to be ordered to refuse him even the accommodation of a seat; and some of the most far-going ad-

vocates for strong measures, declared that his sermon was looked upon as an indictable offence, and that proceedings were to be taken against him for brawling.

The party who were inclined to defend him—the enthusiastically religious young ladies, and the middle-aged spinsters desirous of a move—of course took up his defence the more warmly on account of this attack. If they could not hear Mr. Slope in the cathedral, they would hear him elsewhere; they would leave the dull dean, the dull old prebendaries, and the scarcely less dull young minor canons, to preach to each other: they would work slippers and cushions, and hem bands for Mr. Slope, make him a happy martyr, and stick him up in some new Sion or Bethesda, and put the cathedral quite out of fashion.

Dr. and Mrs. Proudie at once returned to London. They thought it expedient not to have to encounter any personal application from the dean and chapter respecting the sermon, till the violence of the storm had expended itself; but they left Mr. Slope behind them nothing daunted, and he went about his work zealously, flattering such as would listen to his flattery, whispering religious twaddle into the ears of foolish women, ingratiating himself with the few clergy who would receive him, visiting the houses of the poor, inquiring into all people, prying into everything, and searching with his minutest eye into all palatial dilapidations. He did not, however, make any immediate attempt to preach again in the cathedral.

And so all Barchester was by the ears.

CHAPTER VIII.

THE EX-WARDEN REJOICES IN HIS PROBABLE RETURN TO THE HOSPITAL.

AMONG the ladies in Barchester who have hitherto acknowledged Mr. Slope as their spiritual director, must not be reckoned either the widow Bold, or her sister-in-law. On the first outbreak of the wrath of the denizens of the close, none had been more animated against the intruder than these two ladies. And this was natural. Who could be so proud of the musical distinction of their own cathedral as the favourite daughter of the precentor? Who would be so likely to resent an insult offered to the old choir? And in such matters Miss Bold and her sister-in-law had but one opinion.

This wrath, however, had in some degree been mitigated, and I regret to say that these ladies allowed Mr. Slope to be his own apologist. About a fortnight after the sermon had been preached, they were both of them not a little surprised by hearing Mr. Slope announced, as the page in buttons opened Mrs. Bold's drawing-room door. Indeed, what living man could, by a mere morning visit, have surprised them more? Here was the great enemy of all that was good in Barchester coming into their own drawing-room, and they had no strong arm, no ready tongue, near at hand for their protection. The widow snatched her baby out of its cradle into her lap, and Mary Bold stood up ready to die manfully in that baby's behalf, should, under any circumstances, such a sacrifice become necessary.

In this manner was Mr. Slope received. But when he left, he was allowed by each lady to take her hand, and to make his adieux as gentlemen do who have been graciously entertained! Yes; he shook hands with them, and was curtseyed out courteously, the buttoned page opening the door, as he would have done for the best canon of them all. He had touched the baby's little hand and blessed him with a fervid blessing; he had spoken to the widow of her early sorrows, and Eleanor's silent tears had not rebuked him; he had told Mary Bold that her devotion would be rewarded, and Mary Bold had heard the praise without disgust. And how had he done all this? how had he so quickly turned aversion into, at any rate, acquaintance? how had he overcome the enmity with which these ladies had been ready to receive him, and made his peace with them so easily?

My readers will guess from what I have written that I myself do not like Mr. Slope; but I am constrained to admit that he is a man of parts. He knows how to say a soft word in the proper place; he knows how to adapt his flattery to the ears of his hearers; he knows the wiles of the serpent, and he uses them. Could Mr. Slope have adapted his manners to men as well as to women, could he ever have learnt the ways of a gentleman, he might have risen to great things.

He commenced his acquaintance with Eleanor by praising her father. He had, he said, become aware that he had unfortunately offended the feelings of a man of whom he could not speak too highly; he would not now allude to a subject which was probably too serious for drawing-room conversation, but he would say, that it had been very far from him to utter a word in disparagement of a man, of whom all the

world, at least the clerical world, spoke so highly as
it did of Mr. Harding.   And so he went on, unsaying
a great deal of his sermon, expressing his highest admiration for the precentor's musical talents, eulogising
the father and the daughter and the sister-in-law,
speaking in that low silky whisper which he always
had specially prepared for feminine ears, and, ultimately, gaining his object.   When he left, he expressed a hope that he might again be allowed to
call; and though Eleanor gave no verbal assent to this,
she did not express dissent: and so Mr. Slope's right
to visit at the widow's house was established.

The day after this visit Eleanor told her father of
it, and expressed an opinion that Mr. Slope was not
quite so black as he had been painted.   Mr. Harding
opened his eyes rather wider than usual when he
heard what had occurred, but he said little; he could
not agree in any praise of Mr. Slope, and it was not
his practice to say much evil of any one.   He did
not, however, like the visit, and simple-minded as
he was, he felt sure that Mr. Slope had some deeper
motive than the mere pleasure of making soft speeches
to two ladies.

Mr. Harding, however, had come to see his daughter
with other purpose than that of speaking either good
or evil of Mr. Slope.   He had come to tell her that
the place of warden in Hiram's hospital was again to
be filled up, and that in all probability he would
once more return to his old home and his twelve
bedesmen.

"But," said he, laughing, "I shall be greatly shorn
of my ancient glory."

"Why so, papa?"

"This new act of parliament, that is to put us all on our feet again," continued he, "settles my income at four hundred and fifty pounds per annum."

"Four hundred and fifty," said she, "instead of eight hundred! Well; that is rather shabby. But still, papa, you'll have the dear old house and the garden?"

"My dear," said he, "it's worth twice the money;" and as he spoke he showed a jaunty kind of satisfaction in his tone and manner, and in the quick, pleasant way in which he paced Eleanor's drawing-room. "It's worth twice the money. I shall have the house and the garden, and a larger income than I can possibly want."

"At any rate, you'll have no extravagant daughter to provide for;" and as she spoke, the young widow put her arm within his, and made him sit on the sofa beside her; "at any rate you'll not have that expense."

"No, my dear; and I shall be rather lonely without her; but we won't think of that now. As regards income I shall have plenty for all I want. I shall have my old house; and I don't mind owning now that I have felt sometimes the inconvenience of living in a lodging. Lodgings are very nice for young men, but at my time of life there is a want of—I hardly know what to call it, perhaps not respectability—"

"Oh, papa! I'm sure there's been nothing like that. Nobody has thought it; nobody in all Barchester has been more respected than you have been since you took those rooms in High Street. Nobody! Not the dean in his deanery, or the archdeacon out at Plumstead."

6*

"The archdeacon would not be much obliged to you if he heard you," said he, smiling somewhat at the exclusive manner in which his daughter confined her illustration to the church dignitaries of the chapter of Barchester; "but at any rate I shall be glad to get back to the old house. Since I heard that it was all settled, I have begun to fancy that I can't be comfortable without my two sitting-rooms."

"Come and stay with me, papa, till it is settled —there's a dear papa."

"Thank ye, Nelly. But no; I won't do that. It would make two movings. I shall be very glad to get back to my old men again. Alas! alas! There have six of them gone in these few last years. Six out of twelve! And the others I fear have had but a sorry life of it there. Poor Bunce, poor old Bunce!"

Bunce was one of the surviving recipients of Hiram's charity: an old man, now over ninety, who had long been a favourite of Mr. Harding's.

"How happy old Bunce will be," said Mrs. Bold, clapping her soft hands softly. "How happy they all will be to have you back again. You may be sure there will soon be friendship among them again when you are there."

"But," said he, half laughing, "I am to have new troubles, which will be terrible to me. There are to be twelve old women, and a matron. How shall I manage twelve women and a matron!"

"The matron will manage the women of course."

"And who'll manage the matron?" said he.

"She won't want to be managed. She'll be a great lady herself, I suppose. But, papa, where will the matron live? She is not to live in the warden's house with you, is she?"

"Well, I hope not, my dear."

"Oh, papa, I tell you fairly, I won't have a matron for a new step-mother."

"You shan't, my dear; that is, if I can help it. But they are going to build another house for the matron and the women; and I believe they haven't even fixed yet on the site of the building."

"And have they appointed the matron?" said Eleanor.

"They haven't appointed the warden yet," replied he.

"But there's no doubt about that, I suppose," said his daughter.

Mr. Harding explained that he thought there was no doubt; that the archdeacon had declared as much, saying that the bishop and his chaplain between them had not the power to appoint any one else, even if they had the will to do so, and sufficient impudence to carry out such a will. The archdeacon was of opinion, that though Mr. Harding had resigned his wardenship, and had done so unconditionally, he had done so under circumstances which left the bishop no choice as to his re-appointment, now that the affair of the hospital had been settled on a new basis by act of parliament. Such was the archdeacon's opinion, and his father-in-law received it without a shadow of doubt.

Dr. Grantly had always been strongly opposed to Mr. Harding's resignation of the place. He had done all in his power to dissuade him from it. He had considered that Mr. Harding was bound to withstand the

popular clamour with which he was attacked for receiving so large an income as eight hundred a year
from such a charity, and was not even yet satisfied
that his father-in-law's conduct had not been pusillanimous and undignified.　He looked also on this reduction of the warden's income as a shabby, paltry
scheme on the part of government for escaping from a
difficulty into which it had been brought by the public
press.　Dr. Grantly observed that the government had
no more right to dispose of a sum of four hundred and
fifty pounds a year out of the income of Hiram's legacy,
than of nine hundred; whereas, as he said, the bishop,
dean, and chapter clearly had a right to settle what
sum should be paid.　He also declared that the
government had no more right to saddle the charity
with twelve old women than with twelve hundred; and
he was, therefore, very indignant on the matter.　He
probably forgot when so talking that government had
done nothing of the kind, and had never assumed any
such might or any such right.　He made the common
mistake of attributing to the government, which in such
matters is powerless, the doings of parliament, which
in such matters is omnipotent.

But though he felt that the glory and honour of
the situation of warden of Barchester hospital were
indeed curtailed by the new arrangement; that the
whole establishment had to a certain degree been made
vile by the touch of Whig commissioners; that the
place with its lessened income, its old women, and
other innovations, was very different from the hospital
of former days; still the archdeacon was too practical
a man of the world to wish that his father-in-law,
who had at present little more than 200*l.* per annum

for all his wants, should refuse the situation, defiled, undignified, and commission-ridden as it was.

Mr. Harding had, accordingly, made up his mind that he would return to his home at the hospital, and to tell the truth, had experienced almost a childish pleasure in the idea of doing so. The diminished income was to him not even the source of momentary regret. The matron and the old women did rather go against the grain; but he was able to console himself with the reflection, that, after all, such an arrangement might be of real service to the poor of the city. The thought that he must receive his re-appointment as the gift of the new bishop, and probably through the hands of Mr. Slope, annoyed him a little; but his mind was set at rest by the assurance of the archdeacon that there would be no favour in such a presentation. The re-appointment of the old warden would be regarded by all the world as a matter of course. Mr. Harding, therefore, felt no hesitation in telling his daughter that they might look upon his return to his old quarters as a settled matter.

"And you won't have to ask for it, papa."

"Certainly not, my dear. There is no ground on which I could ask for any favour from the bishop, whom, indeed, I hardly know. Nor would I ask a favour, the granting of which might possibly be made a question to be settled by Mr. Slope. No," said he, moved for a moment by a spirit very unlike his own, "I certainly shall be very glad to go back to the hospital; but I should never go there, if it were necessary that my doing so should be the subject of a request to Mr. Slope."

This little outbreak of her father's anger jarred on

the present tone of Eleanor's mind. She had not learnt to like Mr. Slope, but she had learnt to think that he had much respect for her father; and she would, therefore, willingly use her efforts to induce something like good feeling between them.

"Papa," said she, "I think you somewhat mistake Mr. Slope's character."

"Do I?" said he, placidly.

"I think you do, papa. I think he intended no personal disrespect to you when he preached the sermon which made the archdeacon and the dean so angry!"

"I never supposed he did, my dear. I hope I never inquired within myself whether he did or no. Such a matter would be unworthy of any inquiry, and very unworthy of the consideration of the chapter. But I fear he intended disrespect to the ministration of God's services, as conducted in conformity with the rules of the Church of England."

"But might it not be that he thought it his duty to express his dissent from that which you, and the dean, and all of us here so much approve?"

"It can hardly be the duty of a young man rudely to assail the religious convictions of his elders in the church. Courtesy should have kept him silent, even if neither charity nor modesty could do so."

"But Mr. Slope would say that on such a subject the commands of his heavenly Master do not admit of his being silent."

"Nor of his being courteous, Eleanor?"

"He did not say that, papa."

"Believe me, my child, that Christian ministers are never called on by God's word to insult the convictions, or even the prejudices of their brethren; and that religion is at any rate not less susceptible of urbane and courteous conduct among men, than any other study which men may take up. I am sorry to say that I cannot defend Mr. Slope's sermon in the cathedral. But come, my dear, put on your bonnet, and let us walk round the dear old gardens at the hospital. I have never yet had the heart to go beyond the court-yard since we left the place. Now I think I can venture to enter."

Eleanor rang the bell, and gave a variety of imperative charges as to the welfare of the precious baby, whom, all but unwillingly, she was about to leave for an hour or so, and then sauntered forth with her father to revisit the old hospital. It had been forbidden ground to her as well as to him since the day on which they had walked forth together from its walls.

CHAPTER IX.
THE STANHOPE FAMILY.

It is now three months since Dr. Proudie began his reign, and changes have already been effected in the diocese which show at least the energy of an active mind. Among other things absentee clergymen have been favoured with hints much too strong to be overlooked. Poor dear old Bishop Grantly had on this matter been too lenient, and the archdeacon had never been inclined to be severe with those who were absent on reputable pretences, and who provided for their duties in a liberal way.

Among the greatest of the diocesan sinners in this respect was Dr. Vesey Stanhope. Years had now passed since he had done a day's duty; and yet there was no reason against his doing duty except a want of inclination on his own part. He held a prebendal stall in the diocese; one of the best residences in the close; and the two large rectories of Crabtree Canonicorum, and Stogpingum. Indeed, he had the cure of three parishes, for that of Eiderdown was joined to Stogpingum. He had resided in Italy for twelve years. His first going there had been attributed to a sore throat; and that sore throat, though never repeated in any violent manner, had stood him in such stead, that it had enabled him to live in easy idleness ever since.

He had now been summoned home—not, indeed, with rough violence, or by any peremptory command, but by a mandate which he found himself unable to disregard. Mr. Slope had written to him by the bishop's desire. In the first place, the bishop much wanted the valuable co-operation of Dr. Vesey Stanhope in the diocese; in the next, the bishop thought it his imperative duty to become personally acquainted with the most conspicuous of his diocesan clergy; then the bishop thought it essentially necessary for Dr. Stanhope's own interests, that Dr. Stanhope should, at any rate for a time, return to Barchester; and lastly, it was said that so strong a feeling was at the present moment evinced by the hierarchs of the church with reference to the absence of its clerical members, that it behoved Dr. Vesey Stanhope not to allow his name to stand among those which would probably in a few months be submitted to the councils of the nation.

There was something so ambiguously frightful in this last threat that Dr. Stanhope determined to spend two or three summer months at his residence in Barchester. His rectories were inhabited by his curates, and he felt himself from disuse to be unfit for parochial duty; but his prebendal home was kept empty for him, and he thought it probable that he might be able now and again to preach a prebendal sermon. He arrived, therefore, with all his family at Barchester, and he and they must be introduced to my readers.

The great family characteristic of the Stanhopes might probably be said to be heartlessness; but this want of feeling was, in most of them, accompanied by so great an amount of good nature as to make itself but little noticeable to the world. They were so prone to oblige their neighbours that their neighbours failed to perceive how indifferent to them was the happiness and well-being of those around them. The Stanhopes would visit you in your sickness (provided it were not contagious), would bring you oranges, French novels, and the last new bit of scandal, and then hear of your death or your recovery with an equally indifferent composure. Their conduct to each other was the same as to the world; they bore and forbore: and there was sometimes, as will be seen, much necessity for forbearing: but their love among themselves rarely reached above this. It is astonishing how much each of the family was able to do, and how much each did, to prevent the well-being of the other four.

For there were five in all; the doctor, namely, and Mrs. Stanhope, two daughters, and one son. The doctor, perhaps, was the least singular and most estimable of them all, and yet such good qualities as he possessed were all negative. He was a good looking rather plethoric gentleman of about sixty years of age. His hair was snow white, very plentiful, and somewhat like wool of the finest description. His whiskers were very large and very white, and gave to his face the appearance of a benevolent sleepy old lion. His dress was always unexceptionable. Although he had lived so many years in Italy it was invariably of a decent clerical hue, but it never was hyperclerical. He was a man not given to much talking, but what little he did say was generally well said. His reading seldom went beyond romances and poetry of the lightest and not always most moral description. He was thoroughly a *bon vivant;* an accomplished judge of wine, though he never drank to excess; and a most inexorable critic in all affairs touching the kitchen. He had had much to forgive in his own family, since a family had grown up around him, and had forgiven everything—except inattention to his dinner. His weakness in that respect was now fully understood, and his temper but seldom tried. As Dr. Stanhope was a clergyman, it may be supposed that his religious convictions made up a considerable part of his character; but this was not so. That he had religious convictions must be believed; but he rarely obtruded them, even on his children. This abstinence on his part was not systematic, but very characteristic of the man. It was not that he had predetermined never to influence their thoughts; but he was so habitually idle that his time for doing so had never come till the opportunity for doing so was gone for ever. Whatever conviction the father may have had, the children were at any rate but indifferent members of the church from which he drew his income.

Such was Dr. Stanhope. The features of Mrs. Stanhope's character were even less plainly marked than those of her lord. The *far niente* of her Italian life had entered into her very soul, and brought her to regard a state of inactivity as the only earthly good. In manner and appearance she was exceedingly prepossessing. She had been a beauty, and even now, at fifty-five, she was a handsome woman. Her dress was always perfect: she never dressed but once in the day, and never appeared till between three and four; but when she did appear, she appeared at her best. Whether the toil rested partly with her, or wholly with her hand-maid, it is not for such a one as the author even to imagine. The structure of her attire was always elaborate, and yet never over laboured. She was rich in apparel, but not bedizened with finery; her ornaments were costly, rare, and such as could not fail to attract notice, but they did not look as though worn with that purpose. She well knew the great architectural secret of decorating her constructions, and never descended to construct a decoration. But when we have said that Mrs. Stanhope knew how to dress, and used her knowledge daily, we have said all. Other purpose in life she had none. It was something, indeed, that she did not interfere with the purpose of others. In early life she had undergone great trials with reference to the doctor's dinners; but for the last ten or twelve years her eldest daughter Charlotte had taken that labour off her hands, and she had had little to trouble her;—little, that is, till the edict for this terrible English journey had gone forth: since, then, indeed, her life had been laborious enough. For such a one, the toil of being carried from the shores of Como to the city of Barchester is more than labour enough, let the care of the carriers be ever so vigilant.

Mrs. Stanhope had been obliged to have every one of her dresses taken in from the effects of the journey.

Charlotte Stanhope was at this time about thirty-five years old; and, whatever may have been her faults, she had none of those which belong particularly to old young ladies. She neither dressed young, nor talked young, nor indeed looked young. She appeared to be perfectly content with her time of life, and in no way affected the graces of youth. She was a fine young woman; and had she been a man, would have been a very fine young man. All that was done in the house, and that was not done by servants, was done by her. She gave the orders, paid the bills, hired and dismissed the domestics, made the tea, carved the meat, and managed everything in the Stanhope household. She, and she alone, could ever induce her father to look into the state of his worldly concerns. She, and she alone, could in any degree control the absurdities of her sister. She, and she alone, prevented the whole family from falling into utter disrepute and beggary. It was by her advice that they now found themselves very unpleasantly situated in Barchester.

So far, the character of Charlotte Stanhope is not unprepossessing. But it remains to be said, that the influence which she had in her family, though it had been used to a certain extent for their worldly well-being, had not been used to their real benefit, as it might have been. She had aided her father in his in-difference to his professional duties, counselling him that his livings were as much his individual property as the estates of his elder brother were the property of that worthy peer. She had for years past stifled every little rising wish for a return to England which the doctor had from time to time expressed. She had encouraged her mother in her idleness in order that she herself might be mistress and manager of the Stanhope household. She had encouraged and fostered the follies of her sister, though she was always willing, and often able, to protect her from their probable result. She had done her best, and had thoroughly succeeded in spoiling her brother, and turning him loose upon the world an idle man without a profession, and without a shilling that he could call his own.

Miss Stanhope was a clever woman, able to talk on most subjects and quite indifferent as to what the subject was. She prided herself on her freedom from English prejudice, and she might have added, from feminine delicacy. On religion she was a pure freethinker, and with much want of true affection, delighted to throw out her own views before the troubled mind of her father. To have shaken what remained of his Church of England faith would have gratified her much; but the idea of his abandoning his preferment in the church had never once presented itself to her mind. How could he indeed, when he had no income from any other source?

But the two most prominent members of the family still remain to be described. The second child had been christened Madeline, and had been a great beauty. We need not say had been, for she was never more beautiful than at the time of which we write, though her person for many years had been disfigured by an accident. It is unnecessary that we should give in detail the early history of Madeline Stanhope. She had gone to Italy when about seventeen years of age, and had been allowed to make the most of her surpassing beauty in the saloons of Milan, and among the crowded villas along the shores of the Lake of Como. She had become famous for adventures in which her character was just not lost, and had destroyed the hearts of a dozen cavaliers without once being touched in her own. Blood had flowed in quarrels about her charms, and she heard of these encounters with pleasurable excitement. It had been told of her that on one occasion she had stood by in the disguise of a page, and had seen her lover fall.

As is so often the case, she had married the very worst of those who sought her hand. Why she had chosen Paolo Neroni, a man of no birth and no property, a mere captain in the pope's guard, one who had come up to Milan either simply as an adventurer or else as a spy, a man of harsh temper and oily manners, mean in figure, swarthy in face, and so false in words as to be hourly detected, need not now be told. When the moment for doing so came, she had probably no alternative. He, at any rate, had become her husband; and after a prolonged honeymoon among the lakes, they had gone together to Rome, the papal captain having vainly endeavoured to induce his wife to remain behind him.

Six months afterwards she arrived at her father's house a cripple, and a mother. She had arrived without even notice, with hardly clothes to cover her, and without one of those many ornaments which had graced her bridal *trousseau.* Her baby was in the arms of a poor girl from Milan, whom she had taken in exchange for the Roman maid who had accompanied her thus far, and who had then, as her mistress said, become homesick and had returned. It was clear that the lady had determined that there should be no witness to tell stories of her life in Rome.

She had fallen, she said, in ascending a ruin, and had fatally injured the sinews of her knee; so fatally, that when she stood she lost eight inches of her accustomed height; so fatally, that when she essayed to move, she could only drag herself painfully along, with protruded hip and extended foot in a manner less graceful than that of a hunchback. She had consequently made up her mind, once and for ever, that she would never stand, and never attempt to move herself.

Stories were not slow to follow her, averring that she had been cruelly ill used by Neroni, and that to his violence had she owed her accident. Be that as it may, little had been said about her husband, but that little had made it clearly intelligible to the family that Signor Neroni was to be seen and heard of no more. There was no question as to re-admitting the poor ill used beauty to her old family rights, no question as to adopting her infant daughter beneath the Stanhope roof tree. Though heartless, the Stanhopes were not selfish. The two were taken in, petted, made much of, for a time all but adored, and then felt by the two parents to be great nuisances in the house. But in the house the lady was, and there she remained, having her own way, though that way was not very conformable with the customary usages of an English clergyman.

Madame Neroni, though forced to give up all motion in the world, had no intention whatever of giving up the world itself. The beauty of her face was uninjured, and that beauty was of a peculiar kind. Her copious rich brown hair was worn in Grecian *bandeaux* round her head, displaying as much as possible of her forehead and cheeks. Her forehead, though rather low, was very beautiful from its perfect contour and pearly whiteness. Her eyes were long and large, and marvellously bright; might I venture to say, bright as Lucifer's, I should perhaps best express the depth of their brilliancy. They were dreadful eyes to look at, such as would absolutely deter any man of quiet mind and easy spirit from attempting a passage of arms with such foes. There was talent in them, and the fire of passion and the play of wit, but there was no love. Cruelty was there instead, and courage, a desire of masterhood, cunning, and a wish for mischief. And yet, as eyes, they were very beautiful. The eyelashes were long and perfect, and the long steady unabashed gaze, with which she would look into the face of her admirer, fascinated while it frightened him. She was a basilisk from whom an ardent lover of beauty could make no escape. Her nose and teeth and chin and neck and bust were perfect, much more so at twenty-eight than they had been at eighteen. What wonder that with such charms still glowing in her face, and with such deformity destroying her figure, she should resolve to be seen, but only to be seen reclining on a sofa.

Her resolve had not been carried out without difficulty. She had still frequented the opera at Milan; she had still been seen occasionally in the saloons of the *noblesse;* she had caused herself to be carried in and out from her carriage, and that in such a manner as in no wise to disturb her charms, disarrange her dress, or expose her deformities. Her sister always accompanied her and a maid, a man-servant also, and on state occasions, two. It was impossible that her purpose could have been achieved with less: and yet, poor as she was, she had achieved her purpose. And then again the more dissolute Italian youths of Milan frequented the Stanhope villa and surrounded her couch, not greatly to her father's satisfaction. Sometimes his spirit would rise, a dark spot would show itself on his cheek, and he would rebel; but Charlotte would assuage him with some peculiar triumph of her culinary art, and all again would be smooth for a while.

Madeline affected all manner of rich and quaint devices in the garniture of her room, her person, and her feminine belongings. In nothing was this more apparent than in the visiting card which she had prepared for her use. For such an article one would say that she, in her present state, could have but small need, seeing how improbable it was that she should make a morning call: but not such was her own opinion. Her card was surrounded by a deep border of gilding; on this she had imprinted, in three lines,—

> "La Signora Madeline
> "Vesey Neroni.
> —Nata Stanhope."

And over the name she had a bright gilt coronet, which certainly looked very magnificent. How she had come to concoct such a name for herself it would be difficult to explain. Her father had been christened Vesey, as another man is christened Thomas; and she had no more right to assume it than would have the daughter of a Mr. Josiah Jones to call herself Mrs. Josiah Smith, on marrying a man of the latter name. The gold coronet was equally out of place, and perhaps inserted with even less excuse. Paolo Neroni had had not the faintest title to call himself a scion

7 *

of even Italian nobility. Had the pair met in England
Neroni would probably have been a count; but they
had met in Italy, and any such pretence on his part
would have been simply ridiculous. A coronet, however, was a pretty ornament, and if it could solace a
poor cripple to have such on her card, who would begrudge it to her?

Of her husband, or of his individual family, she
never spoke; but with her admirers she would often
allude in a mysterious way to her married life and
isolated state, and, pointing to her daughter, would call
her the last of the blood of the emperors, thus re-
ferring Neroni's extraction to the old Roman family
from which the worst of the Cæsars sprang.

The "Signora" was not without talent, and not
without a certain sort of industry; she was an in-
domitable letter writer, and her letters were worth the
postage: they were full of wit, mischief, satire, love,
latitudinarian philosophy, free religion, and, sometimes,
alas! loose ribaldry. The subject, however, depended
entirely on the recipient, and she was prepared to correspond with any one but moral young ladies or stiff
old women. She wrote also a kind of poetry, generally
in Italian, and short romances, generally in French.
She read much of a desultory sort of literature, and as
a modern linguist had really made great proficiency.
Such was the lady who had now come to wound the
hearts of the men of Barchester.

Ethelbert Stanhope was in some respects like his
younger sister, but he was less inestimable as a man
than she as a woman. His great fault was an entire
absence of that principle which should have induced
him, as the son of a man without fortune, to earn his

own bread. Many attempts had been made to get him to do so, but these had all been frustrated, not so much by idleness on his part, as by a disinclination to exert himself in any way not to his taste. He had been educated at Eton, and had been intended for the Church, but had left Cambridge in disgust after a single term, and notified to his father his intention to study for the bar. Preparatory to that, he thought it well that he should attend a German university, and consequently went to Leipsic. There he remained two years, and brought away a knowledge of German and a taste for the fine arts. He still, however, intended himself for the bar, took chambers, engaged himself to sit at the feet of a learned pundit, and spent a season in London. He there found that all his aptitudes inclined him to the life of an artist, and he determined to live by painting. With this object he returned to Milan, and had himself rigged out for Rome. As a painter he might have earned his bread, for he wanted only diligence to excel; but when at Rome his mind was carried away by other things: he soon wrote home for money, saying that he had been converted to the Mother Church, that he was already an acolyte of the Jesuits, and that he was about to start with others to Palestine on a mission for converting Jews. He did go to Judea, but being unable to convert the Jews, was converted by them. He again wrote home, to say that Moses was the only giver of perfect laws to the world, that the coming of the true Messiah was at hand, that great things were doing in Palestine, and that he had met one of the family of Sidonia, a most remarkable man, who was now on his way to Western Europe, and whom he had induced to deviate from his

route with the object of calling at the Stanhope villa.
Ethelbert then expressed his hope that his mother and
sisters would listen to this wonderful prophet. His
father he knew could not do so from pecuniary considerations. This Sidonia, however, did not take so
strong a fancy to him as another of that family once
did to a young English nobleman. At least he provided him with no heaps of gold as large as lions; so
that the Judaised Ethelbert was again obliged to draw
on the revenues of the Christian Church.

It is needless to tell how the father swore that he
would send no more money and receive no Jew; nor
how Charlotte declared that Ethelbert could not be left
penniless in Jerusalem, and how "La Signora Neroni"
resolved to have Sidonia at her feet. The money was
sent, and the Jew did come. The Jew did come, but
he was not at all to the taste of "La Signora." He
was a dirty little old man, and though he had provided no golden lions, he had, it seems, relieved young
Stanhope's necessities. He positively refused to leave
the villa till he had got a bill from the doctor on his
London bankers.

Ethelbert did not long remain a Jew. He soon reappeared at the villa without prejudices on the subject
of his religion, and with a firm resolve to achieve fame
and fortune as a sculptor. He brought with him some
models which he had originated at Rome, and which
really gave such fair promise that his father was induced to go to further expense in furthering these
views. Ethelbert opened an establishment, or rather
took lodgings and a workshop, at Carrara, and there
spoilt much marble, and made some few pretty images.
Since that period, now four years ago, he had alter-

nated between Carrara and the villa, but his sojourns at the workshop became shorter and shorter, and those at the villa longer and longer. 'Twas no wonder; for Carrara is not a spot in which an Englishman would like to dwell.

When the family started for England he had resolved not to be left behind, and with the assistance of his elder sister had carried his point against his father's wishes. It was necessary, he said, that he should come to England for orders. How otherwise was he to bring his profession to account?

In personal appearance Ethelbert Stanhope was the most singular of beings. He was certainly very handsome. He had his sister Madeline's eyes without their stare, and without their hard cunning cruel firmness. They were also very much lighter, and of so light and clear a blue as to make his face remarkable, if nothing else did so. On entering a room with him, Ethelbert's blue eyes would be the first thing you would see, and on leaving it almost the last you would forget. His light hair was very long and silky, coming down over his coat. His beard had been prepared in holy land, and was patriarchal. He never shaved, and rarely trimmed it. It was glossy, soft, clean, and altogether not unprepossessing. It was such, that ladies might desire to reel it off and work it into their patterns in lieu of floss silk. His complexion was fair and almost pink, he was small in height, and slender in limb, but well-made, and his voice was of peculiar sweetness.

In manner and dress he was equally remarkable. He had none of the *mauvaise honte* of an Englishman. He required no introduction to make himself agreeable to any person. He habitually addressed strangers, ladies as well as men, without any such formality, and in doing so never seemed to meet with rebuke. His costume cannot be described, because it was so various; but it was always totally opposed in every principle of colour and construction to the dress of those with whom he for the time consorted.

He was habitually addicted to making love to ladies, and did so without any scruple of conscience, or any idea that such a practice was amiss. He had no heart to touch himself, and was literally unaware that humanity was subject to such an infliction. He had not thought much about it; but, had he been asked, would have said, that ill-treating a lady's heart meant injuring her promotion in the world. His principles therefore forbade him to pay attention to a girl, if he thought any man was present whom it might suit her to marry. In this manner, his good nature frequently interfered with his amusement; but he had no other motive in abstaining from the fullest declarations of love to every girl that pleased his eye.

Bertie Stanhope, as he was generally called, was, however, popular with both sexes; and with Italians as well as English. His circle of acquaintance was very large, and embraced people of all sorts. He had no respect for rank, and no aversion to those below him. He had lived on familiar terms with English peers, German shopkeepers, and Roman priests. All people were nearly alike to him. He was above, or rather below, all prejudices. No virtue could charm him, no vice shock him. He had about him a natural good manner, which seemed to qualify him for the highest circles, and yet he was never out of place in the lowest.

He had no principle, no regard for others, no self-respect, no desire to be other than a drone in the hive, if only he could, as a drone, get what honey was sufficient for him. Of honey, in his latter days, it may probably be presaged, that he will have but short allowance.

Such was the family of the Stanhopes, who, at this period, suddenly joined themselves to the ecclesiastical circle of Barchester close. Any stranger union, it would be impossible perhaps to conceive. And it was not as though they all fell down into the cathedral precincts hitherto unknown and untalked of. In such case no amalgamation would have been at all probable between the new-comers and either the Proudie set or the Grantly set. But such was far from being the case. The Stanhopes were all known by name in Barchester, and Barchester was prepared to receive them with open arms. The doctor was one of her prebendaries, one of her rectors, one of her pillars of strength; and was, moreover, counted on, as a sure ally, both by Proudies and Grantlys.

He himself was the brother of one peer, and his wife was the sister of another—and both these peers were lords of whiggish tendency, with whom the new bishop had some sort of alliance. This was sufficient to give to Mr. Slope high hope that he might enlist Dr. Stanhope on his side, before his enemies could out-manœuvre him. On the other hand, the old dean had many many years ago, in the days of the doctor's clerical energies, been instrumental in assisting him in his views as to preferment; and many many years ago also, the two doctors, Stanhope and Grantly, had, as young parsons been joyous together in the common rooms of Oxford.   Dr. Grantly, consequently, did not doubt but that the new comer would range himself under his banners.

Little did any of them dream of what ingredients the Stanhope family was now composed.

CHAPTER X.
MRS. PROUDIE'S RECEPTION—COMMENCED.

THE bishop and his wife had only spent three or four days in Barchester on the occasion of their first visit.   His lordship, had, as we have seen, taken his seat on his throne; but his demeanour there, into which it had been his intention to infuse much hierarchal dignity, had been a good deal disarranged by the audacity of his chaplain's sermon.   He had hardly dared to look his clergy in the face, and to declare by the severity of his countenance that in truth he meant all that his factotum was saying on his behalf; nor yet did he dare to throw Mr. Slope over, and show to those around him that he was no party to the sermon, and would resent it.

He had accordingly blessed his people in a shambling manner, not at all to his own satisfaction, and had walked back to his palace with his mind very doubtful as to what he would say to his chaplain on the subject.   He did not remain long in doubt.   He had hardly doffed his lawn when the partner of all his toils entered his study, and exclaimed even before she had seated herself—

"Bishop, did you ever hear a more sublime, more spirit-moving, more appropriate discourse than that?"

"Well, my love; ha—hum—he!" The bishop did not know what to say.

"I hope, my lord, you don't mean to say you disapprove?"

There was a look about the lady's eye which did not admit of my lord's disapproving at that moment. He felt that if he intended to disapprove, it must be now or never; but he also felt that it could not be now. It was not in him to say to the wife of his bosom that Mr. Slope's sermon was ill-timed, impertinent and vexatious.

"No, no," replied the bishop. "No, I can't say I disapprove—a very clever sermon and very well intended, and I dare say will do a great deal of good." This last praise was added, seeing that what he had already said by no means satisfied Mrs. Proudie.

"I hope it will," said she. "I am sure it was well deserved. Did you ever in your life, bishop, hear anything so like play-acting as the way in which Mr. Harding sings the litany? I shall beg Mr. Slope to continue a course of sermons on the subject till all that is altered. We will have at any rate, in our cathedral, a decent, godly, modest morning service. There must be no more play-acting here now;" and so the lady rang for lunch.

The bishop knew more about cathedrals and deans, and precentors and church services than his wife did, and also more of a bishop's powers. But he thought it better at present to let the subject drop.

"My dear," said he, "I think we must go back to London on Tuesday. I find my staying here will be very inconvenient to the Government."

The bishop knew that to this proposal his wife

would not object; and he also felt that by thus retreating from the ground of battle, the heat of the fight might be got over in his absence.

"Mr. Slope will remain here, of course?" said the lady.

"Oh, of course," said the bishop.

Thus, after less than a week's sojourn in his palace, did the bishop fly from Barchester; nor did he return to it for two months, the London season being then over. During that time Mr. Slope was not idle, but he did not again essay to preach in the cathedral. In answer to Mrs. Proudie's letter, advising a course of sermons, he had pleaded that he would at any rate wish to put off such an undertaking till she was there to hear them.

He had employed his time in consolidating a Proudie and Slope party—or rather a Slope and Proudie party, and he had not employed his time in vain. He did not meddle with the dean and chapter, except by giving them little teasing intimations of the bishop's wishes about this and the bishop's feelings about that, in a manner which was to them sufficiently annoying, but which they could not resent. He preached once or twice in a distant church in the suburbs of the city, but made no allusion to the cathedral service. He commenced the establishment of two "Bishop's Barchester Sabbath-day Schools," gave notice of a proposed "Bishop's Barchester Young Men's Sabbath Evening Lecture Room,"—and wrote three or four letters to the manager of the Barchester branch railway, informing him how anxious the bishop was that the Sunday trains should be discontinued.

At the end of two months, however, the bishop

and the lady reappeared; and as a happy harbinger of their return, heralded their advent by the promise of an evening party on the largest scale.   The tickets of invitation were sent out from London—they were dated from Bruton Street, and were despatched by the odious Sabbath breaking railway, in a huge brown paper parcel to Mr. Slope.   Everybody calling himself a gentleman, or herself a lady, within the city of Barchester, and a circle of two miles round it, was included.   Tickets were sent to all the diocesan clergy, and also to many other persons of priestly note, of whose absence the bishop, or at least the bishop's wife, felt tolerably confident.   It was intended, however, to be a thronged and noticeable affair, and preparations were made for receiving some hundreds.

And now there arose considerable agitation among the Grantlyites whether or no they would attend the episcopal bidding.   The first feeling with them all was to send the briefest excuses both for themselves and their wives and daughters.   But by degrees policy prevailed over passion.   The archdeacon perceived that he would be making a false step if he allowed the cathedral clergy to give the bishop just ground of umbrage.   They all met in conclave and agreed to go.   They would show that they were willing to respect the office, much as they might dislike the man.   They agreed to go.   The old dean would crawl in, if it were but for half an hour.   The chancellor, treasurer, archdeacon, prebendaries, and minor canons would all go, and would all take their wives.   Mr. Harding was especially bidden to do so, resolving in his heart to keep himself far removed from Mrs. Proudie.   And Mrs. Bold was determined to go, though assured by her father that

there was no necessity for such a sacrifice on her part.
When all Barchester was to be there, neither Eleanor
nor Mary Bold understood why they should stay away.
Had they not been invited separately? and had not a
separate little note from the chaplain, couched in the
most respectful language, been enclosed with the huge
episcopal card?

And the Stanhopes would be there, one and all.
Even the lethargic mother would so far bestir herself
on such an occasion. They had only just arrived. The
card was at the residence waiting for them; and what
better opportunity could they have of showing themselves to the Barchester world? Some few old friends,
such as the archdeacon and his wife, had called, and
had found the doctor and his eldest daughter; but the
élite of the family were not yet known.

The doctor indeed wished in his heart to prevent
the signora from accepting the bishop's invitation; but
she herself had fully determined that she would accept
it. If her father was ashamed of having his daughter
carried into a bishop's palace, she had no such
feeling.

"Indeed, I shall," she had said to her sister who
had gently endeavoured to dissuade her, by saying that
the company would consist wholly of parsons and parson's wives. "Parsons, I suppose, are much the same
as other men, if you strip them of their black coats;
and as to their wives, I dare say they won't trouble me.
You may tell papa I don't at all mean to be left at
home."

Papa was told, and felt that he could do nothing
but yield. He also felt that it was useless for him now
to be ashamed of his children. Such as they were,

they had become such under his auspices; as he had made his bed, so he must lie upon it; as he had sown his seed, so must he reap his corn. He did not indeed utter such reflections in such language, but such was the gist of his thoughts. It was not because Madeline was a cripple that he shrank from seeing her make one of the bishop's guests; but because he knew that she would practise her accustomed lures, and behave herself in a way that could not fail of being distasteful to the propriety of Englishmen. These things had annoyed but not shocked him in Italy. There they had shocked no one; but here in Barchester, here among his fellow parsons, he was ashamed that they should be seen. Such had been his feelings, but he repressed them. What if his brother clergymen were shocked! They could not take from him his preferment because the manners of his married daughter were too free.

La Signora Neroni had, at any rate, no fear that she would shock anybody. Her ambition was to create a sensation, to have parsons at her feet, seeing that the manhood of Barchester consisted mainly of parsons, and to send, if possible, every parson's wife home with a green fit of jealousy. None could be too old for her, and hardly any too young. None too sanctified, and none too worldly. She was quite prepared to entrap the bishop himself, and then to turn up her nose at the bishop's wife. She did not doubt of success, for she had always succeeded; but one thing was absolutely necessary, she must secure the entire use of a sofa.

The card sent to Dr. and Mrs. Stanhope and family, had been so sent in an envelope, having on the cover Mr. Slope's name. The signora soon learnt that Mrs.

Proudie was not yet at the palace, and that the chaplain was managing everything. It was much more in her line to apply to him than to the lady, and she accordingly wrote him the prettiest little billet in the world. In five lines she explained everything, declared how impossible it was for her not to be desirous to make the acquaintance of such persons as the Bishop of Barchester and his wife, and she might add also of Mr. Slope, depicted her own grievous state, and concluded by being assured that Mrs. Proudie would forgive her extreme hardihood in petitioning to be allowed to be carried to a sofa. She then enclosed one of her beautiful cards. In return she received as polite an answer from Mr. Slope—a sofa should be kept in the large drawing-room, immediately at the top of the grand stairs, especially for her use.

And now the day of the party had arrived. The bishop and his wife came down from town, only on the morning of the eventful day, as behoved such great people to do; but Mr. Slope had toiled day and night to see that everything should be in right order. There had been much to do. No company had been seen in the palace since heaven knows when. New furniture had been required, new pots and pans, new cups and saucers, new dishes and plates. Mrs. Proudie had at first declared that she would condescend to nothing so vulgar as eating and drinking; but Mr. Slope had talked, or rather written her out of economy! Bishops should be given to hospitality, and hospitality meant eating and drinking. So the supper was conceded; the guests, however, were to stand as they consumed it.

There were four rooms opening into each other on the first floor of the house, which were denominated the drawing-rooms, the reception room, and Mrs. Proudie's boudoir. In olden days one of these had been Bishop Grantly's bed-room, and another his common sitting room and study. The present bishop, however, had been moved down into a back parlour, and had been given to understand, that he could very well receive his clergy in the dining-room, should they arrive in too large a flock to be admitted into his small sanctum. He had been unwilling to yield, but after a short debate had yielded.

Mrs. Proudie's heart beat high as she inspected her suite of rooms. They were really very magnificent, or at least would be so by candlelight; and they had nevertheless been got up with commendable economy. Large rooms when full of people and full of light look well, because they are large, and are full, and are light. Small rooms are those which require costly fittings and rich furniture. Mrs. Proudie knew this, and made the most of it; she had therefore a huge gas lamp with a dozen burners hanging from each of the ceilings.

People were to arrive at ten, supper was to last from twelve till one, and at half-past one every body was to be gone. Carriages were to come in at the gate in the town and depart at the gate outside. They were desired to take up at a quarter before one. It was managed excellently, and Mr. Slope was invaluable.

At half-past nine the bishop and his wife and their three daughters entered the great reception room, and very grand and very solemn they were. Mr. Slope was down stairs giving the last orders about the wine. He well understood that curates and country vicars

with their belongings did not require so generous an
article as the dignitaries of the close. There is a useful
gradation in such things, and Marsala at 20*s* a dozen
did very well for the exterior supplementary tables in
the corner.

"Bishop," said the lady, as his lordship sat himself
down, "don't sit on that sofa, if you please; it is to
be kept separate for a lady."

The bishop jumped up and seated himself on a
cane-bottomed chair. "*A* lady?" he inquired meekly;
"do you mean one particular lady, my dear?"

"Yes, Bishop, one particular lady," said his wife,
disdaining to explain.

"She has got no legs, papa," said the youngest
daughter, tittering.

"No legs!" said the bishop, opening his eyes.

"Nonsense, Netta, what stuff you talk," said Olivia.
"She has got legs, but she can't use them. She has
always to be kept lying down, and three or four men
carry her about everywhere."

"Laws, how odd!" said Augusta. "Always carried
about by four men! I'm sure I shouldn't like it. Am
I right behind, mamma? I feel as if I was open;"
and she turned her back to her anxious parent.

"Open! to be sure you are," said she, "and a yard
of petticoat strings hanging out. I don't know why I
pay such high wages to Mrs. Richards, if she can't
take the trouble to see whether or no you are fit to be
looked at," and Mrs. Proudie poked the strings here,
and twitched the dress there, and gave her daughter
a shove and a shake, and then pronounced it all
right.

"But," rejoined the bishop, who was dying with

curiority, about the mysterious lady and her legs, "who is it that is to have the sofa? What's her name, Netta?"

A thundering rap at the front door interrupted the conversation. Mrs. Proudie stood up and shook herself gently, and touched her cap on each side as she looked in the mirror. Each of the girls stood on tiptoe, and re-arranged the bows on their bosoms; and Mr. Slope rushed up stairs three steps at a time.

"But who is it, Netta?" whispered the bishop to his youngest daughter.

"La Signora Madeline Vesey Neroni," whispered back the daughter; "and mind you don't let any one sit upon the sofa."

"La Signora Madeline Vicinironi!" muttered, to himself, the bewildered prelate. Had he been told that the Begum of Oude was to be there, or Queen Pomara of the Western Isles, he could not have been more astonished. La Signora Madeline Vicinironi, who, having no legs to stand on, had bespoken a sofa in his drawing-room!—who could she be? He however could now make no further inquiry, as Dr. and Mrs. Stanhope were announced. They had been sent on out of the way a little before the time, in order that the signora might have plenty of time to get herself conveniently packed into the carriage.

The bishop was all smiles for the prebendary's wife, and the bishop's wife was all smiles for the prebendary. Mr. Slope was presented, and was delighted to make the acquaintance of one of whom he had heard so much. The doctor bowed very low, and then looked as though he could not return the compliment as regarded Mr. Slope, of whom, indeed, he had heard nothing. The doctor, in spite of his long absence, knew an English gentleman when he saw him.

And then the guests came in shoals: Mr. and Mrs. Quiverful and their three grown daughters. Mr. and Mrs. Chadwick and their three daughters. The burly chancellor and his wife and clerical son from Oxford. The meagre little doctor without incumbrance. Mr. Harding with Eleanor and Miss Bold. The dean leaning on a gaunt spinster, his only child now living with him, a lady very learned in stones, ferns, plants, and vermin, and who had written a book about petals. A wonderful woman in her way was Miss Trefoil. Mr. Finnie, the attorney, with his wife, was to be seen, much to the dismay of many who had never met him in a drawing-room before. The five Barchester doctors were all there, and old Scalpen, the retired apothecary and tooth-drawer, who was first taught to consider himself as belonging to the higher orders by the receipt of the bishop's card. Then came the archdeacon and his wife, with their elder daughter Griselda, a slim pale retiring girl of seventeen, who kept close to her mother, and looked out on the world with quiet watchful eyes, one who gave promise of much beauty when time should have ripened it.

And so the rooms became full, and knots were formed, and every new comer paid his respects to my lord and passed on, not presuming to occupy too much of the great man's attention. The archdeacon shook hands very heartily with Doctor Stanhope, and Mrs. Grantly seated herself by the doctor's wife. And Mrs. Proudie moved about with well regulated grace, measuring out the quantity of her favours to the quality of her guests, just as Mr. Slope had been doing with the wine. But the sofa was still empty, and five-and-twenty ladies and five gentlemen had been courteously warned off it by the mindful chaplain.

"Why doesn't she come?" said the bishop to himself. His mind was so preoccupied with the signora, that he hardly remembered how to behave himself *en bishop*.

At last a carriage dashed up to the hall steps with a very different manner of approach from that of any other vehicle that had been there that evening. A perfect commotion took place. The doctor, who heard it as he was standing in the drawing-room, knew that his daughter was coming, and retired into the furthest corner, where he might not see her entrance. Mrs. Proudie perked herself up, feeling that some important piece of business was in hand. The bishop was instinctively aware that La Signora Vicinironi was come at last, and Mr. Slope hurried into the hall to give his assistance.

He was, however, nearly knocked down and trampled on by the cortège that he encountered on the hall steps. He got himself picked up as well as he could, and followed the cortège up stairs. The signora was carried head foremost, her head being the care of her brother and an Italian man servant who was accustomed to the work; her feet were in the care of the lady's maid and the lady's Italian page; and Charlotte Stanhope followed to see that all was done with due grace and decorum. In this manner they climbed easily into the drawing-room, and a broad way through the crowd having been opened, the signora rested safely on her couch. She had sent a servant beforehand to learn whether it was a right or a left hand sofa, for it

required that she should dress accordingly, particularly
as regarded her bracelets.

And very becoming her dress was. It was white
velvet, without any other garniture than rich white lace
worked with pearls across her bosom, and the same
round the armlets of her dress. Across her brow she
wore a band of red velvet, on the centre of which
shone a magnificent Cupid in mosaic, the tints of whose
wings were of the most lovely azure, and the colour of
his chubby cheeks the clearest pink. On the one arm
which her position required her to expose she wore
three magnificent bracelets, each of different stones.
Beneath her on the sofa, and over the cushion and head
of it, was spread a crimson silk mantle or shawl, which
went under her whole body and concealed her feet.
Dressed as she was and looking as she did, so beautiful and yet so motionless, with the pure brilliancy of
her white dress brought out and strengthened by the
colour beneath it, with that lovely head, and those
large bold bright staring eyes, it was impossible that
either man or woman should do other than look at her.

Neither man nor woman for some minutes did do
other.

Her bearers too were worthy of note. The three
servants were Italian, and though perhaps not peculiar
in their own country, were very much so in the palace
at Barchester. The man especially attracted notice,
and created a doubt in the mind of some whether he
were a friend or a domestic. The same doubt was felt
as to Ethelbert. The man was attired in a loose fitting
common black cloth morning coat. He had a jaunty
fat well-pleased clean face, on which no atom of beard
appeared, and he wore round his neck a loose black

silk neckhandkerchief.   The bishop essayed to make him a bow, but the man, who was well-trained, took no notice of him, and walked out of the room quite at his ease, followed by the woman and the boy.

Ethelbert Stanhope was dressed in light blue from head to foot. He had on the loosest possible blue coat, cut square like a shooting coat, and very short. It was lined with silk of azure blue. He had on a blue satin waistcoat, a blue neckhandkerchief which was fastened beneath his throat with a coral ring, and very loose blue trowsers which almost concealed his feet. His soft glossy beard was softer and more glossy than ever.

The bishop who had made one mistake, thought that he also was a servant, and therefore tried to make way for him to pass. But Ethelbert soon corrected the error.

CHAPTER XI.
MRS. PROUDIE'S RECEPTION—CONCLUDED.

"BISHOP OF BARCHESTER, I presume?" said Bertie Stanhope, putting out his hand, frankly; "I am delighted to make your acquaintance. We are in rather close quarters here, a'nt we?"

In truth they were. They had been crowded up behind the head of the sofa: the bishop in waiting to receive his guest, and the other in carrying her; and they now had hardly room to move themselves.

The bishop gave his hand quickly, and made his little studied bow, and was delighted to make———. He couldn't go on, for he did not know whether his friend was a signor, or a count, or a prince.

"My sister really puts you all to great trouble," said Bertie.

"Not at all!" The bishop was delighted to have the opportunity of welcoming the Signora Vicinironi— so at least he said—and attempted to force his way round to the front of the sofa. He had, at any rate, learnt that his strange guests were brother and sister. The man, he presumed, must be Signor Vicinironi,— or count, or prince, as it might be. It was wonderful what good English he spoke. There was just a twang of foreign accent, and no more.

"Do you like Barchester on the whole?" asked Bertie.

The bishop, looking dignified, said that he did like Barchester.

"You've not been here very long, I believe," said Bertie.

"No—not long," said the bishop, and tried again to make his way between the back of the sofa and a heavy rector, who was staring over it at the grimaces of the signora.

"You weren't a bishop before, were you?"

Dr. Proudie explained that this was the first diocese he had held.

"Ah—I thought so," said Bertie; "but you are changed about sometimes, an't you?"

"Translations are occasionally made," said Dr. Proudie; "but not so frequently as in former days."

"They've cut them all down to pretty nearly the same figure, haven't they?" said Bertie.

To this the bishop could not bring himself to make any answer, but again attempted to move the rector.

"But the work, I suppose, is different?" continued

Bertie. "Is there much to do here, at Barchester?" This was said exactly in the tone that a young Admiralty clerk might use in asking the same question of a brother acolyte at the Treasury.

"The work of a bishop of the Church of England," said Dr. Proudie, with considerable dignity, "is not easy. The responsibility which he has to bear is very great indeed."

"Is it?" said Bertie, opening wide his wonderful blue eyes. "Well; I never was afraid of responsibility. I once had thoughts of being a bishop, myself."

"Had thoughts of being a bishop!" said Dr. Prou die, much amazed.

"That is, a parson—a parson first, you know, and a bishop afterwards. If I had once begun, I'd have stuck to it. But, on the whole, I like the Church of Rome the best."

The bishop could not discuss the point, so he remained silent.

"Now, there's my father," continued Bertie; "he hasn't stuck to it. I fancy he didn't like saying the same thing over so often. By the bye, Bishop, have you seen my father?"

The bishop was more amazed than ever. Had he seen his father? "No," he replied; "he had not yet had the pleasure: he hoped he might;" and, as he said so, he resolved to bear heavy on that fat, immovable rector, if ever he had the power of doing so.

"He's in the room somewhere," said Bertie, "and he'll turn up soon. By the bye, do you know much about the Jews?"

At last the bishop saw a way out. "I beg your pardon," said he; "but I'm forced to go round the room."

"Well—I believe I'll follow in your wake," said Bertie. "Terribly hot—isn't it?" This he addressed to the fat rector with whom he had brought himself into the closest contact. "They've got this sofa into the worst possible part of the room; suppose we move it. Take care, Madeline."

The sofa had certainly been so placed that those who were behind it found great difficulty in getting out;—there was but a narrow gangway, which one person could stop. This was a bad arrangement, and one which Bertie thought it might be well to improve.

"Take care, Madeline," said he; and turning to the fat rector, added, "Just help me with a slight push."

The rector's weight was resting on the sofa, and unwittingly lent all its impetus to accelerate and increase the motion which Bertie intentionally originated. The sofa rushed from its moorings, and ran half way into the middle of the room. Mrs. Proudie was standing with Mr. Slope in front of the signora, and had been trying to be condescending and sociable; but she was not in the very best of tempers; for she found that, whenever she spoke to the lady, the lady replied by speaking to Mr. Slope. Mr. Slope was a favourite, no doubt; but Mrs. Proudie had no idea of being less thought of than the chaplain. She was beginning to be stately, stiff, and offended, when unfortunately the castor of the sofa, caught itself in her lace train, and carried away there is no saying how much of her garniture. Gathers were heard to go, stitches to crack, plaits to fly open, flounces were seen to fall, and breadths to expose themselves;—a long ruin of rent lace disfigured the carpet, and still clung to the vile wheel on which the sofa moved.

So, when a granite battery is raised, excellent to the eyes of warfaring men, is its strength and symmetry admired. It is the work of years. Its neat embrasures, its finished parapets, its casemated stories, show all the skill of modern science. But, anon, a small spark is applied to the treacherous fusee—a cloud of dust arises to the heavens—and then nothing is to be seen but dirt and dust and ugly fragments.

We know what was the wrath of Juno when her beauty was despised. We know too what storms of passion even celestial minds can yield. As Juno may have looked at Paris on Mount Ida, so did Mrs. Proudie look on Ethelbert Stanhope when he pushed the leg of the sofa into her lace train.

"Oh, you idiot, Bertie!" said the signora, seeing what had been done, and what were to be the consequences.

"Idiot!" re-echoed Mrs. Proudie, as though the word were not half strong enough to express the required meaning; "I'll let him know——;" and then looking round to learn, at a glance, the worst, she saw that at present it behoved her to collect the scattered *débris* of her dress.

Bertie, when he saw what he had done, rushed over the sofa, and threw himself on one knee before the offended lady. His object, doubtless, was to liberate the torn lace from the castor; but he looked as though he were imploring pardon from a goddess.

"Unhand it, sir!" said Mrs. Proudie. From what scrap of dramatic poetry she had extracted the word cannot be said; but it must have rested on her memory, and now seemed opportunely dignified for the occasion.

"I'll fly to the looms of the fairies to repair the

damage, if you'll only forgive me," said Ethelbert, still on his knees.

"Unhand it, sir!" said Mrs. Proudie, with redoubled emphasis, and all but furious wrath. This allusion to the fairies was a direct mockery, and intended to turn her into ridicule. So at least it seemed to her. "Unhand it, sir!" she almost screamed.

"It's not me; it's the cursed sofa," said Bertie, looking imploringly in her face, and holding up both his hands to show that he was not touching her belongings, but still remaining on his knees.

Hereupon the signora laughed; not loud, indeed, but yet audibly. And as the tigress bereft of her young will turn with equal anger on any within reach, so did Mrs. Proudie turn upon her female guest.

"Madam!" she said—and it is beyond the power of prose to tell of the fire which flashed from her eyes.

The signora stared her full in the face for a moment, and then turning to her brother said, playfully, "Bertie, you idiot, get up."

By this time the bishop, and Mr. Slope, and her three daughters were around her, and had collected together the wide ruins of her magnificence. The girls fell into circular rank behind their mother, and thus following her and carrying out the fragments, they left the reception-rooms in a manner not altogether devoid of dignity. Mrs. Proudie had to retire and re-array herself.

As soon as the constellation had swept by, Ethelbert rose from his knees, and turning with mock anger to the fat rector, said: "After all it was your doing, sir—not mine. But perhaps you are waiting for preferment, and so I bore it."

Whereupon there was a laugh against the fat rector, in which both the bishop and the chaplain joined; and thus things got themselves again into order.

"Oh! my lord, I am so sorry for this accident," said the signora, putting out her hand so as to force the bishop to take it. "My brother is so thoughtless. Pray sit down, and let me have the pleasure of making your acquaintance. Though I am so poor a creature as to want a sofa, I am not so selfish as to require it all." Madeline could always dispose herself so as to make room for a gentleman, though, as she declared, the crinoline of her lady friends was much too bulky to be so accommodated.

"It was solely for the pleasure of meeting you that I have had myself dragged here," she continued. "Of course, with your occupation, one cannot even hope that you should have time to come to us, that is, in the way of calling. And at your English dinner-parties all is so dull and so stately. Do you know, my lord, that in coming to England my only consolation has been the thought that I should know you;" and she looked at him with the look of a she-devil.

The bishop, however, thought that she looked very like an angel, and accepting the proffered seat, sat down beside her. He uttered some platitude as to his deep obligation for the trouble she had taken, and wondered more and more who she was.

"Of course you know my sad story?" she continued.

The bishop didn't know a word of it. He knew, however, or thought he knew, that she couldn't walk into a room like other people, and so made the most of that. He put on a look of ineffable distress, and said that he was aware how God had afflicted her.

The signora just touched the corner of her eyes
with the most lovely of pocket-handkerchiefs. Yes, she
said—she had been sorely tried—tried, she thought,
beyond the common endurance of humanity; but while
her child was left to her, everything was left. "Oh!
my lord," she exclaimed, "you must see that infant—
the last bud of a wondrous tree; you must let a mother
hope that you will lay your holy hands on her innocent
head, and consecrate her for female virtues. May I
hope it?" said she, looking into the bishop's eye, and
touching the bishop's arm with her hand.

The bishop was but a man, and said she might.
After all, what was it but a request that he would confirm her daughter?—a request, indeed, very unnecessary to make, as he should do so as a matter of course,
if the young lady came forward in the usual way.

"The blood of Tiberius," said the signora, in all
but a whisper; "the blood of Tiberius flows in her
veins. She is the last of the Neros!"

The bishop had heard of the last of the Visigoths,
and had floating in his brain some indistinct idea of
the Mohicans, but to have the last of the Neros thus
brought before him for a blessing was very staggering.
Still he liked the lady: she had a proper way of thinking, and talked with more propriety than her brother.
But who were they? It was now quite clear that that
blue madman with the silky beard was not a Prince
Vicinironi. The lady was married, and was of course
one of the Vicinironi's by right of the husband. So
the bishop went on learning.

"When will you see her?" said the signora with
a start.

"See whom?" said the bishop.

"My child," said the mother.

"What is the young lady's age?" asked the bishop.

"She is just seven," said the signora.

"Oh," said the bishop, shaking his head; "she is much too young—very much too young."

"But in sunny Italy you know, we do not count by years," and the signora gave the bishop one of her very sweetest smiles.

"But indeed, she is a great deal too young," persisted the bishop; "we never confirm before——"

"But you might speak to her; you might let her hear from your consecrated lips, that she is not a cast-away because she is a Roman; that she may be a Nero and yet a Christian; that she may owe her black locks and dark cheeks to the blood of the pagan Cæsars, and yet herself be a child of grace; you will tell her this, won't you, my friend?"

The friend said he would, and asked if the child could say her catechism.

"No," said the signora, "I would not allow her to learn lessons such as those in a land ridden over by priests, and polluted by the idolatry of Rome. It is here, here in Barchester, that she must first be taught to lisp those holy words. Oh, that you could be her instructor!"

Now, Dr. Proudie certainly liked the lady, but, seeing that he was a bishop, it was not probable that he was going to instruct a little girl in the first rudiments of her catechism; so he said he'd send a teacher.

"But you'll see her, yourself, my lord?"

The bishop said he would, but where should he call.

"At papa's house," said the signora, with an air of some little surprise at the question.

The bishop actually wanted the courage to ask her who was her papa; so he was forced at last to leave her without fathoming the mystery. Mrs. Proudie, in her second best, had now returned to the rooms, and her husband thought it as well that he should not remain in too close conversation with the lady whom his wife appeared to hold in such slight esteem. Presently he came across his youngest daughter.

"Netta," said he, "do you know who is the father of that Signora Vicinironi?"

"It isn't Vicinironi, papa," said Netta; "but Vesey Neroni, and she's Doctor Stanhope's daughter. But I must go and do the civil to Griselda Grantly; I declare nobody has spoken a word to the poor girl this evening."

Dr. Stanhope! Dr. Vesey Stanhope! Dr. Vesey Stanhope's daughter, of whose marriage with a dissolute Italian scamp he now remembered to have heard something! And that impertinent blue cub who examined him as to his episcopal bearings was old Stanhope's son, and the lady who had entreated him to come and teach her child the catechism was old Stanhope's daughter! the daughter of one of his own prebendaries! As these things flashed across his mind, he was nearly as angry as his wife had been. Nevertheless, he could not but own that the mother of the last of the Neros was an agreeable woman.

Dr. Proudie tripped out into the adjoining room, in which were congregated a crowd of Grantlyite clergymen, among whom the archdeacon was standing pre-eminent, while the old dean was sitting nearly buried in a huge arm-chair by the fire-place. The bishop was very anxious to be gracious, and, if possible, to diminish the bitterness which his chaplain had occasioned.   Let Mr. Slope do the *fortiter in re*, he himself would pour in the *suaviter in modo*.

"Pray don't stir, Mr. Dean, pray don't stir," he said, as the old man essayed to get up: "I take it as a great kindness, your coming to such an *omnium gatherum* as this.   But we have hardly got settled yet, and Mrs. Proudie has not been able to see her friends as she would wish to do.   Well, Mr. Archdeacon, after all, we have not been so hard upon you at Oxford."

"No," said the archdeacon; "you've only drawn our teeth and cut out our tongues; you've allowed us still to breathe and swallow."

"Ha, ha, ha!" laughed the bishop; "it's not quite so easy to cut out the tongue of an Oxford magnate, —and as for teeth,—ha, ha, ha!   Why, in the way we've left the matter, it's very odd if the heads of colleges don't have their own way quite as fully as when the hebdomadal board was in all its glory; what do you say, Mr. Dean?"

"An old man, my lord, never likes changes," said the dean.

"You must have been sad bunglers if it is so," said the archdeacon; "and indeed, to tell the truth, I think you have bungled it.   At any rate, you must own this; you have not done the half what you boasted you would do."

"Now, as regards your system of professors——" began the chancellor slowly.   He was never destined to get beyond such beginning.

"Talking of professors," said a soft clear voice, close behind the chancellor's elbow; "how much you

Englishmen might learn from Germany; only you are
all too proud."

The bishop looking round, perceived that that
abominable young Stanhope had pursued him. The
dean stared at him, as though he were some unearthly
apparition; so also did two or three prebendaries and
minor canons. The archdeacon laughed.

"The German professors are men of learning,"
said Mr. Harding, "but———"

"German professors!" groaned out the chancellor,
as though his nervous system had received a shock
which nothing but a week of Oxford air could cure.

"Yes," continued Ethelbert; not at all understanding
why a German professor should be contemptible in the
eyes of an Oxford don. "Not but what the name is
best earned at Oxford. In Germany the professors do
teach; at Oxford, I believe they only profess to do so,
and sometimes not even that. You'll have those uni-
versities of yours about your ears soon, if you don't
consent to take a lesson from Germany."

There was no answering this. Dignified clergymen
of sixty years of age could not condescend to discuss
such a matter with a young man with such clothes
and such a beard.

"Have you got good water out at Plumstead, Mr.
Archdeacon?" said the bishop by way of changing the
conversation.

"Pretty good," said Dr. Grantly.

"But by no means so good as his wine, my lord!"
said a witty minor canon.

"Nor so generally used," said another; "that is for
inward application."

"Ha, ha, ha!" laughed the bishop, "a good cellar of wine is a very comfortable thing in a house."

"Your German professors, sir, prefer beer, I believe," said the sarcastic little meagre prebendary.

"They don't think much of either," said Ethelbert; "and that perhaps accounts for their superiority. Now the Jewish professor——"

The insult was becoming too deep for the spirit of Oxford to endure, so the archdeacon walked off one way and the chancellor another, followed by their disciples, and the bishop and the young reformer were left together on the hearth-rug.

"I was a Jew once myself," began Bertie.

The bishop was determined not to stand another examination, or be led on any terms into Palestine; so he again remembered that he had to do something very particular, and left young Stanhope with the dean. The dean did not get the worst of it, for Ethelbert gave him a true account of his remarkable doings in the Holy Land.

"Oh, Mr. Harding," said the bishop, overtaking the *ci-devant* warden; "I wanted to say one word about the hospital. You know, of course, that it is to be filled up."

Mr. Harding's heart beat a little, and he said that he had heard so.

"Of course," continued the bishop; "there can be only one man whom I could wish to see in that situation. I don't know what your own views may be, Mr. Harding——"

"They are very simply told, my lord," said the other; "to take the place if it be offered me, and to put up with the want of it should another man get it."

9 *

The bishop professed himself delighted to hear it;
Mr. Harding might be quite sure that no other man
would get it. There were some few circumstances
which would in a slight degree change the nature of
the duties. Mr. Harding was probably aware of this,
and would, perhaps, not object to discuss the matter
with Mr. Slope. It was a subject to which Mr. Slope
had given a good deal of attention.

Mr. Harding felt, he knew not why, oppressed and
annoyed. What could Mr. Slope do to him? He knew
that there were to be changes. The nature of them
must be communicated to the warden through somebody, and through whom so naturally as the bishop's
chaplain. 'Twas thus he tried to argue himself back
to an easy mind, but in vain.

Mr. Slope in the mean time had taken the seat
which the bishop had vacated on the signora's sofa,
and remained with that lady till it was time to mar-
shal the folk to supper. Not with contented eyes had
Mrs. Proudie seen this. Had not this woman laughed
at her distress, and had not Mr. Slope heard it? Was
she not an intriguing Italian woman, half wife and
half not, full of affectation, airs, and impudence? Was
she not horribly bedizened with velvet and pearls, with
velvet and pearls, too, which had not been torn off her
back? Above all, did she not pretend to be more
beautiful than her neighbours? To say that Mrs.
Proudie was jealous would give a wrong idea of her
feelings. She had not the slightest desire that Mr. Slope
should be in love with herself. But she desired the
incense of Mr. Slope's spiritual and temporal services,
and did not choose that they should be turned out of
their course to such an object as Signora Neroni. She

considered also that Mr. Slope ought in duty to hate the signora; and it appeared from his manner that he was very far from hating her.

"Come, Mr. Slope," she said, sweeping by, and looking all that she felt; "can't you make yourself useful? Do pray take Mrs. Grantly down to supper."

Mrs. Grantly heard and escaped. The words were hardly out of Mrs. Proudie's mouth, before the intended victim had stuck her hand through the arm of one of her husband's curates, and saved herself. What would the archdeacon have said had he seen her walking down stairs with Mr. Slope?

Mr. Slope heard also, but was by no means so obedient as was expected. Indeed, the period of Mr. Slope's obedience to Mrs. Proudie was drawing to a close. He did not wish yet to break with her, nor to break with her at all, if it could be avoided. But he intended to be master in that palace, and as she had made the same resolution it was not improbable that they might come to blows.

Before leaving the signora he arranged a little table before her, and begged to know what he should bring her. She was quite indifferent, she said—nothing—anything. It was now she felt the misery of her position, now that she must be left alone. Well, a little chicken, some ham, and a glass of champagne.

Mr. Slope had to explain, not without blushing for his patron, that there was no champagne.

Sherry would do just as well. And then Mr. Slope descended with the learned Miss Trefoil on his arm. Could she tell him, he asked, whether the ferns of Barsetshire were equal to those of Cumberland? His strongest worldly passion was, for ferns—and before she could answer him he left her wedged between the door and the sideboard. It was fifty minutes before she escaped, and even then unfed.

"You are not leaving us, Mr. Slope," said the watchful lady of the house, seeing her slave escaping towards the door, with stores of provisions held high above the heads of the guests.

Mr. Slope explained that the Signora Neroni was in want of her supper.

"Pray, Mr. Slope, let her brother take it to her," said Mrs. Proudie, quite out loud. "It is out of the question that you should be so employed. Pray, Mr. Slope, oblige me; I am sure Mr. Stanhope will wait upon his sister."

Ethelbert was most agreeably occupied in the furthest corner of the room, making himself both useful and agreeable to Mrs. Proudie's youngest daughter.

"I couldn't get out, madam, if Madeline were starving for her supper," said he; "I'm physically fixed, unless I could fly."

The lady's anger was increased by seeing that her daughter also had gone over to the enemy; and when she saw, that in spite of her remonstrances, in the teeth of her positive orders, Mr. Slope went off to the drawing-room, the cup of her indignation ran over, and she could not restrain herself. "Such manners I never saw," she said, muttering. "I cannot, and will not permit it;" and then, after fussing and fuming for a few minutes, she pushed her way through the crowd, and followed Mr. Slope.

When she reached the room above, she found it absolutely deserted, except by the guilty pair. The signora was sitting very comfortably up to her supper, and Mr. Slope was leaning over her and administering to her wants. They had been discussing the merits of Sabbath-day schools, and the lady had suggested that as she could not possibly go to the children, she might be indulged in the wish of her heart by having the children brought to her.

"And when shall it be, Mr. Slope?" said she.

Mr. Slope was saved the necessity of committing himself to a promise by the entry of Mrs. Proudie. She swept close up to the sofa so as to confront the guilty pair, stared full at them for a moment, and then said as she passed on to the next room, "Mr. Slope, his lordship is especially desirous of your attendance below; you will greatly oblige me if you will join him." And so she stalked on.

Mr. Slope muttered something in reply, and prepared to go down stairs. As for the bishop's wanting him, he knew his lady patroness well enough to take that assertion at what it was worth; but he did not wish to make himself the hero of a scene, or to become conspicuous for more gallantry than the occasion required.

"Is she always like this?" said the signora.

"Yes—always—madam," said Mrs. Proudie, returning; "always the same—always equally adverse to impropriety of conduct of every description;" and she stalked back through the room again, following Mr. Slope out of the door.

The signora couldn't follow her, or she certainly would have done so. But she laughed loud, and sent the sound of it ringing through the lobby and down the stairs after Mrs. Proudie's feet. Had she been as active as Grimaldi, she could probably have taken no better revenge.

"Mr. Slope," said Mrs. Proudie, catching the delinquent at the door, "I am surprised that you should leave my company to attend on such a painted Jezebel as that."

"But, she's lame, Mrs. Proudie, and cannot move. Somebody must have waited upon her."

"Lame," said Mrs. Proudie; "I'd lame her if she belonged to me. What business had she here at all? —such impertinence—such affectation."

In the hall and adjacent rooms all manner of cloaking and shawling was going on, and the Barchester folk were getting themselves gone. Mrs. Proudie did her best to smirk at each and every one, as they made their adieux, but she was hardly successful. Her temper had been tried fearfully. By slow degrees, the guests went.

"Send back the carriage quick," said Ethelbert, as Dr. and Mrs. Stanhope took their departure.

The younger Stanhopes were left to the very last, and an uncomfortable party they made with the bishop's family. They all went into the dining room, and then the bishop, observing that "the lady" was alone in the drawing-room, they followed him up. Mrs. Proudie kept Mr. Slope and her daughters in close conversation, resolving that he should not be indulged, nor they polluted. The bishop, in mortal dread of Bertie and the Jews, tried to converse with Charlotte Stanhope about the climate of Italy. Bertie and the signora had no resource but in each other.

"Did you get your supper, at last, Madeline?" said the impudent or else mischievous young man.

"Oh, yes," said Madeline; "Mr. Slope was so very kind as to bring it me. I fear, however, he put himself to more inconvenience than I wished."

Mrs. Proudie looked at her, but said nothing. The meaning of her look might have been thus translated: "If ever you find yourself within these walls again, I'll give you leave to be as impudent and affected, and as mischievous as you please."

At last the carriage returned with the three Italian servants, and La Signora Madeline Vesey Neroni was carried out, as she had been carried in.

The lady of the palace retired to her chamber by no means contented with the result of her first grand party at Barchester.

CHAPTER XII.
SLOPE VERSUS HARDING.

Two or three days after the party, Mr. Harding received a note, begging him to call on Mr. Slope, at the palace, at an early hour the following morning. There was nothing uncivil in the communication, and yet the tone of it was thoroughly displeasing. It was as follows:

"My dear Mr. Harding,—Will you favour me by calling on me at the palace to-morrow morning at 9.30 A.M. The bishop wishes me to speak to you touching the hospital. I hope you will excuse my naming so early an hour. I do so as my time is greatly occupied. If, however, it is positively inconvenient to you, I will change it to 10. You will, perhaps, be kind enough to let me have a note in reply.

        "Believe me to be,
            "My dear Mr. Harding,
                "Your assured friend,
                    "OBH. SLOPE.
" The Palace, Monday morning,
  "20th August, 185—."

Mr. Harding neither could nor would believe anything of the sort; and he thought, moreover, that Mr. Slope was rather impertinent to call himself by such a name. His assured friend, indeed! How many assured friends generally fall to the lot of a man in this world? And by what process are they made? and how much of such process had taken place as yet between Mr. Harding and Mr. Slope? Mr. Harding could not help asking himself these questions as he read and re-read the note before him. He answered it, however, as follows:

"Dear Sir,—I will call at the palace to-morrow at 9.30 A.M. as you desire.

              "Truly yours,
                "S. HARDING.
" High Street, Barchester, Monday."

And on the following morning, punctually at half-past nine, he knocked at the palace door, and asked for Mr. Slope.

The bishop had one small room allotted to him on the groundfloor, and Mr. Slope had another. Into this latter Mr. Harding was shown, and asked to sit down. Mr. Slope was not yet there. The ex-warden stood up at the window looking into the garden, and could not help thinking how very short a time had passed since the whole of that house had been open to him, as though he had been a child of the family, born and bred in it. He remembered how the old servants used to smile as they opened the door to him; how the familiar butler would say, when he had been absent a few hours longer than usual, "A sight of you, Mr. Harding, is good for sore eyes;" how the fussy house-keeper would swear that he couldn't have dined, or couldn't have breakfasted, or couldn't have lunched. And then, above all, he remembered the pleasant gleam of inward satisfaction which always spread itself over the old bishop's face, whenever his friend entered his room.

A tear came into each eye as he reflected that all this was gone. What use would the hospital be to him now? He was alone in the world, and getting old; he would soon, very soon have to go, and leave it all, as his dear old friend had gone;—go, and leave the hospital, and his accustomed place in the cathedral, and his haunts and pleasures, to younger and perhaps wiser men. That chanting of his!—perhaps, in truth, the time for it had gone by. He felt as though the world were sinking from his feet; as though this, this was the time for him to turn with confidence to those hopes which he had preached with confidence to others. "What," said he to himself, "can a man's religion be worth, if it does not support him against the natural melancholy of declining years?" And, as he looked out through his dimmed eyes into the bright parterres of the bishop's garden, he felt that he had the support which he wanted.

Nevertheless, he did not like to be thus kept waiting. If Mr. Slope did not really wish to see him at half-past nine o'clock, why force him to come away from his lodgings with his breakfast in his throat? To tell the truth, it was policy on the part of Mr. Slope. Mr. Slope had made up his mind that Mr. Harding should either accept the hospital with abject submission, or else refuse it altogether; and had calculated that he would probably be more quick to do the latter, if he could be got to enter upon the subject in an ill-humour. Perhaps Mr. Slope was not altogether wrong in his calculation.

It was nearly ten when Mr. Slope hurried into the room, and, muttering something about the bishop and diocesan duties, shook Mr. Harding's hand ruthlessly, and begged him to be seated.

Now the air of superiority which this man assumed, did go against the grain of Mr. Harding; and yet he did not know how to resent it. The whole tendency of his mind and disposition was opposed to any contra-assumption of grandeur on his own part, and he hadn't the worldly spirit or quickness necessary to put down insolent pretensions by downright and open rebuke, as the archdeacon would have. There was nothing for Mr. Harding but to submit, and he accordingly did so.

"About the hospital, Mr. Harding?" began Mr. Slope, speaking of it as the head of a college at Cambridge might speak of some sizarship which had to be disposed of.

Mr. Harding crossed one leg over another, and then one hand over the other on the top of them, and looked Mr. Slope in the face; but he said nothing.

"It's to be filled up again," said Mr. Slope. Mr. Harding said that he had understood so.

"Of course, you know, the income will be very much reduced," continued Mr. Slope. "The bishop wished to be liberal, and he therefore told the government that he thought it ought to be put at not less than 450*l*. I think on the whole the bishop was right; for though the services required will not be of a very onerous nature, they will be more so than they were before. And it is, perhaps, well that the clergy immediately attached to the cathedral town should be made as comfortable as the extent of the ecclesiastical means at our disposal will allow. Those are the bishop's ideas, and I must say mine also."

Mr. Harding sat rubbing one hand on the other, but said not a word.

"So much for the income, Mr. Harding. The house will, of course, remain to the warden, as before. It should, however, I think, be stipulated that he should paint inside every seven years, and outside every three years, and be subject to dilapidations, in the event of vacating, either by death or otherwise. But this is a matter on which the bishop must yet be consulted."

Mr. Harding still rubbed his hands, and still sat silent, gazing up into Mr. Slope's unprepossessing face.

"Then, as to the duties," continued he, "I believe, if I am rightly informed, there can hardly be said to have been any duties hitherto," and he gave a sort of half laugh, as though to pass off the accusation in the guise of a pleasantry.

Mr. Harding thought of the happy, easy years he had passed in his old home; of the worn-out, aged men whom he had succoured; of his good intentions; and of his work, which had certainly been of the lightest. He thought of these things doubting for a moment whether he did or did not deserve the sarcasm. He gave his enemy the benefit of the doubt, and did not rebuke him. He merely observed, very tranquilly, and perhaps with too much humility, that the duties of the situation such as they were, had, he believed, been done to the satisfaction of the late bishop.

Mr. Slope again smiled, and this time the smile was intended to operate against the memory of the late bishop, rather than against the energy of the ex-warden; and so it was understood by Mr. Harding. The colour rose to his cheeks, and he began to feel very angry.

"You must be aware, Mr. Harding, that things are a good deal changed in Barchester," said Mr. Slope.

Mr. Harding said that he was aware of it. "And not only in Barchester, Mr. Harding, but in the world at large. It is not only in Barchester that a new man is carrying out new measures and casting away the useless rubbish of past centuries. The same thing is going on throughout the country. Work is now required from every man who receives wages; and they who have to superintend the doing of work, and the paying of wages, are bound to see that this rule is carried out. New men, Mr. Harding, are now needed, and are now forthcoming in the church, as well as in other professions."

All this was wormwood to our old friend. He had never rated very high his own abilities or activity; but all the feelings of his heart were with the old clergy, and any antipathies of which his heart was susceptible, were directed against those new, busy, uncharitable, self-lauding men, of whom Mr. Slope was so good an example.

"Perhaps," said he, "the bishop will prefer a new man at the hospital?"

"By no means," said Mr. Slope. "The bishop is very anxious that you should accept the appointment; but he wishes you should understand beforehand what will be the required duties. In the first place, a Sabbath-day school will be attached to the hospital."

"What! for the old men?" asked Mr. Harding.

"No, Mr. Harding, not for the old men, but for the benefit of the children of such of the poor of Barchester as it may suit. The bishop will expect that you shall attend this school, and the teachers shall be under your inspection and care."

Mr. Harding slipped his topmost hand off the other, and began to rub the calf of the leg which was supported.

"As to the old men," continued Mr. Slope, "and the old women who are to form a part of the hospital, the bishop is desirous that you shall have morning and evening service on the premises every Sabbath, and one week-day service; that you shall preach to them once at least on Sundays; and that the whole hospital be always collected for morning and evening prayer. The bishop thinks that this will render it unnecessary that any separate seats in the cathedral should be reserved for the hospital immates."

Mr. Slope paused, but Mr. Harding still said nothing.

"Indeed, it would be difficult to find seats for the

women; and, on the whole, Mr. Harding, I may as
well say at once, that for people of that class the
cathedral service does not appear to me the most useful,—even if it be so for any class of people."

"We will not discuss that, if you please," said Mr.
Harding.

"I am not desirous of doing so; at least, not at the
present moment. I hope, however, you fully understand the bishop's wishes about the new establishment
of the hospital; and if, as I do not doubt, I shall receive from you an assurance that you accord with his
lordship's views, it will give me very great pleasure to
be the bearer from his lordship to you of the presentation to the appointment."

"But if I disagree with his lordship's views?"
asked Mr. Harding.

"But I hope you do not," said Mr. Slope.

"But if I do?" again asked the other.

"If such unfortunately should be the case, which I
can hardly conceive, I presume your own feelings will
dictate to you the propriety of declining the appointment."

"But if I accept the appointment, and yet disagree
with the bishop, what then?"

This question rather bothered Mr. Slope. It was
true that he had talked the matter over with the
bishop, and had received a sort of authority for suggesting to Mr. Harding the propriety of a Sunday
school, and certain hospital services; but he had no
authority for saying that these propositions were to be
made peremptory conditions attached to the appointment. The bishop's idea had been that Mr. Harding
would of course consent, and that the school would be-

come, like the rest of those new establishments in the city, under the control of his wife and his chaplain. Mr. Slope's idea had been more correct. He intended that Mr. Harding should refuse the situation, and that an ally of his own should get it; but he had not conceived the possibility of Mr. Harding openly accepting the appointment, and as openly rejecting the conditions.

"It is not, I presume, probable," said he, "that you will accept from the hands of the bishop a piece of preferment, with a fixed predetermination to disacknowledge the duties attached to it."

"If I become warden," said Mr. Harding, "and neglect my duty, the bishop has means by which he can remedy the grievance."

"I hardly expected such an argument from you, or I may say the suggestion of such a line of conduct," said Mr. Slope, with a great look of injured virtue.

"Nor did I expect such a proposition."

"I shall be glad at any rate to know what answer I am to make to his lordship," said Mr. Slope.

"I will take an early opportunity of seeing his lordship myself," said Mr. Harding.

"Such an arrangement," said Mr. Slope, "will hardly give his lordship satisfaction. Indeed, it is impossible that the bishop should himself see every clergyman in the diocese on every subject of patronage that may arise. The bishop, I believe, did see you on the matter, and I really cannot see why he should be troubled to do so again."   ·

"Do you know, Mr. Slope, how long I have been officiating as a clergyman in this city?" Mr. Slope's wish was now nearly fulfilled. Mr. Harding had become angry, and it was probable that he might commit himself.

"I really do not see what that has to do with the question. You cannot think the bishop would be justified in allowing you to regard as a sinecure a situation that requires an active man, merely because you have been employed for many years in the cathedral."

"But it might induce the bishop to see me, if I asked him to do so. I shall consult my friends in this matter, Mr. Slope; but I mean to be guilty of no subterfuge,—you may tell the bishop that as I altogether disagree with his views about the hospital, I shall decline the situation if I find that any such conditions are attached to it as those you have suggested;" and so saying, Mr. Harding took his hat and went his way.

Mr. Slope was contented. He considered himself at liberty to accept Mr. Harding's last speech as an absolute refusal of the appointment. At least, he so represented it to the bishop and to Mrs. Proudie.

"That is very surprising," said the bishop.

"Not at all," said Mrs. Proudie; "you little know how determined the whole set of them are to withstand your authority."

"But Mr. Harding was so anxious for it," said the bishop.

"Yes," said Mr. Slope, "if he can hold it without the slightest acknowledgment of your lordship's jurisdiction."

"That is out of the question," said the bishop.

"I should imagine it to be quite so," said the chaplain.

"Indeed, I should think so," said the lady.

"I really am sorry for it," said the bishop.

"I don't know that there is much cause for sorrow," said the lady. "Mr. Quiverful is a much more deserving man, more in need of it, and one who will make himself much more useful in the close neighbourhood of the palace."

"I suppose I had better see Quiverful?" said the chaplain.

"I suppose you had," said the bishop.

CHAPTER XIII.
THE RUBBISH CART.

MR. HARDING was not a happy man as he walked down the palace pathway, and stepped out into the close. His preferment and pleasant house were a second time gone from him; but that he could endure. He had been schooled and insulted by a man young enough to be his son; but that he could put up with. He could even draw from the very injuries, which had been inflicted on him, some of that consolation, which we may believe martyrs always receive from the injustice of their own sufferings, and which is generally proportioned in its strength to the extent of cruelty with which martyrs are treated. He had admitted to his daughter that he wanted the comfort of his old home, and yet he could have returned to his lodgings in the High Street, if not with exultation, at least with satisfaction, had that been all. But the venom of the chaplain's harangue had worked into his blood, and sapped the life of his sweet contentment.

"New men are carrying out new measures, and are carting away the useless rubbish of past centuries!"

10*

What cruel words these had been; and how often are they now used with all the heartless cruelty of a Slope! A man is sufficiently condemned if it can only be shown that either in politics or religion he does not belong to some new school established within the last score of years. He may then regard himself as rubbish and expect to be carted away. A man is nothing now unless he has within him a full appreciation of the new era; an era in which it would seem that neither honesty nor truth is very desirable, but in which success is the only touchstone of merit. We must laugh at every thing that is established. Let the joke be ever so bad, ever so untrue to the real principles of joking; nevertheless we must laugh—or else beware the cart. We must talk, think, and live up to the spirit of the times, and write up to it too, if that cacoethes be upon us, or else we are nought. New men and new measures, long credit and few scruples, great success or wonderful ruin, such are now the tastes of Englishmen who know how to live. Alas, alas! under such circumstances Mr. Harding could not but feel that he was an Englishman who did not know how to live. This new doctrine of Mr. Slope and the rubbish cart, new at least at Barchester, sadly disturbed his equanimity.

"The same thing is going on throughout the whole country!" "Work is now required from every man who receives wages!" And had he been living all his life receiving wages, and doing no work? Had he in truth so lived as to be now in his old age justly reckoned as rubbish fit only to be hidden away in some huge dust hole? The school of men to whom he professes to belong, the Grantlys, the Gwynnes, and

the old high set of Oxford divines, are afflicted with
no such self-accusations as these which troubled Mr.
Harding. They, as a rule, are as satisfied with the
wisdom and propriety of their own conduct as can be
any Mr. Slope, or any Dr. Proudie, with his own. But
unfortunately for himself Mr. Harding had little of this
self-reliance. When he heard himself designated as
rubbish by the Slopes of the world, he had no other
resource than to make inquiry within his own bosom
as to the truth of the designation. Alas, alas! the
evidence seemed generally to go against him.

He had professed to himself in the bishop's parlour
that in these coming sources of the sorrow of age, in
these fits of sad regret from which the latter years of
few reflecting men can be free, religion would suffice
to comfort him. Yes, religion could console him for
the loss of any worldly good; but was his religion of
that active sort which would enable him so to repent
of misspent years as to pass those that were left to
him in a spirit of hope for the future? And such repentance itself, is it not a work of agony and of tears?
It is very easy to talk of repentance; but a man has
to walk over hot ploughshares before he can complete
it; to be skinned alive as was St. Bartholomew; to be
stuck full of arrows as was St. Sebastian; to lie
broiling on a gridiron like St. Lorenzo! How if his
past life required such repentance as this? had he the
energy to go through with it?

Mr. Harding after leaving the palace, walked
slowly for an hour or so beneath the shady elms of
the close, and then betook himself to his daughter's
house. He had at any rate made up his mind that
he would go out to Plumstead to consult Dr. Grantly,

and that he would in the first instance tell Eleanor
what had occurred.

And now he was doomed to undergo another
misery. Mr. Slope had forestalled him at the widow's
house. He had called there on the preceding afternoon. He could not, he had said, deny himself the
pleasure of telling Mrs. Bold that her father was about
to return to the pretty house at Hiram's hospital. He
had been instructed by the bishop to inform Mr.
Harding that the appointment would now be made at
once. The bishop was of course only too happy to be
able to be the means of restoring to Mr. Harding the
preferment which he had so long adorned. And then
by degrees Mr. Slope had introduced the subject of
the pretty school which he hoped before long to see
attached to the hospital. He had quite fascinated
Mrs. Bold by his description of this picturesque, useful,
and charitable appendage, and she had gone so far
as to say that she had no doubt her father would
approve, and that she herself would gladly undertake
a class.

Any one who had heard the entirely different tone,
and seen the entirely different manner in which Mr.
Slope had spoken of this projected institution to the
daughter and to the father, could not have failed to
own that Mr. Slope was a man of genius. He said
nothing to Mrs. Bold about the hospital sermons and
services, nothing about the exclusion of the old men
from the cathedral, nothing about dilapidation and
painting, nothing about carting away the rubbish.
Eleanor had said to herself that certainly she did not
like Mr. Slope personally, but that he was a very
active, zealous clergyman, and would no doubt be

useful in Barchester. All this paved the way for much additional misery to Mr. Harding.

Eleanor put on her happiest face as she heard her father on the stairs, for she thought she had only to congratulate him; but directly she saw his face, she knew that there was but little matter for congratulation. She had seen him with the same weary look of sorrow on one or two occasions before, and remembered it well. She had seen him when he first read that attack upon himself in the Jupiter which had ultimately caused him to resign the hospital; and she had seen him also when the archdeacon had persuaded him to remain there against his own sense of propriety and honour. She knew at a glance that his spirit was in deep trouble.

"Oh, papa, what is it?" said she, putting down her boy to crawl upon the floor.

"I came to tell you, my dear," said he, "that I am going out to Plumstead: you won't come with me, I suppose?"

"To Plumstead, papa? Shall you stay there?"

"I suppose I shall, to-night: I must consult the archdeacon about this weary hospital. Ah me! I wish I had never thought of it again."

"Why, papa, what is the matter?"

"I've been with Mr. Slope, my dear, and he isn't the pleasantest companion in the world, at least not to me." Eleanor gave a sort of half blush; but she was wrong if she imagined that her father in any way alluded to her acquaintance with Mr. Slope.

"Well, papa."

"He wants to turn the hospital into a Sunday school and a preaching house; and I suppose he will have his way. I do not feel myself adapted for such an establishment, and therefore, I suppose, I must refuse the appointment."

"What would be the harm of the school, papa?"

"The want of a proper schoolmaster, my dear."

"But that would of course be supplied."

"Mr. Slope wishes to supply it by making me his schoolmaster. But as I am hardly fit for such work, I intend to decline."

"Oh! papa! Mr. Slope doesn't intend that. He was here yesterday, and what he intends——"

"He was here yesterday, was he?" asked Mr. Harding.

"Yes, papa."

"And talking about the hospital?"

"He was saying how glad he would be, and the bishop too, to see you back there again. And then he spoke about the Sunday school; and to tell the truth I agreed with him; and I thought you would have done so too. Mr. Slope spoke of a school; not inside the hospital, but just connected with it, of which you would be the patron and visitor; and I thought you would have liked such a school as that; and I promised to look after it and to take a class—and it all seemed so very——. But, oh, papa! I shall be so miserable if I find I have done wrong."

"Nothing wrong at all, my dear," said he, gently, very gently rejecting his daughter's caress. "There can be nothing wrong in your wishing to make yourself useful; indeed, you ought to do so by all means. Every one must now exert himself who would not choose to go to the wall." Poor Mr. Harding thus attempted in his misery to preach the new doctrine to his child. "Himself or herself, it's all the same," he continued; "you will be quite right, my dear, to do something of this sort; but—"

"Well, papa."

"I am not quite sure that if I were you I would select Mr. Slope for my guide."

"But I never have done so, and never shall."

"It would be very wicked of me to speak evil of him, for to tell the truth I know no evil of him; but I am not quite sure that he is honest. That he is not gentleman-like in his manners, of that I am quite sure."

"I never thought of taking him for my guide, papa."

"As for myself, my dear," continued he, "we know the old proverb—'It's bad teaching an old dog tricks.' I must decline the Sunday school, and shall therefore probably decline the hospital also. But I will first see your brother-in-law." So he took up his hat, kissed the baby, and withdrew, leaving Eleanor in as low spirits as himself.

All this was a great aggravation to his misery. He had so few with whom to sympathise, that he could not afford to be cut off from the one whose sympathy was of the most value to him. And yet it seemed probable that this would be the case. He did not own to himself that he wished his daughter to hate Mr. Slope; yet had she expressed such a feeling there would have been very little bitterness in the rebuke he would have given her for so uncharitable a state of mind. The fact, however, was that she was on friendly terms with Mr. Slope, that she coincided with his views, adhered at once to his plans, and listened with delight to his teaching. Mr. Harding hardly wished his daughter to hate the man, but he would have preferred that to her loving him.

He walked away to the inn to order a fly, went home to put up his carpet bag, and then started for Plumstead. There was, at any rate, no danger that the archdeacon would fraternise with Mr. Slope; but then he would recommend internecine war, public appeals, loud reproaches, and all the paraphernalia of open battle. Now that alternative was hardly more to Mr. Harding's taste than the other.

When Mr. Harding reached the parsonage he found that the archdeacon was out, and would not be home till dinner-time, so he began his complaint to his elder daughter. Mrs. Grantly entertained quite as strong an antagonism to Mr. Slope as did her husband; she was also quite as alive to the necessity of combating the Proudie faction, of supporting the old church interest of the close, of keeping in her own set such of the loaves and fishes as duly belonged to it; and was quite as well prepared as her lord to carry on the battle without giving or taking quarter. Not that she was a woman prone to quarrelling, or ill inclined to live at peace with her clerical neighbours; but she felt, as did the archdeacon, that the presence of Mr. Slope in Barchester was an insult to every one connected with the late bishop, and that his assumed dominion in the diocese was a spiritual injury to her husband. Hitherto people had little guessed how bitter Mrs. Grantly could be. She lived on the best of terms with all the rector's wives around her. She had been popular with all the ladies connected with the close. Though much the wealthiest of the ecclesiastical matrons of the county, she had so managed her affairs that her carriage and horses had given umbrage to none. She had never thrown herself among the county grandees so as to excite the envy of other clergymen's wives. She had never talked too loudly of earls and countesses, or boasted that she gave her governess sixty pounds a year, or her cook seventy. Mrs. Grantly had lived the life of a wise, discreet, peace-making woman; and the people of Barchester were surprised at the amount of military vigour she displayed as general of the feminine Grantlyite forces.

Mrs. Grantly soon learnt that her sister Eleanor had promised to assist Mr. Slope in the affairs of the hospital; and it was on this point that her attention soon fixed itself.

"How can Eleanor endure him?" said she.

"He is a very crafty man," said her father, "and his craft has been successful in making Eleanor think that he is a meek, charitable, good clergyman. God forgive me, if I wrong him, but such is not his true character in my opinion."

"His true character, indeed!" said she, with something approaching to scorn for her father's moderation. "I only hope he won't have craft enough to make Eleanor forget herself and her position."

"Do you mean marry him?" said he, startled out of his usual demeanour by the abruptness and horror of so dreadful a proposition.

"What is there so improbable in it? Of course that would be his own object if he thought he had any chance of success. Eleanor has a thousand a year entirely at her own disposal, and what better fortune

could fall to Mr. Slope's lot than the transferring of
the disposal of such a fortune to himself?"

"But you can't think she likes him, Susan?"

"Why not?" said Susan. "Why shouldn't she like
him? He's just the sort of man to get on with a
woman left as she is, with no one to look after her."

"Look after her!" said the unhappy father; "don't
we look after her?"

"Ah, papa, how innocent you are! Of course it
was to be expected that Eleanor should marry again.
I should be the last to advise her against it, if she
would only wait the proper time, and then marry at
least a gentleman."

"But you don't really mean to say that you suppose Eleanor has ever thought of marrying Mr. Slope?
Why, Mr. Bold has only been dead a year."

"Eighteen months," said his daughter. "But I
don't suppose Eleanor has ever thought about it. It
is very probable, though, that he has, and that he
will try and make her do so; and that he will succeed
too, if we don't take care what we are about."

This was quite a new phase of the affair to poor
Mr. Harding. To have thrust upon him as his son-in-
law, as the husband of his favourite child, the only
man in the world whom he really positively disliked,
would be a misfortune which he felt he would not
know how to endure patiently. But then, could there
be any ground for so dreadful a surmise? In all
worldly matters he was apt to look upon the opinion
of his eldest daughter, as one generally sound and
trustworthy. In her appreciation of character, of
motives, and the probable conduct both of men and
women, she was usually not far wrong. She had early

foreseen the marriage of Eleanor and John Bold; she had at a glance deciphered the character of the new bishop and his chaplain; could it possibly be that her present surmise should ever come forth as true?

"But you don't think that she likes him?" said Mr. Harding again.

"Well, papa, I can't say that I think she dislikes him as she ought to do. Why is he visiting there as a confidential friend, when he never ought to have been admitted inside the house? Why is it that she speaks to him about your welfare and your position, as she clearly has done? At the bishop's party the other night, I saw her talking to him for half an hour at the stretch."

"I thought Mr. Slope seemed to talk to nobody there but that daughter of Stanhope's," said Mr. Harding, wishing to defend his child.

"Oh, Mr. Slope is a cleverer man than you think of, papa, and keeps more than one iron in the fire."

To give Eleanor her due, any suspicion as to the slightest inclination on her part towards Mr. Slope was a wrong to her. She had no more idea of marrying Mr. Slope than she had of marrying the bishop; and the idea that Mr. Slope would present himself as a suitor had never occurred to her. Indeed, to give her her due again, she had never thought about suitors since her husband's death. But nevertheless it was true that she had overcome all that repugnance to the man which was so strongly felt for him by the rest of the Grantly faction. She had forgiven him his sermon. She had forgiven him his low church tendencies, his Sabbath schools, and puritanical observances. She had forgiven his pharisaical arrogance, and even his greasy face and oily vulgar manners. Having agreed to overlook such offences as these, why should she not in time be taught to regard Mr. Slope as a suitor?

And as to him, it must also be affirmed that he was hitherto equally innocent of the crime imputed to him. How it had come to pass that a man whose eyes were generally so widely open to everything around him had not perceived that this young widow was rich as well as beautiful, cannot probably now be explained. But such was the fact. Mr. Slope had ingratiated himself with Mrs. Bold, merely as he had done with other ladies, in order to strengthen his party in the city. He subsequently amended his error; but it was not till after the interview between him and Mr. Harding.

CHAPTER XIV.
THE NEW CHAMPION.

THE archdeacon did not return to the parsonage till close upon the hour of dinner, and there was therefore no time to discuss matters before that important ceremony. He seemed to be in an especial good humour, and welcomed his father-in-law with a sort of jovial earnestness that was usual with him when things on which he was intent were going on as he would have them.

"It's all settled, my dear," said he to his wife as he washed his hands in his dressing-room, while she, according to her wont, sat listening in the bedroom; "Arabin has agreed to accept the living." "He'll be here next week." And the archdeacon scrubbed his hands and rubbed his face with a violent alacrity, which showed that Arabin's coming was a great point gained.

"Will he come here to Plumstead?" said the wife.

"He has promised to stay a month with us," said the archdeacon, "so that he may see what his parish is like. You'll like Arabin very much. He's a gentleman in every respect, and full of humour."

"He's very queer, isn't he?" asked the lady.

"Well—he is a little odd in some of his fancies; but there's nothing about him you won't like. He is as staunch a churchman as there is at Oxford. I really don't know what we should do without Arabin. It's a great thing for me to have him so near me; and if anything can put Slope down, Arabin will do it."

The Reverend Francis Arabin was a fellow of Lazarus, the favoured disciple of the great Dr. Gwynne, a high churchman at all points; so high, indeed, that at one period of his career he had all but toppled over into the cesspool of Rome; a poet and also a polemical writer, a great pet in the common rooms at Oxford, an eloquent clergyman, a droll, odd, humorous, energetic, conscientious man, and, as the archdeacon had boasted of him, a thorough gentleman. As he will hereafter be brought more closely to our notice, it is now only necessary to add, that he had just been presented to the vicarage of St. Ewold by Dr. Grantly, in whose gift as archdeacon the living lay. St. Ewold is a parish lying just without the city of Barchester. The suburbs of the new town, indeed, are partly within its precincts, and the pretty church and parsonage are not much above a mile distant from the city gate.

St. Ewold is not a rich piece of preferment—it is worth some three or four hundred a year at most, and has generally been held by a clergyman attached to the cathedral choir. The archdeacon, however, felt, when the living on this occasion became vacant, that it imperatively behoved him to aid the force of his party with some tower of strength, if any such tower could be got to occupy St. Ewold's. He had discussed the matter with his brethren in Barchester; not in any weak spirit as the holder of patronage to be used for his own or his family's benefit, but as one to whom was committed a trust, on the due administration of which much of the church's welfare might depend. He had submitted to them the name of Mr. Arabin, as though the choice had rested with them all in conclave, and they had unanimously admitted that, if Mr. Arabin would accept St. Ewold's, no better choice could possibly be made.

If Mr. Arabin would accept St. Ewold's! There lay the difficulty. Mr. Arabin was a man standing somewhat prominently before the world, that is, before the Church of England world. He was not a rich man, it is true, for he held no preferment but his fellowship; but he was a man not over anxious for riches, not married of course, and one whose time was greatly taken up in discussing, both in print and on platforms, the privileges and practices of the church to which he belonged. As the archdeacon had done battle for its temporalities, so did Mr. Arabin do battle for its spiritualities; and both had done so conscientiously; that is, not so much each for his own benefit as for that of others.

Holding such a position as Mr. Arabin did, there

was much reason to doubt whether he would consent to become the parson of St. Ewold's, and Dr. Grantly had taken the trouble to go himself to Oxford on the matter. Dr. Gwynne and Dr. Grantly together had succeeded in persuading this eminent divine that duty required him to go to Barchester. There were wheels within wheels in this affair. For some time past Mr. Arabin had been engaged in a tremendous controversy with no less a person than Mr. Slope, respecting the apostolic succession. These two gentlemen had never seen each other, but they had been extremely bitter in print. Mr. Slope had endeavoured to strengthen his cause by calling Mr. Arabin an owl, and Mr. Arabin had retaliated by hinting that Mr. Slope was an infidel. This battle had been commenced in the columns of the daily Jupiter, a powerful newspaper, the manager of which was very friendly to Mr. Slope's view of the case. The matter, however, had become too tedious for the readers of the Jupiter, and a little note had therefore been appended to one of Mr. Slope's most telling rejoinders, in which it had been stated that no further letters from the reverend gentlemen could be inserted except as advertisements.

Other methods of publication were, however, found less expensive than advertisements in the Jupiter; and the war went on merrily. Mr. Slope declared that the main part of the consecration of a clergyman was the self-devotion of the inner man to the duties of the ministry. Mr. Arabin contended that a man was not consecrated at all, had, indeed, no single attribute of a clergyman, unless he became so through the imposition of some bishop's hands who had become a bishop through the imposition of other hands, and so on in a direct line to one of the apostles. Each had repeatedly hung the other on the horns of a dilemma; but neither seemed to be a whit the worse for the hanging and so the war went on merrily.

Whether or no the near neighbourhood of the foe may have acted in any way as an inducement to Mr. Arabin to accept the living of St. Ewold, we will not pretend to say; but it had at any rate been settled in Dr. Gwynne's library, at Lazarus, that he would accept it, and that he would lend his assistance towards driving the enemy out of Barchester, or, at any rate, silencing him while he remained there. Mr. Arabin intended to keep his rooms at Oxford, and to have the assistance of a curate at St. Ewold; but he promised to give as much time as possible to the neighbourhood of Barchester, and from so great a man Dr. Grantly was quite satisfied with such a promise. It was no small part of the satisfaction derivable from such an arrangement that Bishop Proudie would be forced to institute into a living, immediately under his own nose, the enemy of his favourite chaplain.

All through dinner the archdeacon's good humour shone brightly in his face. He ate of the good things heartily, he drank wine with his wife and daughter, he talked pleasantly of his doings at Oxford, told his father-in-law that he ought to visit Dr. Gwynne at Lazarus, and launched out again in praise of Mr. Arabin.

"Is Mr. Arabin married, papa?" asked Griselda.

"No, my dear; the fellow of a college is never married."

"Is he a young man, papa?"

"About forty, I believe," said the archdeacon.

"Oh!" said Griselda. Had her father said eighty, Mr. Arabin would not have appeared to her to be very much older.

When the two gentlemen were left alone over their wine, Mr. Harding told his tale of woe. But even this, sad as it was, did not much diminish the archdeacon's good humour, though it greatly added to his pugnacity.

"He can't do it," said Dr. Grantly over and over again, as his father-in-law explained to him the terms on which the new warden of the hospital was to be appointed; "he can't do it. What he says is not worth the trouble of listening to. He can't alter the duties of the place."

"Who can't?" asked the ex-warden.

"Neither the bishop nor the chaplain, nor yet the bishop's wife, who, I take it, has really more to say to such matters than either of the other two. The whole body corporate of the palace together have no power to turn the warden of the hospital into a Sunday schoolmaster."

"But the bishop has the power to appoint whom he pleases, and—"

"I don't know that; I rather think he'll find he has no such power. Let him try it, and see what the press will say. For once we shall have the popular cry on our side. But Proudie, ass as he is, knows the world too well to get such a hornet's nest about his ears."

Mr. Harding winced at the idea of the press. He had had enough of that sort of publicity, and was unwilling to be shown up a second time either as a monster or as a martyr. He gently remarked that he hoped the newspapers would not get hold of his name

11*

again, and then suggested that perhaps it would be better that he should abandon his object. "I am getting old," said he; "and after all I doubt whether I am fit to undertake new duties."

"New duties!" said the archdeacon: "don't I tell you there shall be no new duties?"

"Or, perhaps, old duties either," said Mr. Harding; "I think I will remain content as I am." The picture of Mr. Slope carting away the rubbish was still present to his mind.

The archdeacon drank off his glass of claret, and prepared himself to be energetic. "I do hope," said he, "that you are not going to be so weak as to allow such a man as Mr. Slope to deter you from doing what you know it is your duty to do. You know it is your duty to resume your place at the hospital now that parliament has so settled the stipend as to remove those difficulties which induced you to resign it. You cannot deny this; and should your timidity now prevent you from doing so, your conscience will hereafter never forgive you;" and as he finished this clause of his speech, he pushed over the bottle to his companion.

"Your conscience will never forgive you," he continued. "You resigned the place from conscientious scruples, scruples which I greatly respected, though I did not share them. All your friends respected them, and you left your old house as rich in reputation as you were ruined in fortune. It is now expected that you will return. Dr. Gwynne was saying only the other day—"

"Dr. Gwynne does not reflect how much older a man I am now than when he last saw me."

"Old—nonsense!" said the archdeacon; "you never thought yourself old till you listened to the impudent trash of that coxcomb at the palace."

"I shall be sixty-five if I live till November," said Mr. Harding.

"And seventy-five, if you live till November ten years," said the archdeacon. "And you bid fair to be as efficient then as you were ten years ago. But for heaven's sake let us have no pretence in this matter. Your plea of old age is only a pretence. But you're not drinking your wine. It is only a pretence. The fact is, you are half afraid of this Slope, and would rather subject yourself to comparative poverty and discomfort, than come to blows with a man who will trample on you, if you let him."

"I certainly don't like coming to blows, if I can help it."

"Nor I neither—but sometimes we can't help it. This man's object is to induce you to refuse the hospital, that he may put some creature of his own into it; that he may show his power, and insult us all by insulting you, whose cause and character are so intimately bound up with that of the chapter. You owe it to us all to resist him in this, even if you have no solicitude for yourself. But surely, for your own sake, you will not be so lily-livered as to fall into this trap which he has baited for you, and let him take the very bread out of your mouth without a struggle."

Mr. Harding did not like being called lily-livered, and was rather inclined to resent it. "I doubt there is any true courage," said he, "in squabbling for money."

"If honest men did not squabble for money, in this wicked world of ours, the dishonest men would get it all; and I do not see that the cause of virtue would be much improved. No,—we must use the means which we have. If we were to carry your argument home, we might give away every shilling of revenue which the church has; and I presume you are not prepared to say that the church would be strengthened by such a sacrifice." The archdeacon filled his glass and then emptied it, drinking with much reverence a silent toast to the well-being and permanent security of those temporalities which were so dear to his soul.

"I think all quarrels between a clergyman and his bishop should be avoided," said Mr. Harding.

"I think so too; but it is quite as much the duty of the bishop to look to that as of his inferior. I tell you what, my friend; I'll see the bishop in this matter, that is, if you will allow me; and you may be sure I will not compromise you. My opinion is, that all this trash about the Sunday-schools and the sermons has originated wholly with Slope and Mrs. Proudie, and that the bishop knows nothing about it. The bishop can't very well refuse to see me, and I'll come upon him when he has neither his wife nor his chaplain by him. I think you'll find that it will end in his sending you the appointment without any condition whatever. And as to the seats in the cathedral, we may safely leave that to Mr. Dean. I believe the fool positively thinks that the bishop could walk away with the cathedral if he pleased."

And so the matter was arranged between them. Mr. Harding had come expressly for advice, and therefore felt himself bound to take the advice given him. He had known, moreover, beforehand, that the archdeacon would not hear of his giving the matter up, and accordingly though he had in perfect good faith put forward his own views, he was prepared to yield.

They therefore went into the drawing-room in good humour with each other, and the evening passed pleasantly in prophetic discussions on the future wars of Arabin and Slope. The frogs and the mice would be nothing to them, nor the angers of Agamemnon and Achilles. How the archdeacon rubbed his hands, and plumed himself on the success of his last move. He could not himself descend into the arena with Slope, but Arabin would have no such scruples. Arabin was exactly the man for such work, and the only man whom he knew that was fit for it.

The archdeacon's good humour and high buoyancy continued till, when reclining on his pillow, Mrs. Grantly commenced to give him her view of the state of affairs at Barchester. And then certainly he was startled. The last words he said that night were as follows:—

"If she does, by heaven I'll never speak to her again. She dragged me into the mire once, but I'll not pollute myself with such filth as that—" And the archdeacon gave a shudder which shook the whole room, so violently was he convulsed with the thought which then agitated his mind.

Now in this matter, the widow Bold was scandalously ill-treated by her relatives. She had spoken to the man three or four times, and had expressed her willingness to teach in a Sunday-school. Such was the full extent of her sins in the matter of Mr. Slope. Poor Eleanor! But time will show.

The next morning Mr. Harding returned to Barchester, no further word having been spoken in his hearing respecting Mr. Slope's acquaintance with his younger daughter. But he observed that the arch-deacon at breakfast was less cordial than he had been on the preceding evening.

CHAPTER XV.
THE WIDOW'S SUITORS.

Mr. SLOPE lost no time in availing himself of the bishop's permission to see Mr. Quiverful, and it was in his interview with this worthy pastor that he first learned that Mrs. Bold was worth the wooing. He rode out to Puddingdale to communicate to the embryo warden the good will of the bishop in his favour, and during the discussion on the matter it was not un-natural that the pecuniary resources of Mr. Harding and his family should become the subject of remark.

Mr. Quiverful, with his fourteen children and his four hundred a year, was a very poor man, and the prospect of this new preferment, which was to be held together with his living, was very grateful to him. To what clergyman so circumstanced would not such a prospect be very grateful? But Mr. Quiverful had long been acquainted with Mr. Harding, and had received kindness at his hands, so that his heart misgave him as he thought of supplanting a friend at the hospital. Nevertheless, he was extremely civil, cring-ingly civil, to Mr. Slope; treated him quite as the great man; entreated this great man to do him the honour to drink a glass of sherry, at which, as it was very poor Marsala, the now pampered Slope turned up his nose; and ended by declaring his extreme obliga-tion to the bishop and Mr. Slope, and his great desire to accept the hospital, if—if it were certainly the case that Mr. Harding had refused it.

What man, as needy as Mr. Quiverful, would have been more disinterested?

"Mr. Harding did positively refuse it," said Mr. Slope, with a certain air of offended dignity, "when he heard of the conditions to which the appointment is now subjected. Of course, you understand, Mr. Quiverful, that the same conditions will be imposed on yourself."

Mr. Quiverful cared nothing for the conditions. He would have undertaken to preach any number of sermons Mr. Slope might have chosen to dictate, and to pass every remaining hour of his Sundays within the walls of a Sunday-school. What sacrifices, or, at any rate, what promises, would have been too much to make for such an addition to his income, and for such a house! But his mind still recurred to Mr. Harding.

"To be sure," said he; "Mr. Harding's daughter is very rich, and why should he trouble himself with the hospital?"

"You mean Mrs. Grantly," said Slope.

"I meant his widowed daughter," said the other. "Mrs. Bold has twelve hundred a year of her own, and I suppose Mr. Harding means to live with her."

"Twelve hundred a year of her own!" said Slope, and very shortly afterwards took his leave, avoiding, as far as it was possible for him to do, any further allusion to the hospital. Twelve hundred a year, said he to himself, as he rode slowly home. If it were the fact that Mrs. Bold had twelve hundred a year of her own, what a fool would he be to oppose her father's return to his old place. The train of Mr. Slope's ideas will probably be plain to all my readers. Why should he not make the twelve hundred a year his

own? and if he did so, would it not be well for him
to have a father-in-law comfortably provided with the
good things of this world? would it not, moreover, be
much more easy for him to gain the daughter, if he
did all in his power to forward the father's views?

These questions presented themselves to him in a
very forcible way, and yet there were many points of
doubt. If he resolved to restore to Mr. Harding his
former place, he must take the necessary steps for
doing so at once; he must immediately talk over the
bishop, quarrel on the matter with Mrs. Proudie whom
he knew he could not talk over, and let Mr. Quiverful
know that he had been a little too precipitate as to
Mr. Harding's positive refusal. That he could effect
all this, he did not doubt; but he did not wish to
effect it for nothing. He did not wish to give way to
Mr. Harding, and then be rejected by the daughter.
He did not wish to lose one influential friend before
he had gained another.

And thus he rode home, meditating many things
in his mind. It occurred to him that Mrs. Bold was
sister-in-law to the archdeacon; and that not even for
twelve hundred a year would he submit to that imperious man. A rich wife was a great desideratum to
him, but success in his profession was still greater;
there were, moreover, other rich women who might be
willing to become wives; and after all, this twelve
hundred a year might, when inquired into, melt away
into some small sum utterly beneath his notice. Then
also he remembered that Mrs. Bold had a son.

Another circumstance also much influenced him,
though it was one which may almost be said to have
influenced him against his will. The vision of the

Signora Neroni was perpetually before his eyes. It would be too much to say that Mr. Slope was lost in love, but yet he thought, and kept continually thinking, that he had never seen so beautiful a woman. He was a man whose nature was open to such impulses, and the wiles of the Italianised charmer had been thoroughly successful in imposing upon his thoughts. We will not talk about his heart: not that he had no heart, but because his heart had little to do with his present feelings. His taste had been pleased, his eyes charmed, and his vanity gratified. He had been dazzled by a sort of loveliness which he had never before seen, and had been caught by an easy, free, voluptuous manner which was perfectly new to him. He had never been so tempted before, and the temptation was now irresistible. He had not owned to himself that he cared for this woman more than for others around him; but yet he thought often of the time when he might see her next, and made, almost unconsciously, little cunning plans for seeing her frequently.

He had called at Dr. Stanhope's house the day after the bishop's party, and then the warmth of his admiration had been fed with fresh fuel. If the signora had been kind in her manner and flattering in her speech when lying upon the bishop's sofa, with the eyes of so many on her, she had been much more so in her mother's drawing-room, with no one present but her sister to repress either her nature or her art. Mr. Slope had thus left her quite bewildered, and could not willingly admit into his brain any scheme, a part of which would be the necessity of his abandoning all further special friendship with this lady.

And so he slowly rode along very meditative.

And here the author must beg it to be remembered that Mr. Slope was not in all things a bad man. His motives, like those of most men, were mixed; and though his conduct was generally very different from that which we would wish to praise, it was actuated perhaps as often as that of the majority of the world by a desire to do his duty. He believed in the religion which he taught, harsh, unpalatable, uncharitable as that religion was. He believed those whom he wished to get under his hoof, the Grantlys and Gwynnes of the church, to be the enemies of that religion. He believed himself to be a pillar of strength, destined to do great things; and with that subtle, selfish, ambiguous sophistry to which the minds of all men are so subject, he had taught himself to think that in doing much for the promotion of his own interests he was doing much also for the promotion of religion. But Mr. Slope had never been an immoral man. Indeed, he had resisted temptations to immorality with a strength of purpose that was creditable to him. He had early in life devoted himself to works which were not compatible with the ordinary pleasures of youth, and he had abandoned such pleasures not without a struggle. It must therefore be conceived that he did not admit to himself that he warmly admired the beauty of a married woman without heartfelt stings of conscience; and to pacify that conscience, he had to teach himself that the nature of his admiration was innocent.

And thus he rode along meditative and ill at ease. His conscience had not a word to say against his choosing the widow and her fortune. That he looked upon as a godly work rather than otherwise; as a deed which, if carried through, would redound to his credit as a Christian. On that side lay no future remorse, no conduct which he might probably have to forget, no inward stings. If it should turn out to be really the fact that Mrs. Bold had twelve hundred a year at her own disposal, Mr. Slope would rather look upon it as a duty which he owed his religion to make himself the master of the wife and the money; as a duty too, in which some amount of self-sacrifice would be necessary. He would have to give up his friendship with the signora, his resistance to Mr. Harding, his antipathy— no, he found on mature self-examination, that he could not bring himself to give up his antipathy to Dr. Grantly. He would marry the lady as the enemy of her brother-in-law if such an arrangement suited her; if not, she must look elsewhere for a husband.

It was with such resolve as this that he reached Barchester. He would at once ascertain what the truth might be as to the lady's wealth, and having done this, he would be ruled by circumstances in his conduct respecting the hospital. If he found that he could turn round and secure the place for Mr. Harding without much self-sacrifice, he would do so; but if not, he would woo the daughter in opposition to the father. But in no case would he succumb to the archdeacon.

He saw his horse taken round to the stable, and immediately went forth to commence his inquiries. To give Mr. Slope his due, he was not a man who ever let much grass grow under his feet.

Poor Eleanor! She was doomed to be the intended victim of more schemes than one.

About the time that Mr. Slope was visiting the vicar of Puddingdale, a discussion took place respecting her charms and wealth at Dr. Stanhope's house in the close.

There had been morning callers there, and people had told some truth and also some falsehood respecting the property which John Bold had left behind him. By degrees the visitors went, and as the doctor went with them, and as the doctor's wife had not made her appearance, Charlotte Stanhope and her brother were left together. He was sitting idly at the table, scrawling caricatures of Barchester notables, then yawning, then turning over a book or two, and evidently at a loss how to kill his time without much labour.

"You haven't done much, Bertie, about getting any orders," said his sister.

"Orders!" said he; "who on earth is there at Barchester to give one orders? Who among the people here could possibly think it worth his while to have his head done into marble?"

"Then you mean to give up your profession," said she.

"No, I don't," said he, going on with some absurd portrait of the bishop. "Look at that, Lotte; isn't it the little man all over, apron and all? I'd go on with my profession at once, as you call it, if the governor would set me up with a studio in London; but as to sculpture at Barchester—I suppose half the people here don't know what a torso means."

"The governor will not give you a shilling to start you in London," said Lotte. "Indeed, he can't give you what would be sufficient, for he has not got it. But you might start yourself very well, if you pleased."

"How the deuce am I to do it?" said he.

"To tell you the truth, Bertie, you'll never make a penny by any profession."

"That's what I often think myself," said he, not in

the least offended. "Some men have a great gift of making money, but they can't spend it. Others can't put two shillings together, but they have a great talent for all sorts of outlay. I begin to think that my genius is wholly in the latter line."

"How do you mean to live then?" asked the sister.

"I suppose I must regard myself as a young raven, and look for heavenly manna; besides, we have all got something when the governor goes."

"Yes—you'll have enough to supply yourself with gloves and boots; that is, if the Jews have not got the possession of it all. I believe they have the most of it already. I wonder, Bertie, at your indifference; that you, with your talents and personal advantages, should never try to settle yourself in life. I look forward with dread to the time when the governor must go. Mother, and Madeline, and I,—we shall be poor enough, but you will have absolutely nothing."

"Sufficient for the day is the evil thereof," said Bertie.

"Will you take my advice?" said his sister.

"*Cela dépend*," said the brother.

"Will you marry a wife with money?"

"At any rate," said he, "I won't marry one without: wives with money a'nt so easy to get now-a-days; the parsons pick them all up."

"And a parson will pick up the wife I mean for you, if you do not look quickly about it; the wife I mean is Mrs. Bold."

"Whew-w-w-w!" whistled Bertie, "a widow!"

"She is very beautiful," said Charlotte.

"With a son and heir all ready to my hand," said Bertie.

"A baby that will very likely die," said Charlotte.

"I don't see that," said Bertie. "But however, he may live for me—I don't wish to kill him; only, it must be owned that a ready-made family is a drawback."

"There is only one after all," pleaded Charlotte.

"And that a very little one, as the maid-servant said," rejoined Bertie.

"Beggars mustn't be choosers, Bertie; you can't have everything."

"God knows I am not unreasonable," said he, "nor yet opinionated; and if you'll arrange it all for me, Lotte, I'll marry the lady. Only mark this; the money must be sure, and the income at my own disposal, at any rate for the lady's life."

Charlotte was explaining to her brother that he must make love for himself if he meant to carry on the matter, and was encouraging him to do so, by warm eulogiums on Eleanor's beauty, when the signora was brought into the drawing-room. When at home, and subject to the gaze of none but her own family, she allowed herself to be dragged about by two persons, and her two bearers now deposited her on her sofa. She was not quite so grand in her apparel as she had been at the bishop's party, but yet she was dressed with much care, and though there was a look of care and pain about her eyes, she was, even by day-light, extremely beautiful.

"Well, Madeline; so I'm going to be married," Bertie began, as soon as the servants had withdrawn.

"There's no other foolish thing left, that you haven't done," said Madeline, "and therefore you are quite right to try that."

"Oh, you think it's a foolish thing, do you?" said

he. "There's Lotte advising me to marry by all means. But on such a subject your opinion ought to be the best; you have experience to guide you."

"Yes, I have," said Madeline, with a sort of harsh sadness in her tone, which seemed to say—What is it to you if I am sad? I have never asked your sympathy.

Bertie was sorry when he saw that she was hurt by what he said, and he came and squatted on the floor close before her face to make his peace with her.

"Come, Mad, I was only joking; you know that. But in sobei earnest, Lotte is advising me to marry. She wants me to marry this Mrs. Bold. She's a widow with lots of tin, a fine baby, a beautiful complexion, and the *George and Dragon* hotel up in the High Street. By Jove, Lotte, if I marry her, I'll keep the public house myself—it's just the life to suit me."

"What?" said Madeline, "that vapid swarthy creature in the widow's cap, who looked as though her clothes had been stuck on her back with a pitchfork!" The signora never allowed any woman to be beautiful.

"Instead of being vapid," said Lotte, "I call her a very lovely woman. She was by far the loveliest woman in the rooms the other night; that is, excepting you, Madeline."

Even the compliment did not soften the asperity of the maimed beauty. "Every woman is charming according to Lotte," she said; "I never knew an eye with so little true appreciation. In the first place, what woman on earth could look well in such a thing as that she had on her head?"

"Of course she wears a widow's cap; but she'll put that off when Bertie marries her."

"I don't see any of course in it," said Madeline.
"The death of twenty husbands should not make me
undergo such a penance.   It is as much a relic of
paganism as the sacrifice of a Hindoo woman at the
burning of her husband's body. If not so bloody, it is
quite as barbarous, and quite as useless."

"But you don't blame her for that," said Bertie.
"She does it because it's the custom of the country.
People would think ill of her if she didn't do it."

"Exactly," said Madeline.   "She is just one of
those English nonentities who would tie her head
up in a bag for three months every summer, if
her mother and her grandmother had tied up their
heads before her. It would never occur to her, to
think whether there was any use in submitting to such
a nuisance."

"It's very hard, in a country like England, for a
young woman to set herself in opposition to prejudices
of that sort," said the prudent Charlotte.

"What you mean is, that it's very hard for a fool
not to be a fool," said Madeline.

Bertie Stanhope had been so much knocked about
the world from his earliest years, that he had not retained much respect for the gravity of English customs;
but even to his mind an idea presented itself, that,
perhaps in a wife, true British prejudice would not in
the long run be less agreeable than Anglo-Italian freedom from restraint. He did not exactly say so, but
he expressed the idea in another way.

"I fancy," said he, "that if I were to die, and
then walk, I should think that my widow looked better
in one of those caps than any other kind of head-
dress."

"Yes—and you'd fancy also that she could do nothing better than shut herself up and cry for you, or else burn herself. But she would think differently. She'd probably wear one of those horrid she-helmets, because she'd want the courage not to do so; but she'd wear it with a heart longing for the time when she might be allowed to throw it off. I hate such shallow false pretences. For my part, I would let the world say what it pleased, and show no grief if I felt none; —and perhaps not, if I did."

"But wearing a widow's cap won't lessen her fortune," said Charlotte.

"Or increase it," said Madeline. "Then why on earth does she do it?"

"But Lotte's object is to make her put it off," said Bertie.

"If it be true that she has got twelve hundred a year quite at her own disposal, and she be not utterly vulgar in her manners, I would advise you to marry her. I dare say she is to be had for the asking; and as you are not going to marry her for love, it doesn't much matter whether she is good-looking or not. As to your really marrying a woman for love, I don't believe *you* are fool enough for that."

"Oh, Madeline!" exclaimed her sister.

"And oh, Charlotte!" said the other.

"You don't mean to say that no man can love a woman unless he be a fool?"

"I mean very much the same thing—that any man who is willing to sacrifice his interest to get possession of a pretty face is a fool. Pretty faces are to be had cheaper than that. I hate your mawkish sentimentality, Lotte. You know as well as I do in what

way husbands and wives generally live together; you
know how far the warmth of conjugal affection can
withstand the trial of a bad dinner, of a rainy day, or
of the least privation which poverty brings with it;
you know what freedom a man claims for himself,
what slavery he would exact from his wife if he could!
And you know also how wives generally obey. Marriage means tyranny on one side and deceit on the
other. I say that a man is a fool to sacrifice his
interests for such a bargain. A woman, too generally,
has no other way of living."

"But Bertie has no other way of living," said
Charlotte.

"Then, in God's name, let him marry Mrs. Bold,"
said Madeline. And so it was settled between them.

But let the gentle-hearted reader be under no ap-
prehension whatsoever. It is not destined that Eleanor
shall marry Mr. Slope or Bertie Stanhope. And here,
perhaps, it may be allowed to the novelist to explain
his views on a very important point in the art of
telling tales. He ventures to reprobate that system
which goes so far to violate all proper confidence
between the author and his readers, by maintaining
nearly to the end of the third volume a mystery as to
the fate of their favourite personage. Nay, more, and
worse than this, is too frequently done. Have not
often the profoundest efforts of genius been used to
baffle the aspirations of the reader, to raise false hopes
and false fears, and to give rise to expectations which
are never to be realised? Are not promises all but
made of delightful horrors, in lieu of which the writer
produces nothing but most commonplace realities in his
final chapter? And is there not a species of deceit in

this to which the honesty of the present age should lend no countenance?

And what can be the worth of that solicitude which a peep into the third volume can utterly dissipate? What the value of those literary charms which are absolutely destroyed by their enjoyment? When we have once learnt what was that picture before which was hung Mrs. Ratcliffe's solemn curtain, we feel no further interest about either the frame or the veil. They are to us, merely a receptacle for old bones, an inappropriate coffin, which we would wish to have decently buried out of our sight.

And then, how grievous a thing it is to have the pleasure of your novel destroyed by the ill-considered triumph of a previous reader. "Oh, you needn't be alarmed for Augusta, of course she accepts Gustavus in the end." "How very ill-natured you are, Susan," says Kitty, with tears in her eyes; "I don't care a bit about it now." Dear Kitty, if you will read my book, you may defy the ill-nature of your sister. There shall be no secret that she can tell you. Nay, take the last chapter if you please—learn from its pages all the results of our troubled story, and the story shall have lost none of its interest, if indeed there be any interest in it to lose.

Our doctrine is, that the author and the reader should move along together in full confidence with each other. Let the personages of the drama undergo ever so complete a comedy of errors among them-selves, but let the spectator never mistake the Syra-cusan for the Ephesian; otherwise he is one of the dupes, and the part of a dupe is never dignified.

I would not for the value of this chapter have it

believed by a single reader that my Eleanor could bring herself to marry Mr. Slope, or that she should be sacrificed to a Bertie Stanhope. But among the good folk of Barchester many believed both the one and the other.

CHAPTER XVI.
BABY WORSHIP.

"Diddle, diddle, diddle, diddle, dum, dum, dum," said or sung Eleanor Bold.

"Diddle, diddle, diddle, diddle, dum, dum, dum," continued Mary Bold, taking up the second part in this concerted piece.

The only audience at the concert was the baby, who however gave such vociferous applause, that the performers presuming it to amount to an encore, commenced again.

"Diddle, diddle, diddle, diddle, dum, dum, dum: hasn't he got lovely legs?" said the rapturous mother.

"H'm 'm 'm 'm 'm," simmered Mary, burying her lips in the little fellow's fat neck, by way of kissing him.

"H'm 'm 'm 'm 'm," simmered the mamma, burying her lips also in his fat round short legs. "He's a dawty little bold darling, so he is; and he has the nicest little pink legs in all the world, so he has;" and the simmering and the kissing went on over again, and as though the ladies were very hungry, and determined to eat him.

"Well, then, he's his own mother's own darling: well, he shall—oh, oh—Mary, Mary—did you ever see? What am I to do? My naughty, naughty,

naughty, naughty little Johnny." All these energetic exclamations were elicited by the delight of the mother in finding that her son was strong enough, and mischievous enough, to pull all her hair out from under her cap. "He's been and pulled down all mamma's hair, and he's the naughtiest, naughtiest, naughtiest little man that ever, ever, ever, ever, ever——"

A regular service of baby worship was going on. Mary Bold was sitting on a low easy chair, with the boy in her lap, and Eleanor was kneeling before the object of her idolatry. As she tried to cover up the little fellow's face with her long, glossy, dark brown locks, and permitted him to pull them hither and thither, as he would, she looked very beautiful in spite of the widow's cap which she still wore. There was a quiet, enduring, grateful sweetness about her face, which grew so strongly upon those who knew her, as to make the great praise of her beauty which came from her old friends, appear marvellously exaggerated in those who were only slightly acquainted with her. Her loveliness was like that of many landscapes, which require to be often seen to be fully enjoyed. There was a depth of dark clear brightness in her eyes which was lost upon a quick observer, a character about her mouth which only showed itself to those with whom she familiarly conversed, a glorious form of head the perfect symmetry of which required the eye of an artist for its appreciation. She had none of that dazzling brilliancy, of that voluptuous Rubens beauty, of that pearly whiteness, and those vermilion tints, which immediately entranced with the power of a basilisk men who came within reach of Madeline Neroni. It was all but impossible to resist the signora,

but no one was called upon for any resistance towards
Eleanor. You might begin to talk to her as though
she were your sister, and it would not be till your
head was on your pillow, that the truth and intensity
of her beauty would flash upon you; that the sweetness of her voice would come upon your ear. A sudden
half-hour with the Neroni, was like falling into a pit;
an evening spent with Eleanor like an unexpected
ramble in some quiet fields of asphodel.

"We'll cover him up till there sha'n't be a morsel
of his little 'ittle 'ittle 'ittle nose to be seen," said the
mother, stretching her streaming locks over the infant's
face. The child screamed with delight, and kicked
till Mary Bold was hardly able to hold him.

At this moment the door opened, and Mr. Slope
was announced. Up jumped Eleanor, and with a sudden
quick motion of her hands pushed back her hair over
her shoulders. It would have been perhaps better for
her that she had not, for she thus showed more of her
confusion than she would have done had she remained
as she was. Mr. Slope, however, immediately recognised
her loveliness, and thought to himself, that irrespective
of her fortune, she would be an inmate that a man
might well desire for his house, a partner for his bosom's care very well qualified to make care lie easy.
Eleanor hurried out of the room to re-adjust her cap,
muttering some unnecessary apology about her baby.
And while she is gone, we will briefly go back and
state what had been hitherto the results of Mr. Slope's
meditations on his scheme of matrimony.

His inquiries as to the widow's income had at any
rate been so far successful as to induce him to determine to go on with the speculation. As regarded Mr.

Harding, he had also resolved to do what he could
without injury to himself. To Mrs. Proudie he determined not to speak on the matter, at least not at
present. His object was to instigate a little rebellion on
the part of the bishop. He thought that such a state
of things would be advisable not only in respect to
Messrs. Harding and Quiverful, but also in the affairs
of the diocese generally. Mr. Slope was by no means
of opinion that Dr. Proudie was fit to rule, but he conscientiously thought it wrong that his brother clergy
should be subjected to petticoat government. He therefore made up his mind to infuse a little of his spirit
into the bishop, sufficient to induce him to oppose his
wife, though not enough to make him altogether insubordinate.

He had therefore taken an opportunity of again
speaking to his lordship about the hospital, and had
endeavoured to make it appear that after all it would
be unwise to exclude Mr. Harding from the appointment. Mr. Slope, however, had a harder task than he
had imagined. Mrs. Proudie, anxious to assume to
herself as much as possible of the merit of patronage,
had written to Mrs. Quiverful, requesting her to call at
the palace; and had then explained to that matron,
with much mystery, condescension and dignity, the good
that was in store for her and her progeny. Indeed Mrs.
Proudie had been so engaged at the very time that Mr.
Slope had been doing the same with the husband at
Puddingdale Vicarage, and had thus in a measure
committed herself. The thanks, the humility, the gra-
titude, the surprise of Mrs. Quiverful had been very
overpowering; she had all but embraced the knees of
her patroness, and had promised that the prayers of

fourteen unprovided babes (so Mrs. Quiverful had described her own family, the eldest of which was a stout young woman of three-and-twenty) should be put up to heaven morning and evening for the munificent friend whom God had sent to them. Such incense as this was not unpleasing to Mrs. Proudie, and she made the most of it. She offered her general assistance to the fourteen unprovided babes, if, as she had no doubt, she should find them worthy; expressed a hope that the eldest of them would be fit to undertake tuition in her Sabbath schools, and altogether made herself a very great lady in the estimation of Mrs. Quiverful.

Having done this, she thought it prudent to drop a few words before the bishop, letting him know that she had acquainted the Puddingdale family with their good fortune; so that he might perceive that he stood committed to the appointment. The husband well understood the *ruse* of his wife, but he did not resent it. He knew that she was taking the patronage out of his hands; he was resolved to put an end to her interference, and re-assume his powers. But then he thought this was not the best time to do it. He put off the evil hour, as many a man in similar circumstances has done before him.

Such having been the case, Mr. Slope naturally encountered a difficulty in talking over the bishop, a difficulty indeed which he found could not be overcome except at the cost of a general outbreak at the palace. A general outbreak at the present moment might be good policy, but it also might not. It was at any rate not a step to be lightly taken. He began by whispering to the bishop that he feared that public opinion would be against him if Mr. Harding did not re-appear at the hospital. The bishop answered with some warmth that Mr. Quiverful had been promised the appointment on Mr. Slope's advice. "Not promised!" said Mr. Slope. "Yes, promised," replied the bishop, "and Mrs. Proudie has seen Mrs. Quiverful on the subject." This was quite unexpected on the part of Mr. Slope, but his presence of mind did not fail him, and he turned the statement to his own account.

"Ah, my lord," said he; "we shall all be in scrapes if the ladies interfere."

This was too much in unison with my lord's feelings to be altogether unpalatable, and yet such an allusion to interference demanded a rebuke. My lord was somewhat astounded also, though not altogether made miserable, by finding that there was a point of difference between his wife and his chaplain.

"I don't know what you mean by interference," said the bishop mildly. "When Mrs. Proudie heard that Mr. Quiverful was to be appointed, it was not unnatural that she should .wish to see Mrs. Quiverful about the schools. I really cannot say that I see any interference."

"I only speak, my lord, for your own comfort," said Slope; "for your own comfort and dignity in the diocese. I can have no other motive. As far as personal feelings go, Mrs. Proudie is the best friend I have. I must always remember that. But still, in my present position, my first duty is to your lordship."

"I'm sure of that, Mr. Slope, I am quite sure of that;" said the bishop mollified: "and you really think that Mr. Harding should have the hospital?"

"Upon my word, I'm inclined to think so. I am quite prepared to take upon myself the blame of first

suggesting Mr. Quiverful's name.   But since doing so,
I have found that there is so strong a feeling in the
diocese in favour of Mr. Harding, that I think your
lordship should give way. I hear also that Mr. Harding
has modified the objections he first felt to your lordship's propositions. And as to what has passed between
Mrs. Proudie and Mrs. Quiverful, the circumstance may
be a little inconvenient, but I really do not think that
that should weigh in a matter of so much moment."

And thus the poor bishop was left in a dreadfully
undecided state as to what he should do.   His mind,
however slightly inclined itself to the appointment of
Mr. Harding, seeing that by such a step, he should
have the assistance of Mr. Slope in opposing Mrs.
Proudie.

Such was the state of affairs at the palace, when
Mr. Slope called at Mrs. Bold's house, and found her
playing with her baby.   When she ran out of the
room, Mr. Slope began praising the weather to Mary
Bold, then he praised the baby and kissed him, and
then he praised the mother, and then he praised Miss
Bold herself.   Mrs. Bold, however, was not long before
she came back.

"I have to apologise for calling at so very early
an hour," began Mr. Slope, "but I was really so anxious
to speak to you that I hope you and Miss Bold will
excuse me."

Eleanor muttered something in which the words
"certainly," and "of course," and "not early at all,"
were just audible, and then apologised for her own appearance, declaring with a smile, that her baby was becoming such a big boy that he was quite unmanageable.

"He's a great big naughty boy," said she to the

child; "and we must send him away to a great big rough romping school, were they have great big rods, and do terrible things to naughty boys who don't do what their own mammas tell them;" and she then commenced another course of kissing, being actuated thereto by the terrible idea of sending her child away which her own imagination had depicted.

"And where the masters don't have such beautiful long hair to be dishevelled," said Mr. Slope, taking up the joke and paying a compliment at the same time.

Eleanor thought he might as well have left the compliment alone; but she said nothing and looked nothing, being occupied as she was with the baby.

"Let me take him," said Mary. "His clothes are nearly off his back with his romping," and so saying she left the room with the child. Miss Bold had heard Mr. Slope say he had something pressing to say to Eleanor, and thinking that she might be *de trop*, took this opportunity of getting herself out of the room.

"Don't be long, Mary," said Eleanor, as Miss Bold shut the door.

"I am glad; Mrs. Bold, to have the opportunity of having ten minutes' conversation with you alone," began Mr. Slope. "Will you let me openly ask you a plain question?"

"Certainly," said she.

"And I am sure you will give me a plain and open answer."

"Either that or none at all," said she, laughing.

"My question is this, Mrs. Bold; is your father really anxious to go back to the hospital?"

"Why do you ask me?" said she. "Why don't you ask himself?"

"My dear Mrs. Bold, I'll tell you why. There are wheels within wheels, all of which I would explain to you, only I fear that there is not time. It is essentially necessary that I should have an answer to this question, otherwise I cannot know how to advance your father's wishes; and it is quite impossible that I should ask himself. No one can esteem your father more than I do, but I doubt if this feeling is reciprocal." It certainly was not. "I must be candid with you as the only means of avoiding ultimate consequences, which may be most injurious to Mr. Harding. I fear there is a feeling, I will not even call it a prejudice, with regard to myself in Barchester, which is not in my favour. You remember that sermon——"

"Oh! Mr. Slope, we need not go back to that," said Eleanor.

"For one moment, Mrs. Bold. It is not that I may talk of myself, but because it is so essential that you should understand how matters stand. That sermon may have been ill-judged,—it was certainly misunderstood; but I will say nothing about that now; only this, that it did give rise to a feeling against myself which your father shares with others. It may be that he has proper cause, but the result is that he is not inclined to meet me on friendly terms. I put it to yourself whether you do not know this to be the case."

Eleanor made no answer, and Mr. Slope, in the eagerness of his address, edged his chair a little nearer to the widow's seat, unperceived by her.

"Such being so," continued Mr. Slope, "I cannot ask him this question as I can ask it of you. In spite of my delinquencies since I came to Barchester you have allowed me to regard you as a friend." Eleanor made a little motion with her head which was hardly confirmatory, but Mr. Slope if he noticed it, did not appear to do so. "To you I can speak openly, and explain the feelings of my heart. This your father would not allow. Unfortunately the bishop has thought it right that this matter of the hospital should pass through my hands. There have been some details to get up with which he would not trouble himself, and thus it has come to pass that I was forced to have an interview with your father on the matter."

"I am aware of that," said Eleanor.

"Of course," said he. "In that interview Mr. Harding left the impression on my mind that he did not wish to return to the hospital."

"How could that be?" said Eleanor, at last stirred up to forget the cold propriety of demeanour which she had determined to maintain.

"My dear Mrs. Bold, I give you my word that such was the case," said he, again getting a little nearer to her. "And what is more than that, before my interview with Mr. Harding, certain persons at the palace, I do not mean the bishop, had told me that such was the fact. I own, I hardly believed it; I own, I thought that your father would wish on every ac-count, for conscience' sake, for the sake of those old men, for old association, and the memory of dear days long gone by, on every account I thought that he would wish to resume his duties. But I was told that such was not his wish; and he certainly left me with the impression that I had been told the truth."

"Well!" said Eleanor, now sufficiently roused on the matter.

"I hear Miss Bold's step," said Mr. Slope; "would

it be asking too great a favour to beg you to——I know you can manage anything with Miss Bold."

Eleanor did not like the word manage, but still she went out, and asked Mary to leave them alone for another quarter of an hour.

"Thank you, Mrs. Bold,——I am so very grateful for this confidence. Well, I left your father with this impression. Indeed, I may say that he made me understand that he declined the appointment."

"Not the appointment," said Eleanor. "I am sure he did not decline the appointment. But he said that he would not agree,——that is, that he did not like the scheme about the schools and the services, and all that. I am quite sure he never said that he wished to refuse the place."

"Oh, Mrs. Bold!" said Mr. Slope, in a manner almost impassioned. "I would not, for the world, say to so good a daughter a word against so good a father. But you must, for his sake, let me show you exactly how the matter stands at present. Mr. Harding was a little flurried when I told him of the bishop's wishes about the school. I did so, perhaps, with the less caution because you yourself had so perfectly agreed with me on the same subject. He was a little put out and spoke warmly. 'Tell the bishop,' said he, 'that I quite disagree with him,——and shall not return to the hospital as such conditions are attached to it.' What he said was to that effect; indeed, his words were, if anything, stronger than those. I had no alternative but to repeat them to his lordship, who said that he could look on them in no other light than a refusal. He also had heard the report that your father did not wish for the appointment, and putting all these things together, he thought he had no choice but to look for some one else. He has consequently offered the place to Mr. Quiverful."

"Offered the place to Mr. Quiverful!" repeated Eleanor, her eyes suffused with tears. "Then, Mr. Slope, there is an end of it."

"No, my friend—not so," said he. "It is to prevent such being the end of it that I am now here. I may at any rate presume that I have got an answer to my question, and that Mr. Harding is desirous of returning."

"Desirous of returning—of course he is," said Eleanor; "of course he wishes to have back his house and his income, and his place in the world; to have back what he gave up with such self-denying honesty, if he can have them without restraints on his conduct to which at his age it would be impossible that he should submit. How can the bishop ask a man of his age to turn schoolmaster to a pack of children?"

"Out of the question," said Mr. Slope, laughing slightly; "of course no such demand shall be made on your father. I can at any rate promise you that I will not be the medium of any so absurd a requisition. We wished your father to preach in the hospital, as the inmates may naturally be too old to leave it; but even that shall not be insisted on. We wished also to attach a Sabbath-day school to the hospital, thinking that such an establishment could not but be useful under the surveillance of so good a clergyman as Mr. Harding, and also under your own. But, dear Mrs. Bold; we won't talk of these things now. One thing is clear; we must do what we can to annul this rash offer the bishop has made to Mr. Quiverful. Your

father wouldn't see Quiverful, would he? Quiverful is
an honourable man, and would not, for a moment,
stand in your father's way."

"What?" said Eleanor; "ask a man with fourteen
children to give up his preferment! I am quite sure
he will do no such thing."

"I suppose not," said Slope; and he again drew
near to Mrs. Bold, so that now they were very close
to each other. Eleanor did not think much about it,
but instinctively moved away a little. How greatly
would she have increased the distance could she have
guessed what had been said about her at Plumstead!
"I suppose not. But it is out of the question that
Quiverful should supersede your father,—quite out of
the question. The bishop has been too rash. An idea
occurs to me, which may, perhaps, with God's blessing,
put us right. My dear Mrs. Bold, would you object to
seeing the bishop yourself?"

"Why should not my father see him?" said Eleanor.
She had once before in her life interfered in her father's affairs, and then not to much advantage. She
was older now, and felt that she should take no step
in a matter so vital to him without his consent.

"Why, to tell the truth," said Mr. Slope, with a
look of sorrow, as though he greatly bewailed the
want of charity in his patron, "the bishop fancies that
he has cause of anger against your father. I fear an
interview would lead to further ill will."

"Why," said Eleanor, "my father is the mildest,
the gentlest man living."

"I only know," said Slope, "that he has the best
of daughters. So you would not see the bishop? As

to getting an interview, I could manage that for you without the slightest annoyance to yourself."

"I could do nothing, Mr. Slope, without consulting my father."

"Ah!" said he, "that would be useless; you would then only be your father's messenger. Does anything occur to yourself? Something must be done. Your father shall not be ruined by so ridiculous a misunderstanding."

Eleanor said that nothing occurred to her, but that it was very hard; and the tears came to her eyes and rolled down her cheeks. Mr. Slope would have given much to have had the privilege of drying them; but he had tact enough to know that he had still a great deal to do before he could even hope for any privilege with Mrs. Bold.

"It cuts me to the heart to see you so grieved," said he. "But pray let me assure you that your father's interests shall not be sacrificed if it be possible for me to protect them. I will tell the bishop openly what are the facts. I will explain to him that he has hardly the right to appoint any other than your father, and will show him that if he does so he will be guilty of great injustice,—and you, Mrs. Bold, you will have the charity at any rate to believe this of me, that I am truly anxious for your father's welfare,—for his and for your own."

The widow hardly knew what answer to make. She was quite aware that her father would not be at all thankful to Mr. Slope; she had a strong wish to share her father's feelings; and yet she could not but acknowledge that Mr. Slope was very kind. Her father, who was generally so charitable to all men, who seldom

13*

spoke ill of any one, had warned her against Mr. Slope, and yet she did not know how to abstain from thanking him. What interest could he have in the matter but that which he professed? Nevertheless there was that in his manner which even she distrusted. She felt, she did not know why, that there was something about him which ought to put her on her guard.

Mr. Slope read all this in her hesitating manner just as plainly as though she had opened her heart to him. It was the talent of the man that he could so read the inward feelings of women with whom he conversed. He knew that Eleanor was doubting him, and that if she thanked him she would only do so because she could not help it; but yet this did not make him angry or even annoy him. Rome was not built in a day.

"I did not come for thanks," continued he, seeing her hesitation; "and do not want them—at any rate before they are merited. But this I do want, Mrs. Bold, that I may make to myself friends in this fold to which it has pleased God to call me as one of the humblest of his shepherds. If I cannot do so, my task here must indeed be a sad one. I will at any rate endeavour to deserve them."

"I'm sure," said she, "you will soon make plenty of friends." She felt herself obliged to say something.

"That will be nothing unless they are such as will sympathise with my feelings; unless they are such as I can reverence and admire—and love. If the best and purest turn away from me, I cannot bring myself to be satisfied with the friendship of the less estimable. In such case I must live alone."

"Oh! I'm sure you will not do that, Mr. Slope." Eleanor meant nothing, but it suited him to appear to think some special allusion had been intended.

"Indeed, Mrs. Bold, I shall live alone, quite alone as far as the heart is concerned, if those with whom I yearn to ally myself turn away from me. But enough of this; I have called you my friend, and I hope you will not contradict me. I trust the time may come when I may also call your father so. May God bless you, Mrs. Bold, you and your darling boy. And tell your father from me that what can be done for his interest shall be done."

And so he took his leave, pressing the widow's hand rather more closely than usual. Circumstances, however, seemed just then to make this intelligible, and the lady did not feel called on to resent it.

"I cannot understand him," said Eleanor to Mary Bold, a few minutes afterwards. "I do not know whether he is a good man or a bad man—whether he is true or false."

"Then give him the benefit of the doubt," said Mary, "and believe the best."

"On the whole, I think I do," said Eleanor. "I think I do believe that he means well—and if so, it is a shame that we should revile him, and make him miserable while he is among us. But, oh, Mary, I fear papa will be disappointed in the hospital."

CHAPTER XVII.
WHO SHALL BE COCK OF THE WALK?

ALL this time things were going on somewhat un-easily at the palace. The hint or two which Mr. Slope had given was by no means thrown away upon the bishop. He had a feeling that if he ever meant to oppose the now almost unendurable despotism of his wife, he must lose no further time in doing so; that if he ever meant to be himself master in his own diocese, let alone his own house, he should begin at once. It would have been easier to have done so from the day of his consecration than now, but easier now than when Mrs. Proudie should have succeeded in thoroughly mastering the diocesan details. Then the proffered assistance of Mr. Slope was a great thing for him, a most unexpected and invaluable aid. Hitherto he had looked on the two as allied forces; and had considered that as allies they were impregnable. He had begun to believe that his only chance of escape would be by the advancement of Mr. Slope to some distant and rich preferment. But now it seemed that one of his enemies, certainly the least potent of them, but nevertheless one very important, was willing to desert his own camp. Assisted by Mr. Slope what might he not do? He walked up and down his little study, almost thinking that the time might come when he would be able to appropriate to his own use the big room up stairs, in which his predecessor had always sat.

As he revolved these things in his mind a note was brought to him from Archdeacon Grantly, in which that divine begged his lordship to do him the honour of seeing him on the morrow—would his lordship have the kindness to name an hour? Dr. Grantly's proposed visit would have reference to the reappointment of Mr. Harding to the wardenship of Barchester hospital. The bishop having read his note was informed that the archdeacon's servant was waiting for an answer.

Here at once a great opportunity offered itself to the bishop of acting on his own responsibility. He bethought himself however of his new ally, and rang the bell for Mr. Slope. It turned out that Mr. Slope was not in the house; and then, greatly daring, the bishop with his own unassisted spirit wrote a note to the archdeacon saying that he would see him, and naming an hour for doing so. Having watched from his studywindow that the messenger got safely off from the premises with this despatch, he began to turn over in his mind what step he should next take.

To-morrow he would have to declare to the archdeacon either that Mr. Harding should have the appointment, or that he should not have it. The bishop felt that he could not honestly throw over the Quiverfuls without informing Mrs. Proudie, and he resolved at last to brave the lioness in her den and tell her that circumstances were such that it behoved him to reappoint Mr. Harding. He did not feel that he should at all derogate from his new courage by promising Mrs. Proudie that the very first piece of available preferment at his disposal should be given to Quiverful to atone for the injury done to him. If he could mollify the lioness with such a sop, how happy would he think his first efforts to have been!

Not without many misgivings did he find himself in Mrs. Proudie's boudoir. He had at first thought of sending for her. But it was not at all impossible that she might choose to take such a message amiss, and then also it might be some protection to him to have his daughters present at the interview. He found her sitting with her account books before her nibbling the end of her pencil evidently mersed in pecuniary difficulties, and harassed in mind by the multiplicity of palatial expenses, and the heavy cost of episcopal grandeur. Her daughters were around her. Olivia was reading a novel, Augusta was crossing a note to her bosom friend in Baker Street, and Netta was working diminutive coach wheels for the bottom of a petticoat. If the bishop could get the better of his wife in her present mood, he would be a man indeed. He might then consider the victory his own for ever. After all, in such cases the matter between husband and wife stands much the same as it does between two boys at the same school, two cocks in the same yard, or two armies on the same continent. The conqueror once is generally the conqueror for ever after. The prestige of victory is every thing.

"Ahem—my dear," began the bishop, "if you are disengaged, I wished to speak to you." Mrs. Proudie put her pencil down carefully at the point to which she had dotted her figures, marked down in her memory the sum she had arrived at, and then looked up, sourly enough, into her helpmate's face. "If you are busy, another time will do as well," continued the bishop, whose courage like Bob Acres' had oozed out, now that he found himself on the ground of battle.

"What is it about, Bishop?" asked the lady.

"Well—it was about those Quiverfuls—but I see you are engaged. Another time will do just as well for me."

"What about the Quiverfuls? It is quite understood I believe, that they are to come to the hospital. There is to be no doubt about that, is there?" and as she spoke she kept her pencil sternly and vigorously fixed on the column of figures before her.

"Why, my dear, there is a difficulty," said the bishop.

"A difficulty!" said Mrs. Proudie, "what difficulty? The place has been promised to Mr. Quiverful, and of course he must have it. He has made all his arrangements. He has written for a curate for Puddingdale, he has spoken to the auctioneer about selling his farm, horses, and cows, and in all respects considers the place as his own. Of course he must have it."

Now, bishop, look well to thyself, and call up all the manhood that is in thee. Think how much is at stake. If now thou art not true to thy guns, no Slope can hereafter aid thee. How can he who deserts his own colours at the first smell of gunpowder expect faith in any ally. Thou thyself hast sought the battle-field; fight out the battle manfully now thou art there. Courage, bishop, courage! Frowns cannot kill, nor can sharp words break any bones. After all the apron is thine own. She can appoint no wardens, give away no benefices, nominate no chaplains, an' thou art but true to thyself. Up, man, and at her with a constant heart.

Some little monitor within the bishop's breast so addressed him. But then there was another monitor there which advised him differently, and as follows. Remember, bishop, she is a woman, and such a woman too as thou well knowest: a battle of words with such a woman is the very mischief. Were it not better for thee to carry on this war, if it must be waged, from behind thine own table in thine own study? Does not every cock fight best on his own dunghill? Thy daughters also are here, the pledges of thy love, the fruits of thy loins; is it well that they should see thee in the hour of thy victory over their mother? nay, is it well that they should see thee in the possible hour of thy defeat? Besides, hast thou not chosen thy opportunity with wonderful little skill, indeed with no touch of that sagacity for which thou art famous? Will it not turn out that thou art wrong in this matter, and thine enemy right; that thou hast actually pledged thyself in this matter of the hospital, and that now thou wouldest turn upon thy wife because she requires from thee but the fulfilment of thy promise? Art thou not a Christian bishop, and is not thy word to be held sacred whatever be the result? Return, bishop, to thy sanctum on the lower floor, and postpone thy combative propensities for some occasion in which at least thou mayest fight the battle against odds less tremendously against thee.

All this passed within the bishop's bosom while Mrs. Proudie still sat with her fixed pencil, and the figures of her sum still enduring on the tablets of her memory. "£4 17 s. 7 d." she said to herself. "Of course Mr. Quiverful must have the hospital," she said out loud to her lord.

"Well, my dear, I merely wanted to suggest to you that Mr. Slope seems to think that if Mr. Harding be not appointed, public feeling in the matter would be against us, and that the press might perhaps take it up."

"Mr. Slope seems to think!" said Mrs. Proudie, in a tone of voice which plainly showed the bishop that he was right in looking for a breach in that quarter. "And what has Mr. Slope to do with it? I hope, my lord, you are not going to allow yourself to be governed by a chaplain." And now in her eagerness the lady lost her place in her account.

"Certainly not, my dear. Nothing I can assure you is less probable. But still Mr. Slope may be useful in finding how the wind blows, and I really thought that if we could give something else as good to the Quiverfuls—"

"Nonsense," said Mrs. Proudie; "it would be years before you could give them anything else that could suit them half as well, and as for the press and the public, and all that, remember there are two ways of telling a story. If Mr. Harding is fool enough to tell his tale, we can also tell ours. The place was offered to him, and he refused it. It has now been given to some one else, and there's an end of it. At least, I should think so."

"Well, my dear, I rather believe you are right;" said the bishop, and sneaking out of the room, he went down stairs, troubled in his mind as to how he should receive the archdeacon on the morrow. He felt himself not very well just at present; and began to consider that he might, not improbably, be detained in his room the next morning by an attack of bile. He was, unfortunately, very subject to bilious annoyances.

"Mr. Slope, indeed! I'll Slope him," said the indignant matron to her listening progeny. "I don't know what has come to Mr. Slope. I believe he thinks he is to be Bishop of Barchester himself, because I've taken him by the hand, and got your father to make him his domestic chaplain."

"He was always full of impudence," said Olivia; "I told you so once before, mamma." Olivia, however, had not thought him too impudent when once before he had proposed to make her Mrs. Slope.

"Well, Olivia, I always thought you liked him,"

said Augusta, who at that moment had some grudge against her sister. "I always disliked the man, because I think him thoroughly vulgar."

"There you're wrong," said Mrs. Proudie; "he's not vulgar at all; and what is more, he is a soul-stirring, eloquent preacher; but he must be taught to know his place if he is to remain in this house."

"He has the horridest eyes I ever saw in a man's head," said Netta; "and I tell you what, he's terribly greedy; did you see all the currant pie he ate yesterday?"

When Mr. Slope got home he soon learnt from the bishop, as much from his manner as his words, that Mrs. Proudie's behests in the matter of the hospital were to be obeyed. Dr. Proudie let fall something as to "this occasion only," and "keeping all affairs about patronage exclusively in his own hands." But he was quite decided about Mr. Harding; and as Mr. Slope did not wish to have both the prelate and the prelatess against him, he did not at present see that he could do anything but yield.

He merely remarked that he would of course carry out the bishop's views, and that he was quite sure that if the bishop trusted to his own judgment things in the diocese would certainly be well ordered. Mr. Slope knew that if you hit a nail on the head often enough, it will penetrate at last.

He was sitting alone in his room on the same evening when a light knock was made on his door, and before he could answer it the door was opened, and his patroness appeared. He was all smiles in a moment, but so was not she also. She took, however, the chair that was offered to her, and thus began her expostulation:—

"Mr. Slope, I did not at all approve your conduct the other night with that Italian woman. Any one would have thought that you were her lover."

"Good gracious, my dear madam," said Mr. Slope, with a look of horror. "Why, she is a married woman."

"That's more than I know," said Mrs. Proudie; "however she chooses to pass for such. But married or not married, such attention as you paid to her was improper. I cannot believe that you would wish to give offence in my drawing-room, Mr. Slope; but I owe it to myself and my daughters to tell you that I disapprove your conduct."

Mr. Slope opened wide his huge protruding eyes, and stared out of them with a look of well-feigned surprise. "Why, Mrs. Proudie," said he, "I did but fetch her something to eat when she said she was hungry."

"And you have called on her since," continued she, looking at the culprit with the stern look of a detective policeman in the act of declaring himself.

Mr. Slope turned over in his mind whether it would be well for him to tell this termagant at once that he should call on whom he liked, and do what he liked; but he remembered that his footing in Barchester was not yet sufficiently firm, and that it would be better for him to pacify her.

"I certainly called since at Dr. Stanhope's house, and certainly saw Madame Neroni."

"Yes, and you saw her alone," said the episcopal Argus.

"Undoubtedly, I did," said Mr. Slope, "but that was because nobody else happened to be in the room. Surely it was no fault of mine if the rest of the family were out."

"Perhaps not; but I assure you, Mr. Slope, you will fall greatly in my estimation if I find that you allow yourself to be caught by the lures of that woman. I know women better than you do, Mr. Slope, and you may believe me that that signora, as she calls herself, is not a fitting companion for a strict evangelical, unmarried young clergyman."

How Mr. Slope would have liked to laugh at her, had he dared! But he did not dare. So he merely said, "I can assure you, Mrs. Proudie, the lady in question is nothing to me."

"Well, I hope not, Mr. Slope. But I have considered it my duty to give you this caution; and now there is another thing I feel myself called on to speak about; it is your conduct to the bishop, Mr. Slope."

"My conduct to the bishop," said he, now truly surprised and ignorant what the lady alluded to.

"Yes, Mr. Slope; your conduct to the bishop. It is by no means what I would wish to see it."

"Has the bishop said anything, Mrs. Proudie?"

"No, the bishop has said nothing. He probably thinks that any remarks on the matter will come better from me, who first introduced you to his lordship's notice. The fact is, Mr. Slope, you are a little inclined to take too much upon yourself."

An angry spot showed itself on Mr. Slope's cheeks, and it was with difficulty that he controlled himself. But he did do so, and sat quite silent while the lady went on.

"It is the fault of many young men in your position, and therefore the bishop is not inclined at present to resent it. You will, no doubt, soon learn what is required from you, and what is not. If you will take my advice, however, you will be careful not to obtrude advice upon the bishop in any matter touching patronage. If his lordship wants advice, he knows where to look for it." And then having added to her counsel a string of platitudes as to what was desirable and what not desirable in the conduct of a strictly evangelical, unmarried young clergyman, Mrs. Proudie retreated, leaving the chaplain to his thoughts.

The upshot of his thoughts was this, that there certainly was not room in the diocese for the energies of both himself and Mrs. Proudie, and that it behoved him quickly to ascertain whether his energies or hers were to prevail.

CHAPTER XVIII.
THE WIDOW'S PERSECUTION.

EARLY on the following morning Mr. Slope was summoned to the bishop's dressing-room, and went there fully expecting that he should find his lordship very indignant, and spirited up by his wife to repeat the rebuke which she had administered on the previous day. Mr. Slope had resolved that at any rate from him he would not stand it, and entered the dressing-room in rather a combative disposition; but he found the bishop in the most placid and gentlest of humours. His lordship complained of being rather unwell, had a slight headache, and was not quite the thing in his stomach; but there was nothing the matter with his temper.

"Oh, Slope," said he, taking the chaplain's proffered hand, "Archdeacon Grantly is to call on me this morning, and I really am not fit to see him. I fear I must trouble

you, to see him for me;" and then Dr. Proudie proceeded to explain what it was that must be said to
Dr. Grantly. He was to be told in fact in the civilest
words in which the tidings could be conveyed, that
Mr. Harding having refused the wardenship, the appointment had been offered to Mr. Quiverful and accepted by him.

Mr. Slope again pointed out to his patron that he
thought he was perhaps not quite wise in his decision,
and this he did *sotto voce*. But even with this precau-
tion it was not safe to say much, and during the little
that he did say, the bishop made a very slight, but
still a very ominous gesture with his thumb towards
the door which opened from his dressing-room to some
inner sanctuary. Mr. Slope at once took the hint, and
said no more; but he perceived that there was to be
confidence between him and his patron, that the league
desired by him was to be made, and that this appointment of Mr. Quiverful was to be the last sacrifice
offered on the altar of conjugal obedience. All this
Mr. Slope read in the slight motion of the bishop's
thumb, and he read it correctly. There was no need
of parchments and seals, of attestations, explanations,
and professions. The bargain was understood between
them, and Mr. Slope gave the bishop his hand upon it.
The bishop understood the little extra squeeze, and an
intelligible gleam of assent twinkled in his eye.

"Pray be civil to the archdeacon, Mr. Slope," said
he out loud; "but make him quite understand that in
this matter Mr. Harding has put it out of my power to
oblige him."

It would be a calumny on Mrs. Proudie to suggest
that she was sitting in her bed-room with her ear at

the keyhole during this interview. She had within her a spirit of decorum which prevented her from descending to such baseness. To put her ear to a key-hole or to listen at a chink, was a trick for a housemaid.

Mrs. Proudie knew this, and therefore she did not do it; but she stationed herself as near to the door as she well could, that she might, if possible, get the advantage which the housemaid would have had, without descending to the housemaid's artifice.

It was little, however, that she heard, and that little was only sufficient to deceive her. She saw nothing of that friendly pressure, perceived nothing of that concluded bargain; she did not even dream of the treacherous resolves which those two false men had made together to upset her in the pride of her station, to dash the cup from her lip before she had drank of it, to sweep away all her power before she had tasted its sweets! Traitors that they were; the husband of her bosom, and the outcast whom she had fostered and brought to the warmth of the world's brightest fireside! But neither of them had the magnanimity of this woman. Though two men have thus leagued themselves together against her, even yet the battle is not lost.

Mr. Slope felt pretty sure that Dr. Grantly would decline the honour of seeing him, and such turned out to be the case. The archdeacon, when the palace door was opened to him, was greeted by a note. Mr. Slope presented his compliments, &c. &c. The bishop was ill in his room, and very greatly regretted, &c. &c. Mr. Slope had been charged with the bishop's views, and if agreeable to the archdeacon, would do himself the honour, &c. &c. The archdeacon, however, was not agreeable, and having read his note in the hall, crumpled it up in his hand, and muttering something about sorrow for his lordship's illness, took his leave, without sending as much as a verbal message in answer to Mr. Slope's note.

"Ill!" said the archdeacon to himself as he flung himself into his brougham. "The man is absolutely a coward. He is afraid to see me. Ill, indeed!" The archdeacon was never ill himself, and did not therefore understand that any one else could in truth be prevented by illness from keeping an appointment. He regarded all such excuses as subterfuges, and in the present instance he was not far wrong.

Dr. Grantly desired to be driven to his father-in-law's lodgings in the High Street, and hearing from the servant that Mr. Harding was at his daughter's, followed him to Mrs. Bold's house, and there found him. The archdeacon was fuming with rage when he got into the drawing-room, and had by this time nearly forgotten the pusillanimity of the bishop in the villany of the chaplain.

"Look at that," said he, throwing Mr. Slope's crumpled note to Mr. Harding. "I am to be told that if I choose I may have the honour of seeing Mr. Slope, and that too, after a positive engagement with the bishop."

"But he says the bishop is ill," said Mr. Harding.

"Pshaw! You don't mean to say that you are deceived by such an excuse as that. He was well enough yesterday. Now I tell you what, I will see the bishop; and I will tell him also very plainly what I think of his conduct. I will see him, or else Barchester will soon be too hot to hold him."

Eleanor was sitting in the room, but Dr. Grantly had hardly noticed her in his anger. Eleanor now said to him, with the greatest innocence, "I wish you had seen Mr. Slope, Dr. Grantly, because I think perhaps it might have done good."

The archdeacon turned on her with almost brutal wrath. Had she at once owned that she had accepted Mr. Slope for her second husband, he could hardly have felt more convinced of her belonging body and soul to the Slope and Proudie party than he now did on hearing her express such a wish as this. Poor Eleanor!

"See him!" said the archdeacon glaring at her; "and why am I to be called on to lower myself in the world's esteem and my own by coming in contact with such a man as that? I have hitherto lived among gentlemen, and do not mean to be dragged into other company by anybody."

Poor Mr. Harding well knew what the archdeacon meant, but Eleanor was as innocent as her own baby. She could not understand how the archdeacon could consider himself to be dragged into bad company by condescending to speak to Mr. Slope for a few minutes when the interests of her father might be served by his doing so.

"I was talking for a full hour yesterday to Mr. Slope," said she, with some little assumption of dignity, "and I did not find myself lowered by it."

"Perhaps not," said he. "But if you'll be good enough to allow me, I shall judge for myself in such matters. And I tell you what, Eleanor; it will be much better for you if you will allow yourself to be guided also by the advice of those who are your

14*

friends. If you do not you will be apt to find that you have no friends left who can advise you."

Eleanor blushed up to the roots of her hair. But even now she had not the slightest idea of what was passing in the archdeacon's mind. No thought of love-making or love-receiving had yet found its way to her heart since the death of poor John Bold; and if it were possible that such a thought should spring there, the man must be far different from Mr. Slope that could give it birth.

Nevertheless Eleanor blushed deeply, for she felt she was charged with improper conduct, and she did so with the more inward pain because her father did not instantly rally to her side; that father for whose sake and love she had submitted to be the receptacle of Mr. Slope's confidence. She had given a detailed account of all that had passed to her father; and though he had not absolutely agreed with her about Mr. Slope's views touching the hospital, yet he had said nothing to make her think that she had been wrong in talking to him.

She was far too angry to humble herself before her brother-in-law. Indeed, she had never accustomed herself to be very abject before him, and they had never been confidential allies. "I do not the least understand what you mean, Dr. Grantly," said she. "I do not know that I can accuse myself of doing anything that my friends should disapprove. Mr. Slope called here expressly to ask what papa's wishes were about the hospital; and as I believe he called with friendly intentions I told him."

"Friendly intentions!" sneered the archdeacon.

"I believe you greatly wrong Mr. Slope," continued

Eleanor; "but I have explained this to papa already; and as you do not seem to approve of what I say, Dr. Grantly, I will with your permission leave you and papa together," and so saying she walked slowly out of the room.

All this made Mr. Harding very unhappy. It was quite clear that the archdeacon and his wife had made up their minds that Eleanor was going to marry Mr. Slope. Mr. Harding could not really bring himself to think that she would do so, but yet he could not deny that circumstances made it appear that the man's company was not disagreeable to her. She was now constantly seeing him, and yet she received visits from no other unmarried gentleman. She always took his part when his conduct was canvassed, although she was aware how personally objectionable he was to her friends. Then, again, Mr. Harding felt that if she should choose to become Mrs. Slope, he had nothing that he could justly urge against her doing so. She had full right to please herself, and he, as a father, could not say that she would disgrace herself by marrying a clergyman who stood so well before the world as Mr. Slope did. As for quarrelling with his daughter on account of such a marriage, and separating himself from her as the archdeacon had threatened to do, that, with Mr. Harding, would be out of the question. If she should determine to marry this man, he must get over his aversion as best he could. His Eleanor, his own old companion in their old happy home, must still be the friend of his bosom, the child of his heart. Let who would cast her off, he would not. If it were fated that he should have to sit in his old age at the same table with that man whom of all men he disliked the most, he would meet his fate as best he might. Anything to him would be preferable to the loss of his daughter.

Such being his feelings, he hardly knew how to take part with Eleanor against the archdeacon or with the archdeacon against Eleanor. It will be said that he should never have suspected her.—Alas! he never should have done so. But Mr. Harding was by no means a perfect character. In his indecision, his weakness, his proneness to be led by others, his want of self-confidence, he was very far from being perfect. And then it must be remembered that such a marriage as that which the archdeacon contemplated with disgust, which we who know Mr. Slope so well would regard with equal disgust, did not appear so monstrous to Mr. Harding, because in his charity he did not hate the chaplain as the archdeacon did, and as we do.

He was, however, very unhappy when his daughter left the room, and he had recourse to an old trick of his that was customary to him in his times of sadness. He began playing some slow tune upon an imaginary violoncello, drawing one hand slowly backwards and forwards as though he held a bow in it, and modulating the unreal cords with the other.

"She'll marry that man as sure as two and two make four," said the practical archdeacon.

"I hope not, I hope not," said the father. "But if she does, what can I say to her? I have no right to object to him."

"No right!" exclaimed Dr. Grantly.

"No right as her father. He is in my own profession, and for aught we know a good man."

To this the archdeacon would by no means assent. It

was not well, however, to argue the case against Eleanor in her own drawing-room, and so they both walked forth and discussed the matter in all its bearings under the elm trees of the close. Mr. Harding also explained to his son-in-law what had been the purport, at any rate the alleged purport, of Mr. Slope's last visit to the widow. He, however, stated that he could not bring himself to believe that Mr. Slope had any real anxiety such as that he had pretended. "I cannot forget his demeanour to myself," said Mr. Harding, "and it is not possible that his ideas should have changed so soon."

"I see it all," said the archdeacon. "The sly *tartufe!* He thinks to buy the daughter by providing for the father. He means to show how powerful he is, how good he is, and how much he is willing to do for her *beaux yeux;* yes, I see it all now. But we'll be too many for him yet, Mr. Harding;" he said, turning to his companion with some gravity, and pressing his hand upon the other's arm. "It would, perhaps, be better for you to lose the hospital than get it on such terms."

"Lose it!" said Mr. Harding; "why I've lost it already. I don't want it. I've made up my mind to do without it. I'll withdraw altogether. I'll just go and write a line to the bishop and tell him that I withdraw my claim altogether."

Nothing would have pleased him better than to be allowed to escape from the trouble and difficulty in such a manner. But he was now going too fast for the archdeacon.

"No — no — no! we'll do no such thing," said Dr. Grantly; "we'll still have the hospital. I hardly doubt but that we'll have it. But not by Mr. Slope's assistance. If that be necessary we'll lose it; but we'll have it, spite of his teeth, if we can. Arabin will be at Plumstead to-morrow; you must come over and talk to him."

The two now turned into the cathedral library, which was used by the clergymen of the close as a sort of ecclesiastical club-room, for writing sermons and sometimes letters; also for reading theological works, and sometimes magazines and newspapers. The theological works were not disturbed, perhaps, quite as often as from the appearance of the building the outside public might have been led to expect. Here the two allies settled on their course of action. The archdeacon wrote a letter to the bishop, strongly worded, but still respectful, in which he put forward his father-in-law's claim to the appointment, and expressed his own regret that he had not been able to see his lordship when he called. Of Mr. Slope he made no mention whatsoever. It was then settled that Mr. Harding should go out to Plumstead on the following day; and after considerable discussion on the matter, the archdeacon proposed to ask Eleanor there also, so as to withdraw her, if possible, from Mr. Slope's attentions. "A week or two," said he, "may teach her what he is, and while she is there she will be out of harm's way. Mr. Slope won't come there after her."

Eleanor was not a little surprised when her brother-in-law came back and very civilly pressed her to go out to Plumstead with her father. She instantly perceived that her father had been fighting her battles for her behind her back. She felt thankful to him, and for his sake she would not show her resentments to the archdeacon by refusing his invitation. But she could not, she said, go on the morrow; she had an invitation to drink tea at the Stanhopes which she had promised to accept. She would, she added, go with her father on the next day, if he would wait; or she would follow him.

"The Stanhopes!" said Dr. Grantly; "I did not know you were so intimate with them."

"I did not know it myself," said she, "till Miss Stanhope called yesterday. However, I like her very much, and I have promised to go and play chess with some of them."

"Have they a party there?" said the archdeacon, still fearful of Mr. Slope.

"Oh, no," said Eleanor; "Miss Stanhope said there was to be nobody at all. But she had heard that Mary had left me for a few weeks, and she had learnt from some one that I play chess, and so she came over on purpose to ask me to go in."

"Well, that's very friendly," said the ex-warden. "They certainly do look more like foreigners than English people, but I dare say they are none the worse for that."

The archdeacon was inclined to look upon the Stanhopes with favourable eyes, and had nothing to object on the matter. It was therefore arranged that Mr. Harding should postpone his visit to Plumstead for one day, and then take with him Eleanor, the baby, and the nurse.

Mr. Slope is certainly becoming of some importance in Barchester.

CHAPTER XIX.
BARCHESTER BY MOONLIGHT.

THERE was much cause for grief and occasional perturbation of spirits in the Stanhope family, but yet they rarely seemed to be grieved or to be disturbed. It was the peculiar gift of each of them that each was able to bear his or her own burden without complaint, and perhaps without sympathy. They habitually looked on the sunny side of the wall, if there was a gleam on either side for them to look at; and, if there was none, they endured the shade with an indifference which, if not stoical, answered the end at which the Stoics aimed. Old Stanhope could not but feel that he had ill-performed his duties as a father and a clergyman; and could hardly look forward to his own death without grief at the position in which he would leave his family. His income for many years had been as high as 3000*l.* a year, and yet they had among them no other provision than their mother's fortune of 10,000*l.* He had not only spent his income, but was in debt. Yet with all this, he seldom showed much outward sign of trouble.

It was the same with the mother. If she added little to the pleasures of her children she detracted still less: she neither grumbled at her lot, nor spoke much of her past or future sufferings; as long as she had a maid to adjust her dress, and had those dresses well made, nature with her was satisfied. It was the same with the children. Charlotte never rebuked her father with the prospect of their future poverty, nor did it seem to grieve her that she was becoming an old maid so quickly; her temper was rarely ruffled, and, if we might judge by her appearance, she was always happy. The signora was not so sweet-tempered, but she possessed much enduring courage; she seldom complained —never, indeed, to her family. Though she had a cause for affliction which would have utterly broken down the heart of most women as beautiful as she and as devoid of all religious support, yet, she bore her suffering in silence, or alluded to it only to elicit the sympathy and stimulate the admiration of the men with whom she flirted. As to Bertie, one would have imagined from the sound of his voice and the gleam of his eye that he had not a sorrow nor a care in the world. Nor had he. He was incapable of anticipating to-morrow's griefs. The prospect of future want no more disturbed his appetite than does that of the butcher's knife disturb the appetite of the sheep.

Such was the usual tenour of their way; but there were rare exceptions. Occasionally the father would allow an angry glance to fall from his eye, and the lion would send forth a low dangerous roar as though he meditated some deed of blood. Occasionally also Madame Neroni would become bitter against mankind, more than usually antagonistic to the world's decencies, and would seem as though she was about to break from her moorings and allow herself to be carried forth by the tide of her feelings to utter ruin and shipwreck. She, however, like the rest of them, had no real feelings, could feel no true passion. In that was her security. Before she resolved on any contemplated escapade she would make a small calculation, and generally summed up that the Stanhope villa or even Barchester close was better than the world at large.

They were most irregular in their hours. The father

was generally the earliest in the breakfast-parlour, and
Charlotte would soon follow and give him his coffee;
but the others breakfasted anywhere, anyhow, and at
any time. On the morning after the archdeacon's futile
visit to the palace, Dr. Stanhope came down stairs
with an ominously dark look about his eyebrows; his
white locks were rougher than usual, and he breathed
thickly and loudly as he took his seat in his arm-chair.
He had open letters in his hand, and when Charlotte
came into the room he was still reading them. She
went up and kissed him as was her wont, but he
hardly noticed her as she did so, and she knew at
once that something was the matter.

"What's the meaning of that?" said he, throwing
over the table a letter with a Milan post-mark. Charlotte was a little frightened as she took it up, but her
mind was relieved when she saw that it was merely
the bill of their Italian milliner. The sum total was
certainly large, but not so large as to create an important row.

"It's for our clothes, papa, for six months before
we came here. The three of us can't dress for nothing you know."

"Nothing, indeed!" said he, looking at the figures,
which in Milanese denominations were certainly monstrous.

"The man should have sent it to me," said Charlotte.

"I wish he had with all my heart—if you would
have paid it. I see enough in it, to know that three
quarters of it are for Madeline."

"She has little else to amuse her, sir," said Charlotte with true good nature.

"And I suppose he has nothing else to amuse him," said the doctor, throwing over another letter to his daughter. It was from some member of the family of Sidonia, and politely requested the father to pay a small trifle of 700*l.*, being the amount of a bill discounted in favour of Mr. Ethelbert Stanhope, and now overdue for a period of nine months.

Charlotte read the letter, slowly folded it up, and put it under the edge of the tea-tray.

"I suppose he has nothing to amuse him but discounting bills with Jews. Does he think I'll pay that?"

"I am sure he thinks no such thing," said she.

"And who does he think will pay it?"

"As far as honesty goes I suppose it won't much matter if it is never paid," said she. "I dare say he got very little of it."

"I suppose it won't much matter either," said the father, "if he goes to prison and rots there. It seems to me that that's the other alternative."

Dr. Stanhope spoke of the custom of his youth. But his daughter, though she had lived so long abroad, was much more completely versed in the ways of the English world. "If the man arrests him," said she, "he must go through the court."

It is thus, thou great family of Sidonia—it is thus that we Gentiles treat thee, when, in our extremest need, thou and thine have aided us with mountains of gold as big as lions,—and occasionally with wine-warrants and orders for dozens of dressing-cases.

"What, and become an insolvent?" said the doctor.

"He's that already," said Charlotte, wishing always to get over a difficulty.

"What a condition," said the doctor, "for the son of a clergyman of the Church of England."

"I don't see why clergymen's sons should pay their debts more than other young men," said Charlotte.

"He's had as much from me since he left school as is held sufficient for the eldest son of many a nobleman," said the angry father.

"Well, sir," said Charlotte, "give him another chance."

"What!" said the doctor, "do you mean that I am to pay that Jew?"

"Oh no! I wouldn't pay him, he must take his chance; and if the worst comes to the worst, Bertie must go abroad. But I want you to be civil to Bertie, and let him remain here as long as we stop. He has a plan in his head, that may put him on his feet after all."

"Has he any plan for following up his profession?"

"Oh, he'll do that too; but that must follow. He's thinking of getting married."

Just at that moment the door opened, and Bertie came in whistling. The doctor immediately devoted himself to his egg, and allowed Bertie to whistle himself round to his sister's side without noticing him.

Charlotte gave a sign to him with her eye, first glancing at her father, and then at the letter, the corner of which peeped out from under the tea-tray. Bertie saw and understood, and with the quiet motion of a cat abstracted the letter, and made himself acquainted with its contents. The doctor, however, had seen him, deep as he appeared to be mersed in his egg-shell, and said in his harshest voice, "Well, sir, do you know that gentleman?"

"Yes, sir," said Bertie. "I have a sort of ac-, quaintance with him, but none that can justify him in troubling you. If you will allow me, sir, I will answer this."

"At any rate I sha'n't," said the father, and then he added, after a pause, "Is it true, sir, that you owe the man 700*l.*?"

"Well," said Bertie, "I think I should be inclined to dispute the amount, if I were in a condition to pay him such of it as I really do owe him."

"Has he your bill for 700*l.*?" said the father, speaking very loudly and very angrily.

"Well, I believe he has," said Bertie; "but all the money I ever got from him was 150*l.*"

"And what became of the 550*l.*?"

"Why, sir; the commission was 100*l.* or so, and I took the remainder in paving stones and rocking-, horses."

"Paving-stones and rocking-horses!" said the doctor, "where are they?"

"Oh, sir, I suppose they are in London somewhere —but I'll inquire if you wish for them."

"He's an idiot," said the doctor, "and it's sheer folly to waste more money on him. Nothing can save him from ruin," and so saying, the unhappy father walked out of the room.

"Would the governor like to have the paving-stones?" said Bertie to his sister.

"I'll tell you what," said she. "If you don't take care, you will find yourself loose upon the world without even a house over your head: you don't know him as well as I do. He's very angry."

Bertie stroked his big beard, sipped his tea, chatted

over his misfortunes in a half comic, half serious tone, and ended by promising his sister that he would do his very best to make himself agreeable to the widow Bold. Then Charlotte followed her father to his own room and softened down his wrath, and persuaded him to say nothing more about the Jew bill discounter, at any rate for a few weeks. He even went so far as to say he would pay the 700*l.*, or at any rate settle the bill, if he saw a certainty of his son's securing for himself anything like a decent provision in life. Nothing was said openly between them about poor Eleanor: but the father and the daughter understood each other.

They all met together in the drawing-room at nine o'clock, in perfect good humour with each other; and about that hour Mrs. Bold was announced. She had never been in the house before, though she had of course called; and now she felt it strange to find herself there in her usual evening dress, entering the drawing-room of these strangers in this friendly unceremonious way, as though she had known them all her life. But in three minutes they made her at home. Charlotte tripped down stairs and took her bonnet from her, and Bertie came to relieve her from her shawl, and the signora smiled on her as she could smile when she chose to be gracious, and the old doctor shook hands with her in a kind benedictory manner that went to her heart at once, and made her feel that he must be a good man.

She had not been seated for above five minutes when the door again opened, and Mr. Slope was announced. She felt rather surprised, because she was told that nobody was to be there, and it was very evident from the manner of some of them, that Mr.

Slope was unexpected.   But still there was not much in it.   In such invitations a bachelor or two more or less are always spoken of as nobodies, and there was no reason why Mr. Slope should not drink tea at Dr. Stanhope's as well as Eleanor herself.   He, however, was very much surprised and not very much gratified at finding that his own embryo spouse made one of the party.   He had come there to gratify himself by gazing on Madame Neroni's beauty, and listening to and returning her flattery: and though he had not owned as much to himself, he still felt that if he spent the evening as he had intended to do, he might probably not thereby advance his suit with Mrs. Bold.

The signora, who had no idea of a rival, received Mr. Slope with her usual marks of distinction.   As he took her hand, she made some confidential communication to him in a low voice, declaring that she had a plan to communicate to him after tea, and was evidently prepared to go on with her work of reducing the chaplain to a state of captivity.   Poor Mr. Slope was rather beside himself.   He thought that Eleanor could not but have learnt from his demeanour that he was an admirer of her own, and he had also flattered himself that the idea was not unacceptable to her. What would she think of him if he now devoted himself to a married woman!

But Eleanor was not inclined to be severe in her criticisms on him in this respect, and felt no annoyance of any kind, when she found herself seated between Bertie and Charlotte Stanhope.   She had no suspicion of Mr. Slope's intentions; she had no suspicion even of the suspicion of other people; but still she felt well pleased not to have Mr. Slope too near to her.

And she was not ill-pleased to have Bertie Stanhope near her. It was rarely indeed that he failed to
make an agreeable impression on strangers. With a
bishop indeed who thought much of his own dignity it
was possible that he might fail, but hardly with a
young and pretty woman. He possessed the tact of
becoming instantly intimate with women without giving
rise to any fear of impertinence. He had about him
somewhat of the propensities of a tame cat. It seemed
quite natural that he should be petted, caressed, and
treated with familiar good nature, and that in return
he should purr, and be sleek and graceful, and above all
never show his claws. Like other tame cats, however,
he had his claws, and sometimes made them dangerous.

When tea was over Charlotte went to the open
window and declared loudly that the full harvest moon
was much too beautiful to be disregarded, and called
them all to look at it. To tell the truth, there was
but one there who cared much about the moon's beauty,
and that one was not Charlotte; but she knew how
valuable an aid to her purpose the chaste goddess
might become, and could easily create a little enthusiasm
for the purpose of the moment. Eleanor and Bertie
were soon with her. The doctor was now quiet in his
arm-chair, and Mrs. Stanhope in hers, both prepared
for slumber.

"Are you a Whewellite or a Brewsterite, or a
t'othermanite, Mrs. Bold?" said Charlotte, who knew
a little about everything, and had read about a third
of each of the books to which she alluded.

"Oh!" said Eleanor; "I have not read any of the
books, but I feel sure that there is one man in the
moon at least, if not more."

"You don't believe in the pulpy gelatinous matter?" said Bertie.

"I heard about that," said Eleanor; "and I really think it's almost wicked to talk in such a manner. How can we argue about God's power in the other stars from the laws which he has given for our rule in this one?"

"How indeed!" said Bertie. "Why shouldn't there be a race of salamanders in Venus? and even if there be nothing but fish in Jupiter, why shouldn't the fish there be as wide awake as the men and women here?"

"That would be saying very little for them," said Charlotte. "I am for Dr. Whewell myself; for I do not think that men and women are worth being repeated in such countless worlds. There may be souls in other stars, but I doubt their having any bodies attached to them. But come, Mrs. Bold, let us put our bonnets on and walk round the close. If we are to discuss sidereal questions, we shall do so much better under the towers of the cathedral, than stuck in this narrow window."

Mrs. Bold made no objection, and a party was made to walk out. Charlotte Stanhope well knew the rule as to three being no company, and she had therefore to induce her sister to allow Mr. Slope to accompany them.

"Come, Mr. Slope," she said; "I'm sure you'll join us. We shall be in again in a quarter of an hour, Madeline."

Madeline read in her eye all that she had to say, knew her object, and as she had to depend on her sister for so many of her amusements, she felt that she must yield. It was hard to be left alone while others

15*

of her own age walked out to feel the soft influence of the bright night, but it would be harder still to be without the sort of sanction which Charlotte gave to all her flirtation and intrigues. Charlotte's eye told her that she must give up just at present for the good of the family, and so Madeline obeyed.

But Charlotte's eyes said nothing of the sort to Mr. Slope. He had no objection at all to the *tête-à-tête* with the signora, which the departure of the other three would allow him, and gently whispered to her, "I shall not leave you alone."

"Oh, yes," said she; "go—pray go, pray go, for my sake. Do not think that I am so selfish. It is understood that nobody is kept within for me. You will understand this too when you know me better. Pray join them, Mr. Slope, but when you come in speak to me for five minutes before you leave us."

Mr. Slope understood that he was to go, and he therefore joined the party in the hall. He would have had no objection at all to this arrangement, if he could have secured Mrs. Bold's arm; but this of course was out of the question. Indeed, his fate was very soon settled, for no sooner had he reached the hall-door than Miss Stanhope put her hand within his arm, and Bertie walked off with Eleanor just as naturally as though she were already his own property.

And so they sauntered forth: first they walked round the close, according to their avowed intent; then they went under the old arched gateway below St. Cuthbert's little church, and then they turned behind the grounds of the bishop's palace, and so on till they came to the bridge just at the edge of the town, from which passers-by can look down into the gardens of Hiram's

Hospital; and here Charlotte and Mr. Slope, who were in advance, stopped till the other two came up to them. Mr. Slope knew that the gable-ends and old brick chimneys which stood up so prettily in the moonlight, were those of Mr. Harding's late abode, and would not have stopped on such a spot, in such company, if he could have avoided it; but Miss Stanhope would not take the hint which he tried to give.

"This is a very pretty place, Mrs. Bold," said Charlotte; "by far the prettiest place near Barchester. I wonder your father gave it up."

It was a very pretty place, and now by the deceitful light of the moon looked twice larger, twice prettier, twice more antiquely picturesque than it would have done in truth-telling daylight. Who does not know the air of complex multiplicity and the mysterious interesting grace which the moon always lends to old gabled buildings half surrounded, as was the hospital, by fine trees! As seen from the bridge on the night of which we are speaking, Mr. Harding's late abode did look very lovely; and though Eleanor did not grieve at her father's having left it, she felt at the moment an intense wish that he might be allowed to return.

"He is going to return to it almost immediately, is he not?" asked Bertie.

Eleanor made no immediate reply. Many such a question passes unanswered, without the notice of the questioner; but such was not now the case. They all remained silent as though expecting her to reply, and after a moment or two, Charlotte said, "I believe it is settled that Mr. Harding returns to the hospital, is it not?"

"I don't think anything about it is settled yet," said Eleanor.

"But it must be a matter of course," said Bertie; "that is, if your father wishes it; who else on earth could hold it after what has occurred?"

Eleanor quietly made her companion understand that the matter was one which she could not discuss in the present company; and then they passed on; Charlotte said she would go a short way up the hill out of the town so as to look back upon the towers of the cathedral, and as Eleanor lent upon Bertie's arm for assistance in the walk, she told him how the matter stood between her father and the bishop.

"And, he," said Bertie, pointing on to Mr. Slope, "what part does he take in it?"

Eleanor explained how Mr. Slope had at first endeavoured to tyrannise over her father, but how he had latterly come round, and done all he could to talk the bishop over in Mr. Harding's favour. "But my father," said she, "is hardly inclined to trust him; they all say he is so arrogant to the old clergymen of the city."

"Take my word for it," said Bertie, "your father is right. If I am not very much mistaken, that man is both arrogant and false."

They strolled up to the top of the hill, and then returned through the fields by a footpath which leads by a small wooden bridge, or rather a plank with a rustic rail to it, over the river to the other side of the cathedral from that at which they had started. They had thus walked round the bishop's grounds, through which the river runs, and round the cathedral and adjacent fields, and it was past eleven before they reached the doctor's door.

"It is very late," said Eleanor, "it will be a shame to disturb your mother again at such an hour."

"Oh," said Charlotte, laughing, "you won't disturb mamma; I dare say she is in bed by this time, and Madeline would be furious if you did not come in and see her. Come, Bertie, take Mrs. Bold's bonnet from her."

They went up stairs, and found the signora alone, reading. She looked somewhat sad and melancholy, but not more so perhaps than was sufficient to excite additional interest in the bosom of Mr. Slope; and she was soon deep in whispered intercourse with that happy gentleman, who was allowed to find a resting-place on her sofa. The signora had a way of whispering that was peculiarly her own, and was exactly the reverse of that which prevails among great tragedians. The great tragedian hisses out a positive whisper, made with bated breath, and produced by inarticulated tongue-formed sounds, but yet he is audible through the whole house. The signora however used no hisses, and produced all her words in a clear silver tone, but they could only be heard by the ear into which they were poured.

Charlotte hurried and skurried about the room hither and thither, doing, or pretending to do many things; and then saying something about seeing her mother, ran up stairs. Eleanor was thus left alone with Bertie, and she hardly felt an hour fly by her. To give Bertie his due credit, he could not have played his cards better. He did not make love to her, nor sigh, nor look languishing; but he was amusing and familiar, yet respectful; and when he left Eleanor at her own door at one o'clock, which he did by the bye with the assistance of the now jealous Slope, she thought that he was one of the most agreeable men, and the Stanhopes decidedly the most agreeable family, that she had ever met.

CHAPTER XX.

MR. ARABIN.

THE Rev. Francis Arabin, fellow of Lazarus, late professor of poetry at Oxford, and present vicar of St. Ewold, in the diocese of Barchester, must now be introduced personally to the reader. And as he will fill a conspicuous place in the volume, it is desirable that he should be made to stand before the reader's eye by the aid of such portraiture as the author is able to produce.

It is to be regretted that no mental method of daguerreotype or photography has yet been discovered, by which the characters of men can be reduced to writing and put into grammatical language with an unerring precision of truthful description. How often does the novelist feel, ay, and the historian also and the biographer, that he has conceived within his mind and accurately depicted on the tablet of his brain the full character and personage of a man, and that nevertheless, when he flies to pen and ink to perpetuate the portrait, his words forsake, elude, disappoint, and play the deuce with him, till at the end of a dozen pages the man described has no more resemblance to the man conceived than the sign-board at the corner of the street has to the Duke of Cambridge?

And yet such mechanical descriptive skill would hardly give more satisfaction to the reader than the skill of the photographer does to the anxious mother desirous to possess an absolute duplicate of her beloved child. The likeness is indeed true; but it is a dull, dead, unfeeling, inauspicious likeness. The face is indeed there, and those looking at it will know at once whose image it is; but the owner of the face will not be proud of the resemblance.

There is no royal road to learning; no short cut to the acquirement of any valuable art. Let photographers and daguerreotypers do what they will, and improve as they may with further skill on that which skill has already done, they will never achieve a portrait of the human face divine. Let biographers, novelists, and the rest of us groan as we may under the burdens which we so often feel too heavy for our shoulders; we must either bear them up like men, or own ourselves too weak for the work we have undertaken. There is no way of writing well and also of writing easily.

Labor omnia vincit improbus. Such should be the chosen motto of every labourer, and it may be that labour, if adequately enduring, may suffice at last to produce even some not untrue resemblance of the Rev. Francis Arabin.

Of his doings in the world, and of the sort of fame which he has achieved, enough has been already said. It has also been said that he is forty years of age, and still unmarried. He was the younger son of a country gentleman of small fortune in the north of England. At an early age he went to Winchester, and was intended by his father for New College; but though studious as a boy, he was not studious within the prescribed limits; and at the age of eighteen he left school with a character for talent, but without a scholarship. All that he had obtained, over and above the advantage of his character, was a gold medal for English verse, and hence was derived a strong presumption on the part of his friends that he was destined to add another name to the imperishable list of English poets.

From Winchester he went to Oxford, and was entered as a commoner at Balliol. Here his special career very soon commenced. He utterly eschewed the society of fast men, gave no wine parties, kept no horses, rowed no boats, joined no rows, and was the pride of his college tutor. Such at least was his career till he had taken his little go; and then he commenced a course of action which, though not less creditable to himself as a man, was hardly so much to the taste of the tutor. He became a member of a vigorous debating society, and rendered himself remarkable there for humorous energy. Though always in earnest, yet his earnestness was always droll. To be true in his ideas, unanswerable in his syllogisms, and just in his aspirations was not enough for him. He had failed, failed in his own opinion as well as that of others when others came to know him, if he could not reduce the arguments of his opponents to an absurdity, and conquer both by wit and reason. To say that his object was ever to raise a laugh, would be most untrue. He hated such common and unnecessary evidence of satisfaction on the part of his hearers. A joke that required to be laughed at was, with him, not worth uttering. He could appreciate by a keener sense than that of his ears the success of his wit, and would see in the eyes of his auditory whether or no he was understood and appreciated.

He had been a religious lad before he left school. That is, he had addicted himself to a party in religion, and having done so had received that benefit which most men do who become partisans in such a cause. We are much too apt to look at schism in our church as an unmitigated evil. Moderate schism, if there may be such a thing, at any rate calls attention to the subject, draws in supporters who would otherwise have been inattentive to the matter, and teaches men to think upon religion. How great an amount of good of this description has followed that movement in the Church of England which commenced with the publication of Froude's Remains!

As a boy young Arabin took up the cudgels on the side of the Tractarians, and at Oxford he sat for a while at the feet of the great Newman. To this cause he lent all his faculties. For it he concocted verses, for it he made speeches, for it he scintillated the brightest sparks of his quiet wit. For it he ate and drank and dressed, and had his being. In due process of time he took his degree, and wrote himself B. A., but he did not do so with any remarkable amount of academical éclat. He had occupied himself too much with high church matters, and the polemics, politics, and outward demonstrations usually concurrent with high churchmanship, to devote himself with sufficient vigour to the acquisition of a double first. He was not a double first, nor even a first class man; but he revenged himself on the university by putting firsts and double firsts out of fashion for the year, and laughing down a species of pedantry which at the age of twenty-three leaves no room in a man's mind for graver subjects than conic sections or Greek accents.

Greek accents, however, and conic sections were esteemed necessaries at Balliol, and there was no admittance there for Mr. Arabin within the list of its fellows. Lazarus, however, the richest and most comfortable abode of Oxford dons, opened its bosom to the young champion of a church militant. Mr. Arabin was ordained, and became a fellow soon after taking his degree, and shortly after that was chosen professor of poetry.

And now came the moment of his great danger. After many mental struggles, and an agony of doubt which may be well surmised, the great prophet of the Tractarians confessed himself a Roman Catholic. Mr. Newman left the Church of England, and with him carried many a waverer. He did not carry off Mr. Arabin, but the escape which that gentleman had was a very narrow one. He left Oxford for a while that he might meditate in complete peace on the step which appeared to him to be all but unavoidable, and shut himself up in a little village on the seashore of one of our remotest counties, that he might learn by communing with his own soul whether or no he could with a safe conscience remain within the pale of his mother church.

Things would have gone badly with him there had he been left entirely to himself. Every thing was against him: all his worldly interests required him to remain a Protestant; and he looked on his worldly interests as a legion of foes, to get the better of whom was a point of extremest honour. In his then state of ecstatic agony such a conquest would have cost him little; he could easily have thrown away all his livelihood; but it cost him much to get over the idea that

by choosing the Church of England he should be open
in his own mind to the charge that he had been led
to such a choice by unworthy motives. Then his heart
was against him: he loved with a strong and eager
love the man who had hitherto been his guide, and
yearned to follow his footsteps. His tastes were against
him: the ceremonies and pomps of the Church of Rome,
their august feasts and solemn fasts, invited his imagination and pleased his eye. His flesh was against
him: how great an aid would it be to a poor, weak,
wavering man to be constrained to high moral duties,
self-denial, obedience, and chastity by laws which were
certain in their enactments, and not to be broken
without loud, palpable, unmistakable sin! Then his
faith was against 'him: he required to believe so much;
panted so eagerly to give signs of his belief; deemed
it so insufficient to wash himself simply in the waters
of Jordan; that some great deed, such as that of for-
saking everything for a true church, had for him allure-
ments almost past withstanding.

Mr. Arabin was at this time a very young man,
and when he left Oxford for his far retreat was much
too confident in his powers of fence, and too apt to
look down on the ordinary sense of ordinary people, to
expect aid in the battle that he had to fight from any
chance inhabitants of the spot which he had selected.
But Providence was good to him; and there, in that
all but desolate place, on the storm-beat shore of that
distant sea, he met one who gradually calmed his
mind, quieted his imagination, and taught him something of a Christian's duty. When Mr. Arabin left
Oxford, he was inclined to look upon the rural clergymen of most English parishes almost with contempt.

It was his ambition, should he remain within the fold
of their church, to do somewhat towards redeeming
and rectifying their inferiority, and to assist in infus-
ing energy and faith into the hearts of Christian
ministers, who were, as he thought, too often satisfied
to go through life without much show of either.

And yet it was from such a one that Mr. Arabin
in his extremest need received that aid which he so
much required. It was from the poor curate of a small
Cornish parish that he first learnt to know that the
highest laws for the governance of a Christian's duty
must act from within and not from without; that no
man can become a serviceable servant solely by obedience to written edicts; and that the safety which he
was about to seek within the gates of Rome was no
other than the selfish freedom from personal danger
which the bad soldier attempts to gain who counter-
feits illness on the eve of battle.

Mr. Arabin returned to Oxford a humbler but a
better and a happier man; and from that time forth he
put his shoulder to the wheel as a clergyman of the
Church for which he had been educated. The intercourse of those among whom he familiarly lived kept
him staunch to the principles of that system of the
Church to which he had always belonged. Since his
severance from Mr. Newman, no one had had so strong
an influence over him as the head of his college.
During the time of his expected apostasy, Dr. Gwynne
had not felt much predisposition in favour of the young
fellow. Though a High Churchman himself within
moderate limits, Dr. Gwynne felt no sympathy with
men who could not satisfy their faiths with the Thirty-
nine articles. He regarded the enthusiasm of such as

Newman as a state of mind more nearly allied to mad-
ness than to religion and when he saw it evinced by
very young men, was inclined to attribute a good deal
of it to vanity. Dr. Gwynne himself, though a religious
man, was also a thoroughly practical man of the world,
and he regarded with no favourable eye the tenets of
any one who looked on the two things as incompatible.
When ·he found that Mr. Arabin was a half Roman, he
began to regret all he had done towards bestowing a
fellowship on so unworthy a recipient; and when again
he learnt that Mr. Arabin would probably complete his
journey to Rome, he regarded with some satisfaction
the fact that in such case the fellowship would be
again vacant.

When, however, Mr. Arabin returned and professed
himself a confirmed Protestant, the master of Lazarus
again opened his arms to him, and gradually he became the pet of the college. For some little time he
was saturnine, silent, and unwilling to take any prominent part in university broils; but gradually his
mind recovered, or rather made its tone, and he became
known as a man always ready at a moment's notice to
take up the cudgels in opposition to anything that
savoured of an evangelical bearing. He was great in
sermons, great on platforms, great at after dinner con-
versations, and always pleasant as well as great. He
took delight in elections, served on committees, opposed tooth and nail all projects of university reform,
and talked jovially over his glass of port of the ruin
to be anticipated by the Church, and of the sacrilege
daily committed by the Whigs. The ordeal through
which he had gone, in resisting the blandishments of
the lady of Rome, had certainly done much towards

the strengthening of his character. Although in small and outward matters he was self-confident enough, nevertheless in things affecting the inner man he aimed at a humility of spirit which would never have been attractive to him but for that visit to the coast of Cornwall. This visit he now repeated every year.

Such is an interior view of Mr. Arabin at the time when he accepted the living of St. Ewold. Exteriorly, he was not a remarkable person. He was above the middle height, well made, and very active. His hair which had been jet black, was now tinged with gray, but his face bore no sign of years. It would perhaps be wrong to say that he was handsome, but his face was, nevertheless, pleasant to look upon. The cheek bones were rather too high for beauty, and the formation of the forehead too massive and heavy: but the eyes, nose, and mouth were perfect. There was a continual play of lambent fire about his eyes, which gave promise of either pathos or humour whenever he essayed to speak, and that promise was rarely broken. There was a gentle play about his mouth which declared that his wit never descended to sarcasm, and that there was no ill-nature in his repartee.

Mr. Arabin was a popular man among women, but more so as a general than a special favourite. Living as a fellow at Oxford, marriage with him had been out of the question, and it may be doubted whether he had ever allowed his heart to be touched. Though belonging to a Church in which celibacy is not the required lot of its ministers, he had come to regard himself as one of those clergymen to whom to be a bachelor is almost a necessity. He had never looked for parochial duty, and his career at Oxford was utterly incompatible with such domestic joys as a wife and nursery. He looked on women, therefore, in the same light that one sees them regarded by many Romish priests. He liked to have near him that which was pretty and amusing, but women generally were little more to him than children. He talked to them without putting out all his powers, and listened to them without any idea that what he should hear from them could either actuate his conduct or influence his opinion.

Such was Mr. Arabin, the new vicar of St. Ewold, who is going to stay with the Grantlys, at Plumstead Episcopi.

Mr. Arabin reached Plumstead the day before Mr. Harding and Eleanor, and the Grantly family were thus enabled to make his acquaintance and discuss his qualifications before the arrival of the other guests. Griselda was surprised to find that he looked so young; but she told Florinda her younger sister, when they had retired for the night, that he did not talk at all like a young man; and she decided with the authority that seventeen has over sixteen, that he was not at all nice, although his eyes were lovely. As usual, sixteen implicitly acceded to the dictum of seventeen in such a matter, and said that he certainly was not nice. They then branched off on the relative merits of other clerical bachelors in the vicinity, and both determined without any feeling of jealousy between them that a certain Rev. Augustus Green was by many degrees the most estimable of the lot. The gentleman in question had certainly much in his favour, as, having a comfortable allowance from his father, he could devote the whole proceeds of his curacy to violet gloves and unexceptionable neck ties. Having thus fixedly resolved that the new comer had nothing about him to shake the pre-eminence of the exalted Green, the two girls went to sleep in each other's arms, contented with themselves and the world.

Mrs. Grantly at first sight came to much the same conclusion about her husband's favourite as her daughters had done, though, in seeking to measure his relative value, she did not compare him to Mr. Green; indeed, she made no comparison by name between him and any one else; but she remarked to her husband that one person's swans were very often another person's geese, thereby clearly showing that Mr. Arabin had not yet proved his qualifications in swanhood to her satisfaction.

"Well, Susan," said he, rather offended at hearing his friend spoken of so disrespectfully, "if you take Mr. Arabin for a goose, I cannot say that I think very highly of your discrimination."

"A goose! No, of course, he's not a goose. I've no doubt he's a very clever man. But you're so matter-of-fact, archdeacon, when it suits your purpose, that one can't trust oneself to any *façon de parler*. I've no doubt Mr. Arabin is a very valuable man—at Oxford, and that he'll be a good vicar at St. Ewold. All I mean is, that having passed one evening with him, I don't find him to be absolutely a paragon. In the first place, if I am not mistaken, he is a little inclined to be conceited."

"Of all the men that I know intimately," said the archdeacon, "Arabin is, in my opinion, the most free from any taint of self-conceit. His fault is that he's too diffident."

"Perhaps so," said the lady; "only I must own I did not find it out this evening."

Nothing further was said about him. Dr. Grantly thought that his wife was abusing Mr. Arabin merely because he had praised him; and Mrs. Grantly knew that it was useless arguing for or against any person in favour or in opposition to whom the archdeacon had already pronounced a strong opinion.

In truth they were both right. Mr. Arabin was a diffident man in social intercourse with those whom he did not intimately know; when placed in situations which it was his business to fill, and discussing matters with which it was his duty to be conversant, Mr. Arabin was from habit brazen-faced enough. When standing on a platform in Exeter Hall, no man would be less mazed than he by the eyes of the crowd before him; for such was the work which his profession had called on him to perform; but he shrank from a strong expression of opinion in general society, and his doing so not uncommonly made it appear that he considered the company not worth the trouble of his energy. He was averse to dictate when the place did not seem to him to justify dictation; and as those subjects on which people wished to hear him speak were such as he was accustomed to treat with decision, he generally shunned the traps there were laid to allure him into discussion, and, by doing so, not unfrequently subjected himself to such charges as those brought against him by Mrs. Grantly.

Mr. Arabin, as he sat at his open window, enjoying the delicious moonlight and gazing at the gray towers of the church, which stood almost within the rectory grounds, little dreamed that he was the subject of so many friendly or unfriendly criticisms. Considering how much we are all given to discuss the characters of

16*

others, and discuss them often not in the strictest spirit of charity, it is singular how little we are inclined to think that others can speak ill-naturedly of us, and how angry and hurt we are when proof reaches us that they have done so. It is hardly too much to say that we all of us occasionally speak of our dearest friends in a manner in which those dearest friends would very little like to hear themselves mentioned; and that we nevertheless expect that our dearest friends shall invariably speak of us as though they were blind to all our faults, but keenly alive to every shade of our virtues.

It did not occur to Mr. Arabin that he was spoken of at all. It seemed to him, when he compared himself with his host, that he was a person of so little consequence to any, that he was worth no one's words or thoughts. He was utterly alone in the world as regarded domestic ties and those inner familiar relations which are hardly possible between others than husbands and wives, parents and children, or brothers and sisters. He had often discussed with himself the necessity of such bonds for a man's happiness in this world, and had generally satisfied himself with the answer that happiness in this world is not a necessity. Herein he deceived himself, or rather tried to do so. He, like others, yearned for the enjoyment of whatever he saw enjoyable; and though he attempted, with the modern stoicism of so many Christians, to make himself believe that joy and sorrow were matters which here should be held as perfectly indifferent, these things were not indifferent to him. He was tired of his Oxford rooms and his college life. He regarded the wife and children of his friend with something like envy; he all but coveted the pleasant drawing-room, with its pretty windows opening on to lawns and flower-beds, the apparel of the comfortable house, and—above all—the air of home which encompassed it all.

It will be said that no time can have been so fitted for such desires on his part as this, when he had possessed himself of a country parish, of a living among fields and gardens, of a house which a wife would grace. It is true there was a difference between the opulence of Plumstead and the modest economy of St. Ewold; but surely Mr. Arabin was not a man to sigh after wealth! Of all men, his friends would have unanimously declared he was the last to do so. But how little our friends know us! In his period of stoical rejection of this world's happiness, he had cast from him as utter dross all anxiety as to fortune. He had, as it were, proclaimed himself to be indifferent to promotion, and those who chiefly admired his talents, and would mainly have exerted themselves to secure to them their deserved reward, had taken him at his word. And now, if the truth must out, he felt himself disappointed—disappointed not by them but by himself. The day-dream of his youth was over, and at the age of forty he felt that he was not fit to work in the spirit of an apostle. He had mistaken himself, and learned his mistake when it was past remedy. He had professed himself indifferent to mitres and diaconal residences, to rich livings and pleasant glebes, and now he had to own to himself that he was sighing for the good things of other men, on whom in his pride he had ventured to look down.

Not for wealth, in its vulgar sense, had he ever sighed; not for the enjoyment of rich things had he ever longed; but for the allotted share of worldly bliss, which a wife, and children, and happy home could give him, for that usual amount of comfort which he had ventured to reject as unnecessary for him, he did now feel that he would have been wiser to have searched.

He knew that his talents, his position, and his friends would have won for him promotion, had he put himself in the way of winning it. Instead of doing so, he had allowed himself to be persuaded to accept a living which would give him an income of some 300*l.* a year, should he, by marrying, throw up his fellowship. Such, at the age of forty, was the worldly result of labour, which the world had chosen to regard as successful. The world also thought that Mr. Arabin was, in his own estimation, sufficiently paid. Alas! alas! the world was mistaken; and Mr. Arabin was beginning to ascertain that such was the case.

And here, may I beg the reader not to be hard in his judgment upon this man. Is not the state at which he has arrived, the natural result of efforts to reach that which is not the condition of humanity? Is not modern stoicism, built though it be on Christianity, as great an outrage on human nature as was the stoicism of the ancients? The philosophy of Zeno was built on true laws, but on true laws misunderstood, and therefore misapplied. It is the same with our Stoics here, who would teach us that wealth and worldly comfort and happiness on earth are not worth the search. Alas, for a doctrine which can find no believing pupils and no true teachers!

The case of Mr. Arabin was the more singular, as he belonged to a branch of the Church of England well inclined to regard its temporalities with avowed favour, and had habitually lived with men who were accustomed to much worldly comfort. But such was his idiosyncrasy, that these very facts had produced within him, in early life, a state of mind that was not natural to him. He was content to be a High Churchman, if he could be so on principles of his own, and could strike out a course showing a marked difference from those with whom he consorted. He was ready to be a partisan as long as he was allowed to have a course of action and of thought unlike that of his party. His party had indulged him, and he began to feel that his party was right and himself wrong, just when such a conviction was too late to be of service to him. He discovered, when such discovery was no longer serviceable, that it *would* have been worth his while to have worked for the usual pay assigned to work in this world, and have earned a wife and children, with a carriage for them to sit in; to have earned a pleasant dining-room, in which his friends could drink his wine, and the power of walking up the high street of his country town, with the knowledge that all its tradesmen would have gladly welcomed him within their doors. Other men arrived at those convictions in their start in life, and so worked up to them. To him they had come when they were too late to be of use.

It has been said that Mr. Arabin was a man of pleasantry; and it may be thought that such a state of mind as that described, would be antagonistic to humour. But surely such is not the case. Wit is the outward mental casing of the man, and has no more to do with the inner mind of thoughts and feelings than have the rich brocaded garments of the priest at the altar with the asceticism of the anchorite below them, whose skin is tormented with sackcloth, and whose body is half flayed with rods. Nay, will not such a one often rejoice more than any other in the rich show of his outer apparel? Will it not be food for his pride to feel that he groans inwardly, while he shines outwardly? So it is with the mental efforts which men make. Those which they show forth daily to the world are often the opposites of the inner workings of the spirit.

In the archdeacon's drawing-room, Mr. Arabin had sparkled with his usual unaffected brilliancy, but when he retired to his bed-room, he sat there sad, at his open window, repining within himself that he also had no wife, no bairns, no soft sward of lawn duly mown for him to lie on, no herd of attendant curates, no bowings from the banker's clerks, no rich rectory. That apostleship that he had thought of had evaded his grasp, and he was now only vicar of St. Ewold's, with a taste for a mitre. Truly he had fallen between two stools.

CHAPTER XXI.
ST. EWOLD'S PARSONAGE.

When Mr. Harding and Mrs. Bold reached the rectory on the following morning, the archdeacon and his friend were at St. Ewold's. They had gone over that the new vicar might inspect his church, and be introduced to the squire, and were not expected back before dinner. Mr. Harding rambled out by himself, and strolled, as was his wont at Plumstead, about the lawn and round the church; and as he did so, the two sisters naturally fell into conversation about Barchester.

There was not much sisterly confidence between them. Mrs. Grantly was ten years older than Eleanor, and had been married while Eleanor was yet a child. They had never, therefore, poured into each other's ears their hopes and loves; and now that one was a wife and the other a widow, it was not probable that they would begin to do so. They lived too much asunder to be able to fall into that kind of intercourse which makes confidence between sisters almost a necessity; and, moreover, that which is so easy at eighteen is often very difficult at twenty-eight. Mrs. Grantly knew this, and did not, therefore, expect confidence from her sister; and yet she longed to ask her whether in real truth Mr. Slope was agreeable to her.

It was by no means difficult to turn the conversation to Mr. Slope. That gentleman had become so famous at Barchester, had so much to do with all clergymen connected with the city, and was so specially concerned in the affairs of Mr. Harding, that it would have been odd if Mr. Harding's daughters had not talked about him. Mrs. Grantly was soon abusing him, which she did with her whole heart; and Mrs. Bold was nearly as eager to defend him. She positively disliked the man, would have been delighted to learn that he had taken himself off so that she should never see him again, had indeed almost a fear of him, and yet she constantly found herself taking his part. The abuse of other people, and abuse of a nature that she felt to be unjust, imposed this necessity on her, and at last made Mr. Slope's defence an habitual course of argument with her.

From Mr. Slope the conversation turned to the Stanhopes, and Mrs. Grantly was listening with some interest to Eleanor's account of the family, when it dropped out that Mr. Slope made one of the party.

"What!" said the lady of the rectory, "was Mr. Slope there too?"

Eleanor merely replied that such had been the case.

"Why, Eleanor, he must be very fond of you, I think; he seems to follow you everywhere."

Even this did not open Eleanor's eyes. She merely laughed, and said that she imagined Mr. Slope found other attraction at Dr. Stanhope's. And so they parted. Mrs. Grantly felt quite convinced that the odious match would take place; and Mrs. Bold as convinced that that unfortunate chaplain, disagreeable as he must be allowed to be, was more sinned against than sinning.

The archdeacon of course heard before dinner that Eleanor had remained the day before in Barchester with the view of meeting Mr. Slope, and that she had so met him. He remembered how she had positively stated that there were to be no guests at the Stanhopes, and he did not hesitate to accuse her of deceit. Moreover, the fact, or rather presumed fact, of her being deceitful on such a matter, spoke but too plainly in evidence against her as to her imputed crime of receiving Mr. Slope as a lover.

"I am afraid that anything we can do will be too late," said the archdeacon. "I own I am fairly surprised. I never liked your sister's taste with regard to men; but still I did not give her credit for——ugh!"

"And so soon, too," said Mrs. Grantly, who thought more, perhaps, of her sister's indecorum in having a lover before she had put off her weeds, than her bad taste in having such a lover as Mr. Slope.

"Well, my dear, I shall be sorry to be harsh, or to do anything that can hurt your father; but, positively, neither that man nor his wife shall come within my doors."

Mrs. Grantly sighed, and then attempted to console herself and her lord by remarking that, after all, the thing was not accomplished yet. Now that Eleanor was at Plumstead, much might be done to wean her from her fatal passion. Poor Eleanor!

The evening passed off without anything to make it remarkable. Mr. Arabin discussed the parish of St. Ewold with the Archdeacon, and Mrs. Grantly and Mr. Harding, who knew the personages of the parish, joined in. Eleanor also knew them, but she said little. Mr. Arabin did not apparently take much notice of her, and she was not in a humour to receive at that time with any special grace any special favourite of her brother-in-law. Her first idea on reaching her bedroom was that a much pleasanter family party might be met at Dr. Stanhope's than at the rectory. She began to think that she was getting tired of clergymen and their respectable humdrum wearisome mode of living, and that after all, people in the outer world, who had lived in Italy, London, or elsewhere, need not necessarily be regarded as atrocious and abominable. The Stanhopes, she had thought, were a giddy, thoughtless, extravagant set of people; but she had seen nothing wrong about them, and had, on the other hand, found that they thoroughly knew how to make their house agreeable. It was a thousand pities, she thought, that the archdeacon should not have a little of the same *savoir vivre*. Mr. Arabin, as we have said, did not apparently take much notice of her; but yet he did not go to bed without feeling that he had been in company with a very pretty woman; and as is the case with most bachelors, and some married men, regarded the prospect of his month's visit at Plumstead in a pleasanter light, when he learnt that a very pretty woman was to share it with him.

Before they all retired it was settled that the whole party should drive over on the following day to inspect the parsonage at St. Ewold. The three clergymen were to discuss dilapidations, and the two ladies were to lend their assistance in suggesting such changes as might be necessary for a bachelor's abode. Accordingly, soon after breakfast, the carriage was at the door. There was only room for four inside, and the archdeacon got upon the box. Eleanor found herself opposite to Mr. Arabin, and was, therefore, in a manner forced into conversation with him. They were soon on comfortable terms together; and had she thought about it, she would have thought that, in spite of his black cloth, Mr. Arabin would not have been a bad addition to the Stanhope family party.

Now that the archdeacon was away, they could all trifle. Mr. Harding began by telling them in the most innocent manner imaginable an old legend about Mr. Arabin's new parish. There was, he said, in days of yore, an illustrious priestess of St. Ewold, famed through the whole country for curing all manner of diseases. She had a well, as all priestesses have ever had, which well was extant to this day, and shared in the minds of many of the people the sanctity which belonged to the consecrated ground of the parish church. Mr. Arabin declared that he should look on such tenets on the part of his parishioners as anything but orthodox. And Mrs. Grantly replied that she so entirely disagreed with him as to think that no parish was in a proper state that had not its priestess as well at its priest. "The duties are never well done," said she, "unless they are so divided."

"I suppose, papa," said Eleanor, "that in the olden times the priestess bore all the sway herself. Mr. Arabin, perhaps, thinks that such might be too much the case now if a sacred lady were admitted within the parish."

"I think, at any rate," said he, "that it is safer to run no such risk. No priestly pride has ever exceeded that of sacerdotal females. A very lowly curate I might, perhaps, essay to rule; but a curatess would be sure to get the better of me."

"There are certainly examples of such accidents happening," said Mrs. Grantly. "They do say that there is a priestess at Barchester who is very imperious in all things touching the altar. Perhaps the fear of such a fate as that is before your eyes."

When they were joined by the archdeacon on the gravel before the vicarage, they descended again to grave dulness. Not that Archdeacon Grantly was a dull man; but his frolic humours were of a cumbrous kind; and his wit, when he was witty, did not generally extend itself to his auditory. On the present occasion he was soon making speeches about wounded roofs and walls, which he declared to be in want of some surgeon's art. There was not a partition that he did not tap, nor a block of chimneys that he did not narrowly examine; all water-pipes, flues, cisterns, and sewers underwent an investigation; and he even descended, in the care of his friend, so far as to bore sundry boards in the floors with a bradawl.

Mr. Arabin accompanied him through the rooms, trying to look wise in such domestic matters, and the other three also followed. Mrs. Grantly showed that she had not herself been priestess of a parish twenty years for nothing, and examined the bells and window panes in a very knowing way.

"You will, at any rate, have a beautiful prospect out of your own window, if this is to be your private sanctum," said Eleanor. She was standing at the lattice of a little room up stairs, from which the view certainly was very lovely. It was from the back of the vicarage, and there was nothing to interrupt the eye between the house and the glorious gray pile of the cathedral. The intermediate ground, however, was beautifully studded with timber. In the immediate foreground ran the little river which afterwards skirted the city; and, just to the right of the cathedral, the pointed gables and chimneys of Hiram's Hospital peeped out of the elms which encompass it.

"Yes," said he, joining her. "I shall have a beautifully complete view of my adversaries. I shall sit down before the hostile town, and fire away at them at a very pleasant distance. I shall just be able to lodge a shot in the hospital, should the enemy ever get possession of it; and as for the palace, I have it within full range."

"I never saw anything like you clergymen," said Eleanor; "you are always thinking of fighting each other."

"Either that," said he, "or else supporting each other. The pity is that we cannot do the one without the other. But are we not here to fight? Is not ours a church militant? What is all our work but fighting, and hard fighting, if it be well done?"

"But not with each other."

"That's as it may be. The same complaint which you make of me for battling with another clergyman of our own church, the Mohammedan would make against me for battling with the error of a priest of Rome. Yet, surely, you would not be inclined to say that I should be wrong to do battle with such as him. A pagan, too, with his multiplicity of gods, would think it equally odd that the Christian and the Mohammedan should disagree."

"Ah! but you wage your wars about trifles so bitterly."

"Wars about trifles," said he, "are always bitter, especially among neighbours. When the differences are great, and the parties comparative strangers, men quarrel with courtesy. What combatants are ever so eager as two brothers?"

"But do not such contentions bring scandal on the church?"

"More scandal would fall on the church if there were no such contentions. We have but one way to avoid them—that of acknowledging a common head of our church, whose word on all points of doctrine shall be authoritative. Such a termination of our difficulties is alluring enough. It has charms which are irresistible to many, and all but irresistible, I own, to me."

"You speak now of the Church of Rome?" said Eleanor.

"No," said he, "not necessarily of the Church of

Rome; but of *a* church with *a* head.   Had it pleased
God to vouchsafe to us such a church our path would
have been easy.   But easy paths have not been thought
good for us."   He paused and stood silent for a while,
thinking of the time when he had so nearly sacrificed
all he had, his powers of mind, his free agency, the
fresh running waters of his mind's fountain, his very
inner self, for an easy path in which no fighting would
be needed; and then he continued:—"What you say
is partly true; our contentions do bring on us some
scandal.   The outer world, though it constantly reviles
us for our human infirmities, and throws in our teeth
the fact that being clergymen we are still no more
than men, demands of us that we should do our work
with godlike perfection.   There is nothing godlike
about us: we differ from each other with the acerbity
common to man—we triumph over each other with
human frailty—we allow differences on subjects of
divine origin to produce among us antipathies and
enmities which are anything but divine.   This is all
true.   But what would you have in place of it?   There
is no infallible head for a church on earth.   This
dream of believing man has been tried, and we see
in Italy and in Spain what has come of it.   Grant
that there are and have been no bickerings within
the pale of the Pope's Church.   Such an assumption
would be utterly untrue; but let us grant it, and then
let us say which church has incurred the heavier
scandals."

There was a quiet earnestness about Mr. Arabin,
as he half acknowledged and half defended himself
from the charge brought against him, which surprised
Eleanor.   She had been used all her life to listen to

clerical discussion; but the points at issue between the disputants had so seldom been of more than temporal significance as to have left on her mind no feeling of reverence for such subjects. There had always been a hard worldly leaven of the love either of income or of power in the strains she had heard; there had been no panting for the truth; no aspirations after religious purity. It had always been taken for granted by those around her that they were indubitably right, that there was no ground for doubt, that the hard uphill work of ascertaining what the duty of a clergyman should be had been already accomplished in full; and that what remained for an active militant parson to do, was to hold his own against all comers. Her father, it is true, was an exception to this; but then he was so essentially antimilitant in all things, that she classed him in her own mind apart from all others. She had never argued the matter within herself, or considered whether this common tone was or was not faulty; but she was sick of it without knowing that she was so. And now she found to her surprise and not without a certain pleasurable excitement, that this new comer among them spoke in a manner very different from that to which she was accustomed.

"It is so easy to condemn," said he, continuing the thread of his thoughts. "I know no life that must be so delicious as that of a writer for newspapers, or a leading member of the opposition—to thunder forth accusations against men in power; show up the worst side of everything that is produced; to pick holes in every coat; to be indignant, sarcastic, jocose, moral, or supercilious; to damn with faint praise, or crush, with open calumny! What can be so easy as this

when the critic has to be responsible for nothing?
You condemn what I do; but put yourself in my position and do the reverse, and then see if I cannot
condemn you."

"Oh! Mr. Arabin, I do not condemn you."

"Pardon me, you do, Mrs. Bold—you as one of
the world; you are now the opposition member; you
are now composing your leading article, and well and
bitterly you do it. 'Let dogs delight to bark and
bite;' you fitly begin with an elegant quotation; 'but
if we are to have a church at all, in heaven's name
let the pastors who preside over it keep their hands
from each other's throats. Lawyers can live without
befouling each other's names; doctors do not fight
duels. Why is it that clergymen alone should indulge
themselves in such unrestrained liberty of abuse against
each other?' and so you go on reviling us for our un-
godly quarrels, our sectarian propensities, and scandalous
difference. It will, however, give you no trouble to
write another article next week in which we, or some
of us, shall be twitted with an unseemly apathy in
matters of our vocation. It will not fall on you to
reconcile the discrepancy; your reader will never ask
you how the poor parson is to be urgent in season
and out of season, and yet never come in contact with
men who think widely differently from him. You,
when you condemn this foreign treaty, or that official
arrangement, will have to incur no blame for the
graver faults of any different measure. It is so easy
to condemn; and so pleasant too; for eulogy charms
no listeners as detraction does."

Eleanor only half followed him in his raillery, but
she caught his meaning. "I know I ought to apologise

for presuming to criticise you," she said; "but I was thinking with sorrow of the ill-will that has lately come among us at Barchester, and I spoke more freely than I should have done."

"Peace on earth and good-will among men, are, like heaven, promises for the future;" said he, following rather his own thoughts than hers. "When that prophecy is accomplished, there will no longer be any need for clergymen."

Here they were interrupted by the archdeacon, whose voice was heard from the cellar shouting to the vicar.

"Arabin, Arabin,"—and then turning to his wife, who was apparently at his elbow—"where has he gone to? This cellar is perfectly abominable. It would be murder to put a bottle of wine into it till it has been roofed, walled, and floored. How on earth old Goodenough ever got on with it, I cannot guess. But then Goodenough never had a glass of wine that any man could drink."

"What is it, archdeacon?" said the vicar, running down stairs, and leaving Eleanor above to her meditations.

"This cellar must be roofed, walled, and floored," repeated the archdeacon. "Now mind what I say, and don't let the architect persuade you that it will do; half of these fellows know nothing about wine. This place as it is now would be damp and cold in winter, and hot and muggy in summer. I wouldn't give a straw for the best wine that ever was vinted, after it had lain here a couple of years."

Mr. Arabin assented, and promised that the cellar should be reconstructed according to the archdeacon's receipt.

17*

"And, Arabin, look here; was such an attempt at
a kitchen grate ever seen?"

"The grate is really very bad," said Mrs. Grantly;
"I am sure the priestess won't approve of it, when she
is brought home to the scene of her future duties.
Really, Mr. Arabin, no priestess accustomed to such an
excellent well as that above could put up with such a
grate as this."

"If there must be a priestess at St. Ewold's at all,
Mrs. Grantly, I think we will leave her to her well,
and not call down her divine wrath on any of the im-
perfections rising from our human poverty. However,
I own I am amenable to the attractions of a well-
cooked dinner, and the grate shall certainly be changed."

By this time the archdeacon had again ascended,
and was now in the dining-room. "Arabin," said he,
speaking in his usual loud clear voice, and with that
tone of dictation which was so common to him; "you
must positively alter this dining-room, that is, remodel
it altogether; look here, it is just sixteen feet by
fifteen; did anybody ever hear of a dining-room of
such proportions!" and the archdeacon stepped the
room long-ways and cross-ways with ponderous steps,
as though a certain amount of ecclesiastical dignity
could be imparted even to such an occupation as that
by the manner of doing it. "Barely sixteen; you may
call it a square."

"It would do very well for a round table," suggested the ex-warden.

Now there was something peculiarly unorthodox in
the archdeacon's estimation in the idea of a round table.
He had always been accustomed to a goodly board of
decent length, comfortably elongating itself according

to the number of the guests, nearly black with perpetual rubbing, and as bright as a mirror. Now round dinner tables are generally of oak, or else of such new construction as not to have acquired the peculiar hue which was so pleasing to him. He connected them with what he called the nasty new fangled method of leaving a cloth on the table, as though to warn people that they were not to sit long. In his eyes there was something democratic and parvenue in a round table. He imagined that dissenters and calico-printers chiefly used them, and perhaps a few literary lions more conspicuous for their wit than their gentility. He was a little flurried at the idea of such an article being introduced into the diocese by a protégé of his own, and at the instigation of his father in-law.

"A round dinner-table," said he, with some heat, "is the most abominable article of furniture that ever was invented. I hope that Arabin has more taste than to allow such a thing in his house."

Poor Mr. Harding felt himself completely snubbed, and of course said nothing further; but Mr. Arabin who had yielded submissively in the small matters of the cellar and kitchen grate, found himself obliged to oppose reforms which might be of a nature too expensive for his pocket.

"But it seems to me, archdeacon, that I can't very well lengthen the room without pulling down the wall, and if I pull down the wall, I must build it up again; then if I throw out a bow on this side, I must do the same on the other, then if I do it for the ground floor, I must carry it up to the floor above. That will be putting a new front to the house, and will cost, I suppose a couple of hundred pounds. The ecclesiastical commissioners will hardly assist me when they hear that my grievance consists in having a dining room only sixteen feet long."

The archdeacon proceeded to explain that nothing would be easier than adding six feet to the front of the dining-room, without touching any other room in the house. Such irregularities of construction in small country houses were, he said, rather graceful than otherwise, and he offered to pay for the whole thing out of his own pocket if it cost more than forty pounds. Mr. Arabin, however, was firm, and, although the archdeacon fussed and fumed about it, would not give way.

Forty pounds, he said, was a matter of serious moment to him, and his friends, if under such circumstances they would be good-natured enough to come to him at all, must put up with the misery of a square room. He was willing to compromise matters by disclaiming any intention of having a round table.

"But," said Mrs. Grantly, "what if the priestess insists on having both the rooms enlarged?"

"The priestess in that case must do it for herself, Mrs. Grantly."

"I have no doubt she will be well able to do so," replied the lady; "to do that and many more wonderful things. I am quite sure that the priestess of St. Ewold, when she does come, won't come empty-handed."

Mr. Arabin, however, did not appear well inclined to enter into speculative expenses on such a chance as this, and therefore, any material alterations in the house, the cost of which could not fairly be made to lie at the door either of the ecclesiastical commissioners or of the estate of the late incumbent, were tabooed.

With this essential exception, the archdeacon ordered, suggested, and carried all points before him in a manner very much to his own satisfaction. A close observer, had there been one there, might have seen that his wife had been quite as useful in the matter as himself. No one knew better than Mrs. Grantly the appurtenances necessary to a comfortable house. She did not, however, think it necessary to lay claim to any of the glory which her lord and master was so ready to appropriate as his own.

Having gone through their work effectually and systematically, the party returned to Plumstead well satisfied with their expedition.

CHAPTER XXII.

THE THORNES OF ULLATHORNE.

On the following Sunday Mr. Arabin was to read himself in at his new church. It was agreed at the rectory that the archdeacon should go over with him and assist at the reading-desk, and that Mr. Harding should take the archdeacon's duty at Plumstead Church. Mrs. Grantly had her school and her buns to attend to, and professed that she could not be spared; but Mrs. Bold was to accompany them. It was further agreed also, that they would lunch at the squire's house, and return home after the afternoon service.

Wilfred Thorne, Esq., of Ullathorne, was the squire of St. Ewold's; or rather the squire of Ullathorne; for the domain of the modern landlord was of wider notoriety than the fame of the ancient saint. He was a fair specimen of what that race has come to in our days, which a century ago was, as we are told, fairly represented by Squire Western. If that representation be a true one, few classes of men can have made faster strides in improvement. Mr. Thorne, however, was a man possessed of quite a sufficient number of foibles to lay him open to much ridicule. He was still a bachelor, being about fifty, and was not a little proud of his person. When living at home at Ullathorne there was not much room for such pride, and there therefore he always looked like a gentleman, and like that which he certainly was, the first man in his parish. But during the month or six weeks which he annually spent in London, he tried so hard to look like a great man there also, which he certainly was not, that he was put down as a fool by many at his club. He was a man of considerable literary attainment in a certain way and on certain subjects. His favourite authors were Montaigne and Burton, and he knew more perhaps than any other man in his own county, and the next to it, of the English essayists of the two last centuries. He possessed complete sets of the "Idler," the "Spectator," the "Tatler," the "Guardian," and the "Rambler;" and would discourse by hours together on the superiority of such publications to anything which has since been produced in our Edinburghs and Quarterlies. He was a great proficient in all questions of genealogy, and knew enough of almost every gentleman's family in England to say of what blood and lineage were descended all those who had any claim to be considered as possessors of any such luxuries. For blood and lineage he himself had a most profound respect. He counted back his own ancestors to some period long antecedent to the Conquest; and could tell you, if you would listen to him, how it had come to pass that they, like Cedric the Saxon, had been permitted to hold their own among the Norman barons. It was not, according to his showing, on account of any weak complaisance on the part of his family towards their Norman neighbours. Some Ealfried of Ullathorne once fortified his own castle, and held out, not only that, but the then existing cathedral of Barchester also, against one Geoffrey De Burgh, in the time of King John; and Mr. Thorne possessed the whole history of the siege written on vellum, and illuminated in a most costly manner. It little signified that no one could read the writing, as, had that been possible, no one could have understood the language. Mr. Thorne could, however, give you all the particulars in good English, and had no objection to do so.

It would be unjust to say that he looked down on men whose families were of recent date. He did not do so. He frequently consorted with such, and had chosen many of his friends from among them. But he looked on them as great millionaires are apt to look on those who have small incomes; as men who have Sophocles at their fingers' ends regard those who know nothing of Greek. They might doubtless be good sort of people, entitled to much praise for virtue, very admirable for talent, highly respectable in every way; but they were without the one great good gift. Such was Mr. Thorne's way of thinking on this matter; nothing could atone for the loss of good blood; nothing could neutralise its good effects. Few indeed were now possessed of it, but the possession was on that account the more precious. It was very pleasant to hear Mr. Thorne descant on this matter. Were you in your ignorance to surmise that such a one was of a good

family because the head of his family was a baronet of
an old date, he would open his eyes with a delightful
look of affected surprise, and modestly remind you that
baronetcies only dated from James I. He would gently
sigh if you spoke of the blood of the Fitzgeralds and
De Burghs; would hardly allow the claims of the How-
ards and Lowthers; and has before now alluded to
the Talbots as a family who had hardly yet achieved
the full honours of a pedigree.

In speaking once of a wide spread race whose
name had received the honours of three coronets, scions
from which sat for various constituencies, some one of
whose members had been in almost every cabinet
formed during the present century, a brilliant race such
as there are few in England, Mr. Thorne had called
them all "dirt." He had not intended any disrespect
to these men. He admired them in many senses, and
allowed them their privileges without envy. He had
merely meant to express his feeling that the streams
which ran through their veins were not yet purified by
time to that perfection, had not become so genuine an
ichor, as to be worthy of being called blood in the
genealogical sense.

When Mr. Arabin was first introduced to him, Mr.
Thorne had immediately suggested that he was one of
the Arabins of Uphill Stanton. Mr. Arabin replied that
he was a very distant relative of the family alluded to.
To this Mr. Thorne surmised that the relationship could
not be very distant. Mr. Arabin assured him that it
was so distant that the families knew nothing of each
other. Mr. Thorne laughed his gentle laugh at this,
and told Mr. Arabin that there was now existing no
branch of his family separated from the parent stock

at an earlier date than the reign of Elizabeth; and that therefore Mr. Arabin could not call himself distant. Mr. Arabin himself was quite clearly an Arabin of Uphill Stanton.

"But," said the vicar, "Uphill Stanton has been sold to the De Greys, and has been in their hands for the last fifty years."

"And when it has been there one hundred and fifty, if it unluckily remain there so long," said Mr. Thorne, "your descendants will not be a whit the less entitled to describe themselves as being of the family of Uphill Stanton. Thank God, no De Grey can buy that—and, thank God—no Arabin, and no Thorne, can sell it."

In politics, Mr. Thorne was an unflinching conservative. He looked on those fifty-three Trojans, who, as Mr. Dod tells us, censured free trade in November, 1852, as the only patriots left among the public men of England. When that terrible crisis of free trade had arrived, when the repeal of the corn laws was carried by those very men whom Mr. Thorne had hitherto regarded as the only possible saviours of his country, he was for a time paralysed. His country was lost; but that was comparatively a small thing. Other countries had flourished and fallen, and the human race still went on improving under God's providence. But now all trust in human faith must for ever be at an end. Not only must ruin come, but it must come through the apostasy of those who had been regarded as the truest of true believers. Politics in England, as a pursuit for gentlemen, must be at an end. Had Mr. Thorne been trodden under foot by a Whig, he could have borne it as a Tory and a martyr; but to be so

utterly thrown over and deceived by those he had so
earnestly supported, so thoroughly trusted, was more
than he could endure and live. He therefore ceased
to live as a politician, and refused to hold any converse with the world at large on the state of the
country.

Such were Mr. Thorne's impressions for the first
two or three years after Sir Robert Peel's apostasy;
but by degrees his temper, as did that of others, cooled
down. He began once more to move about, to frequent
the bench and the market, and to be seen at dinners,
shoulder to shoulder with some of those who had so
cruelly betrayed him. It was a necessity for him to
live, and that plan of his for avoiding the world did
not answer. He, however, and others around him who
still maintained the same staunch principles of protection—men like himself, who were too true to flinch
at the cry of a mob—had their own way of consoling
themselves. They were, and felt themselves to be, the
only true depositaries left of certain Eleusinian mysteries, of certain deep and wondrous services of worship
by which alone the gods could be rightly approached.
To them and them only was it now given to know
these things, and to perpetuate them, if that might
still be done, by the careful and secret education of
their children.

We have read how private and peculiar forms of
worship have been carried on from age to age in
families, which to the outer world have apparently
adhered to the services of some ordinary church. And
so by degrees it was with Mr. Thorne. He learnt at
length to listen calmly while protection was talked of
as a thing dead, although he knew within himself that

it was still quick with a mystic life. Nor was he without a certain pleasure that such knowledge though given to him should be debarred from the multitude. He became accustomed to hear, even among country gentlemen, that free trade was after all not so bad, and to hear this without dispute, although conscious within himself that everything good in England had gone with his old palladium. He had within him something of the feeling of Cato, who gloried that he could kill himself because Romans were no longer worthy of their name. Mr. Thorne had no thought of killing himself, being a Christian, and still possessing his 4000 *l.* a year; but the feeling was not on that account the less comfortable.

Mr. Thorne was a sportsman, and had been active though not outrageous in his sports. Previous to the great downfall of politics in his county, he had supported the hunt by every means in his power. He had preserved game till no goose or turkey could show a tail in the parish of St. Ewold's. He had planted gorse covers with more care than oaks and larches. He had been more anxious for the comfort of his foxes than of his ewes and lambs. No meet had been more popular than Ullathorne; no man's stables had been more liberally open to the horses of distant men than Mr. Thorne's; no man had said more, written more, or done more to keep the club up. The theory of protection could expand itself so thoroughly in the practices of a county hunt! But when the great ruin came; when the noble master of the Barsetshire hounds supported the recreant minister in the House of Lords, and basely surrendered his truth, his manhood, his friends, and his honour for the hope of a garter, then Mr. Thorne gave up the hunt. He did not cut his covers, for that would not have been the act of a gentleman. He did not kill his foxes, for that according to his light would have been murder. He did not say that his covers should not be drawn, or his earths stopped, for that would have been illegal according to the by-laws prevailing among country gentlemen. But he absented himself from home on the occasion of every meet at Ullathorne, left the covers to their fate, and could not be persuaded to take his pink coat out of the press, or his hunters out of his stable. This lasted for two years, and then by degrees he came round. He first appeared at a neighbouring meet on a pony, dressed in his shooting coat, as though he had trotted in by accident; then he walked up one morning on foot to see his favourite gorse drawn, and when his groom brought his mare out by chance, he did not refuse to mount her. He was next persuaded, by one of the immortal fifty-three, to bring his hunting materials over to the other side of the county, and take a fortnight with the hounds there; and so gradually he returned to his old life. But in hunting as in other things he was only supported by an inward feeling of mystic superiority to those with whom he shared the common breath of outer life.

Mr. Thorne did not live in solitude at Ullathorne. He had a sister, who was ten years older than himself, and who participated in his prejudices and feelings so strongly, that she was a living caricature of all his foibles. She would not open a modern quarterly, did not choose to see a magazine in her drawing-room, and would not have polluted her fingers with a shred of the "Times" for any consideration. She spoke of Addison, Swift, and Steele, as though they were still living, regarded De Foe as the best known novelist of his country, and thought of Fielding as a young but meritorious novice in the fields of romance. In poetry, she was familiar with names as late as Dryden, and had once been seduced into reading the "Rape of the Lock;" but she regarded Spenser as the purest type of her country's literature in this line. Genealogy was her favourite insanity. Those things which are the pride of most genealogists were to her contemptible. Arms and mottoes set her beside herself. Ealfried of Ullathorne had wanted no motto to assist him in cleaving to the brisket Geoffrey De Burgh; and Ealfried's great grandfather, the gigantic Ullafrid, had required no other arms than those which nature gave him to hurl from the top of his own castle a cousin of the base invading Norman. To her all modern English names were equally insignificant: Hengist, Horsa, and such like, had for her ears the only true savour of nobility. She was not contented unless she could go beyond the Saxons; and would certainly have christened her children, had she had children, by the names of the ancient Britons. In some respects she was not unlike Scott's Ulrica, and had she been given to cursing, she would certainly have done so in the names of Mista, Skogula, and Zernebock. Not having submitted to the embraces of any polluting Norman, as poor Ulrica had done, and having assisted no parricide, the milk of human kindness was not curdled in her bosom. She never cursed, therefore, but blessed rather. This, however, she did in a strange uncouth Saxon manner that would have been unintelligible to any peasants but her own.

As a politician, Miss Thorne had been so thoroughly

disgusted with public life by base deeds long antecedent to the Corn Law question, that that had but little
moved her. In her estimation her brother had been a
fast young man, hurried away by a too ardent tempera-
ment into democratic tendencies. Now happily he was
brought to sounder views by seeing the iniquity of the
world. She had not yet reconciled herself to the Reform Bill, and still groaned in spirit over the defalca-
tions of the Duke as touching the Catholic Emancipa-
tion. If asked whom she thought the Queen should
take as her counsellor, she would probably have named
Lord Eldon; and when reminded that that venerable
man was no longer present in the flesh to assist us, she
would probably have answered with a sigh that none
now could help us but the dead.

In religion, Miss Thorne was a pure Druidess. We
would not have it understood by that, that she did
actually in these latter days assist at any human sacrifices, or that she was in fact hostile to the Church
of Christ. She had adopted the Christian religion as a
milder form of the worship of her ancestors, and always
appealed to her doing so as evidence that she had no
prejudices against reform, when it could be shown that
reform was salutary. This reform was the most modern
of any to which she had as yet acceded, it being presumed that British ladies had given up their paint and
taken to some sort of petticoats before the days of St.
Augustine. That further feminine step in advance
which combines paint and petticoats together, had not
found a votary in Miss Thorne.

But she was a Druidess in this, that she regretted
she knew not what in the usages and practices of her
Church. She sometimes talked and constantly thought

of good things gone by, though she had but the faintest idea of what those good things had been. She imagined that a purity had existed which was now gone; that a piety had adorned our pastors and a simple docility our people, for which it may be feared history gave her but little true warrant. She was accustomed to speak of Cranmer as though he had been the firmest and most simple-minded of martyrs, and of Elizabeth as though the pure Protestant faith of her people had been the one anxiety of her life. It would have been cruel to undeceive her, had it been possible; but it would have been impossible to make her believe that the one was a time-serving priest, willing to go any length to keep his place, and that the other was in heart a papist, with this sole proviso, that she should be her own pope.

And so Miss Thorne went on sighing and regretting, looking back to the divine right of kings as the ruling axiom of a golden age, and cherishing, low down in the bottom of her heart of hearts, a dear unmentioned wish for the restoration of some exiled Stuart. Who would deny her the luxury of her sighs, or the sweetness of her soft regrets!

In her person and her dress she was perfect, and well she knew her own perfection. She was a small elegantly made old woman, with a face from which the glow of her youth had not departed without leaving some streaks of a roseate hue. She was proud of her colour, proud of her grey hair which she wore in short crisp curls peering out all around her face from the dainty white lace cap. To think of all the money that she spent in lace used to break the heart of poor Mrs. Quiverful with her seven daughters. She was proud of her teeth, which were still white and numerous, proud of her bright cheery eye, proud of her short jaunty step, and very proud of the neat, precise, small feet with which those steps were taken. She was proud also, ay, very proud, of the rich brocaded silk in which it was her custom to ruffle through her drawing-room.

We know what was the custom of the lady of Branksome—

> "Nine-and-twenty knights of fame
> Hung their shields in Branksome Hall."

The lady of Ullathorne was not so martial in her habits, but hardly less costly. She might have boasted that nine-and-twenty silken skirts might have been produced in her chamber, each fit to stand alone. The nine-and-twenty shields of the Scottish heroes were less independent, and hardly more potent to withstand any attack that might be made on them. Miss Thorne when fully dressed might be said to have been armed cap-a-pie, and she was always fully dressed, as far as was ever known to mortal man.

For all this rich attire Miss Thorne was not indebted to the generosity of her brother. She had a very comfortable independence of her own, which she divided among juvenile relatives, the milliners, and the poor, giving much the largest share to the latter. It may be imagined, therefore, that with all her little follies she was not unpopular. All her follies have, we believe, been told. Her virtues were too numerous to describe, and not sufficiently interesting to deserve description.

While we are on the subject of the Thornes, one word must be said of the house they lived in. It was not a large house, nor a fine house, nor perhaps to modern ideas a very commodious house; but by those

who love the peculiar colour and peculiar ornaments
of genuine Tudor architecture it was considered a perfect gem. We beg to own ourselves among the number,
and therefore take this opportunity to express our surprise that so little is known by English men and women
of the beauties of English architecture. The ruins of
the Colosseum, the Campanile at Florence, St. Mark's,
Cologne, the Bourse and Notre Dame, are with our
tourists as familiar as household words; but they know
nothing of the glories of Wiltshire, Dorsetshire, and
Somersetshire. Nay, we much question whether many
noted travellers, men who have pitched their tents perhaps under Mount Sinai, are not still ignorant that
there are glories in Wiltshire, Dorsetshire, and Somersetshire. We beg that they will go and see.

Mr. Thorne's house was called Ullathorne Court,
and was properly so called; for the house itself formed
two sides of a quadrangle, which was completed on
the other two sides by a wall about twenty feet high.
This wall was built of cut stone, rudely cut indeed,
and now much worn, but of a beautiful rich tawny
yellow colour, the effect of that stonecrop of minute
growth, which it had taken three centuries to produce.
The top of this wall was ornamented by huge round
stone balls of the same colour as the wall itself. Entrance into the court was had through a pair of iron
gates, so massive that no none could comfortably open
or close them, consequently they were rarely disturbed.
From the gateway two paths led obliquely across the
court; that to the left reaching the hall-door, which was
in the corner made by the angle of the house, and that
to the right leading to the back entrance, which was at
the further end of the longer portion of the building.

With those who are now adepts in contriving house accommodation, it will militate much against Ullathorne Court, that no carriage could be brought to the hall-door. If you enter Ullathorne at all, you must do so, fair reader, on foot, or at least in a bath-chair. No vehicle drawn by horses ever comes within that iron gate. But this is nothing to the next horror that will encounter you. On entering the front door, which you do by no very grand portal, you find yourself immediately in the dining-room. What,—no hall? exclaims my luxurious friend, accustomed to all the comfortable appurtenances of modern life. Yes, kind sir; a noble hall, if you will but observe it; a true old English hall of excellent dimensions for a country gentleman's family; but, if you please, no dining-parlour.

Both Mr. and Miss Thorne were proud of this peculiarity of their dwelling, though the brother was once all but tempted by his friends to alter it. They delighted in the knowledge that they, like Cedric, positively dined in their true hall, even though they so dined tête-à-tête. But though they had never owned, they had felt and endeavoured to remedy the discomfort of such an arrangement. A huge screen partitioned off the front door and a portion of the hall, and from the angle so screened off a second door led into a passage, which ran along the larger side of the house next to the courtyard. Either my reader or I must be a bad hand at topography, if it be not clear that the great hall forms the ground-floor of the smaller portion of the mansion, that which was to your left as you entered the iron gate, and that it occupies the whole of this wing of the building. It must be equally clear that it looks out on a trim mown lawn, through three quadrangular windows with stone mullions, each window divided into a larger portion at the bottom, and a smaller portion at the top, and each portion again divided into five by perpendicular stone supporters. There may be windows which give a better light than such as these, and it may be, as my utilitarian friend observes, that the giving of light is the desired object of a window. I will not argue the point with him. Indeed I cannot. But I shall not the less die in the assured conviction that no sort or description of window is capable of imparting half so much happiness to mankind as that which had been adopted at Ullathorne Court. What—not an oriel? says Miss Diana de Midellage. No, Miss Diana; not even an oriel, beautiful as is an oriel window. It has not about it so perfect a feeling of quiet English homely comfort. Let oriel windows grace a college, or the half public mansion of a potent peer; but for the sitting room of quiet country ladies, of ordinary homely folk, nothing can equal the square mullioned windows of the Tudor architects.

The hall was hung round with family female insipidities by Lely, and unprepossessing male Thornes in red coats by Kneller; each Thorne having been let into a panel in the wainscoting, in the proper manner. At the further end of the room was a huge fire-place, which afforded much ground of difference between the brother and sister. An antiquated grate that would hold about a hundred weight of coal, had been stuck on to the hearth, by Mr. Thorne's father. This hearth had of course been intended for the consumption of wood fagots, and the iron dogs for the purpose were still standing, though half buried in the masonry of the grate. Miss Thorne was very anxious to revert to the dogs. The dear good old creature was always glad to revert to anything, and had she been systematically indulged, would doubtless in time have reflected that fingers were made before forks, and have reverted accordingly. But in the affairs of the fire-place, Mr. Thorne would not revert. Country gentlemen around him, all had comfortable grates in their dining-rooms. He was not exactly the man to have suggested a modern usage; but he was not so far prejudiced as to banish those which his father had prepared for his use. Mr. Thorne had, indeed, once suggested that with very little contrivance the front door might have been so altered, as to open at least into the passage; but on hearing this, his sister Monica, such was Miss Thorne's name, had been taken ill, and had remained so for a week. Before she came down stairs she received a pledge from her brother that the entrance should never be changed in her lifetime.

At the end of the hall opposite to the fire-place a door led into the drawing-room, which was of equal size, and lighted with precisely similar windows. But yet the aspect of the room was very different. It was papered, and the ceiling, which in the hall showed the old rafters, was whitened and finished with a modern cornice. Miss Thorne's drawing-room, or, as she always called it, withdrawing-room, was a beautiful apartment. The windows opened on to the full extent of the lovely trim garden; immediately before the windows were plots of flowers in stiff, stately, stubborn little beds, each bed surrounded by a stone coping of its own; beyond, there was a low parapet wall, on which stood urns and images, fawns, nymphs, satyrs, and a whole tribe of Pan's followers; and then again, beyond that, a beautiful lawn sloped away to a sunk fence which divided the garden from the park. Mr. Thorne's study was at the end of the drawing-room, and beyond that were the kitchen and the offices. Doors opened into both Miss Thorne's withdrawing-room and Mr. Thorne's sanctum from the passage above alluded to; which, as it came to the latter room, widened itself so as to make space for the huge black oak stairs, which led to the upper regions.

Such was the interior of Ullathorne Court. But having thus described it, perhaps somewhat too tediously, we beg to say that it is not the interior to which we wish to call the English tourist's attention, though we advise him to lose no legitimate opportunity of becoming acquainted with it in a friendly manner. It is the outside of Ullathorne that is so lovely. Let the tourist get admission at least into the garden, and fling himself on that soft sward just opposite to the exterior angle of the house. He will there get the double frontage, and enjoy that which is so lovely—the expanse of architectural beauty without the formal dulness of one long line.

It is the colour of Ullathorne that is so remarkable. It is all of that delicious tawny hue which no stone can give, unless it has on it the vegetable richness of centuries. Strike the wall with your hand, and you will think that the stone has on it no covering, but rub it carefully, and you will find that the colour comes off upon your finger. No colourist that ever yet worked from a palette has been able to come up to this rich colouring of years crowding themselves on years.

Ullathorne is a high building for a country house, for it possesses three stories; and in each story, the windows are of the same sort as that described, though varying in size, and varying also in their lines athwart the house. Those of the ground floor are all uniform in size and position. But those above are irregular both in size and place, and this irregularity gives a bizarre and not unpicturesque appearance to the building. Along the top, on every side, runs a low parapet, which nearly hides the roof, and at the corners are more figures of fawns and satyrs.

Such is Ullathorne House. But we must say one word of the approach to it, which shall include all the description which we mean to give of the church also. The picturesque old church of St. Ewold's stands immediately opposite to the iron gates which open into the court, and is all but surrounded by the branches of the lime trees, which form the avenue leading up to the house from both sides. This avenue is magnificent, but it would lose much of its value in the eyes of many proprietors, by the fact that the road through it is not private property. It is a public lane between hedge rows, with a broad grass margin on each side of the road, from which the lime trees spring. Ullathorne Court, therefore, does not stand absolutely surrounded by its own grounds, though Mr. Thorne is owner of all the adjacent land. This, however, is the source of very little annoyance to him. Men, when they are acquiring property, think much of such things, but they who live where their ancestors have lived for years, do not feel the misfortune. It never occurred either to Mr. or Miss Thorne that they were not sufficiently private, because the world at large might, if it so wished, walk or drive by their iron gates. That part of the world which availed itself of the privilege was however very small.

Such a year or two since were the Thornes of Ullathorne. Such, we believe, are the inhabitants of many an English country home. May it be long before their number diminishes.

CHAPTER XXIII.

MR. ARABIN READS HIMSELF IN AT ST. EWOLD'S.

ON the Sunday morning the archdeacon with his sister-in-law and Mr. Arabin drove over to Ullathorne, as had been arranged. On their way thither the new vicar declared himself to be considerably disturbed in his mind at the idea of thus facing his parishioners for the first time. He had, he said, been always subject to *mauvaise honte* and an annoying degree of bashfulness, which often unfitted him for any work of a novel description; and now he felt this so strongly that he feared he should acquit himself badly in St. Ewold's reading-desk. He knew, he said, that those sharp little eyes of Miss Thorne would be on him, and that they would not approve. All this the archdeacon greatly ridiculed. He himself knew not, and had never known, what it was to be shy. He could not conceive that Miss Thorne, surrounded as she would be by the peasants of Ullathorne and a few of the poorer inhabitants of the suburbs of Barchester, could in any way affect the composure of a man well accustomed to address the learned congregation of St. Mary's at Oxford, and he laughed accordingly at the idea of Mr. Arabin's modesty.

Thereupon Mr. Arabin commenced to subtilise. The change, he said, from St. Mary's to St. Ewold's was quite as powerful on the spirits as would be that from St. Ewold's to St. Mary's. Would not a peer who, by chance of fortune, might suddenly be driven to herd among navvies, be as afraid of the jeers of his companions, as would any navvy suddenly exalted to a seat among the peers? Whereupon the archdeacon declared with a loud laugh that he would tell Miss Thorne that her new minister had likened her to a navvy. Eleanor, however, pronounced such a conclusion to be unfair; a comparison might be very just in its proportions which did not all assimilate the things compared. But Mr. Arabin went on subtilising, regarding neither the archdeacon's raillery nor Eleanor's defence. A young lady, he said, would execute with most perfect self-possession a difficult piece of music in a room crowded with strangers, who would not be able to express herself in intelligible language, even on any ordinary subject and among her most intimate friends, if she were required to do so standing on a box somewhat elevated among them. It was all an affair of education, and he at forty found it difficult to educate himself anew.

Eleanor dissented on the matter of the box; and averred she could speak very well about dresses, or babies, or legs of mutton from any box, provided it were big enough for her to stand upon without fear, even though all her friends were listening to her. The archdeacon was sure she would not be able to say a word; but this proved nothing in favour of Mr. Arabin. Mr. Arabin said that he would try the question out with Mrs. Bold, and get her on a box some day when the rectory might be full of visitors. To this Eleanor assented, making condition that the visitors should be of their own set, and the archdeacon cogitated in his mind, whether by such a condition it was intended that Mr. Slope should be included, resolving also that, if so, the trial would certainly never take place in the rectory drawing-room at Plumstead.

And so arguing, they drove up to the iron gates of Ullathorne Court.

Mr. and Miss Thorne were standing ready dressed for church in the hall, and greeted their clerical visitors with cordiality. The archdeacon was an old favourite. He was a clergyman of the old school, and this recommended him to the lady. He had always been an opponent of free trade as long as free trade was an open question; and now that it was no longer so, he, being a clergyman, had not been obliged, like most of his lay Tory companions, to read his recantation. He could therefore be regarded as a supporter of the immaculate fifty-three, and was on this account a favourite with Mr. Thorne. The little bell was tinkling, and the rural population of the parish were standing about the lane, leaning on the church stile, and against the walls of the old court, anxious to get a look at their new minister as he passed from the house to the rectory. The archdeacon's servant had already preceded them thither with the vestments.

They all went forth together; and when the ladies passed into the church the three gentlemen tarried a moment in the lane, that Mr. Thorne might name to the vicar with some kind of one-sided introduction, the most leading among his parishioners.

"Here are our churchwardens, Mr. Arabin; Farmer

Greenacre and Mr. Stiles. Mr. Stiles has the mill as you go into Barchester; and very good churchwardens they are."

"Not very severe, I hope," said Mr. Arabin: the two ecclesiastical officers touched their hats, and each made a leg in the approved rural fashion, assuring the vicar that they were very glad to have the honour of seeing him, and adding that the weather was very good for the harvest. Mr. Stiles being a man somewhat versed in town life, had an impression of his own dignity, and did not quite like leaving his pastor under the erroneous idea that he being a churchwarden kept the children in order during church time. 'Twas thus he understood Mr. Arabin's allusion to his severity, and hastened to put matters right by observing that "Sexton Clodheve looked to the younguns, and perhaps sometimes there may be a thought too much stick going on during sermon." Mr. Arabin's bright eye twinkled as he caught that of the archdeacon's; and he smiled to himself as he observed how ignorant his officers were of the nature of their authority, and of the surveillance which it was their duty to keep even over himself.

Mr. Arabin read the lessons and preached. It was enough to put a man a little out, let him have been ever so used to pulpit reading, to see the knowing way in which the farmers cocked their ears, and set about a mental criticism as to whether their new minister did or did not fall short of the excellence of him who had lately departed from them. A mental and silent criticism it was for the existing moment, but soon to be made public among the elders of St. Ewold's over the green graves of their children and forefathers. The excellence, however, of poor old Mr. Goodenough had not been wonderful, and there were few there who did not deem that Mr. Arabin did his work sufficiently well, in spite of the slightly nervous affection which at first impeded him, and which nearly drove the archdeacon beside himself.

But the sermon was the thing to try the man. It often surprises us that very young men can muster courage to preach for the first time to a strange congregation. Men who are as yet but little more than boys, who have but just left, what indeed we may not call a school, but a seminary intended for their tuition as scholars, whose thoughts have been mostly of boating, cricketing, and wine parties, ascend a rostrum high above the heads of the submissive crowd, not that they may read God's word to those below, but that they may preach their own word for the edification of their hearers. It seems strange to us that they are not stricken dumb by the new and awful solemnity of their position. How am I, just turned twenty-three, who have never yet passed ten thoughtful days since the power of thought first came to me, how am I to instruct these greybeards, who with the weary thinking of so many years have approached so near the grave? Can I teach them their duty? Can I explain to them that which I so imperfectly understand, that which years of study may have made so plain to them? Has my newly acquired privilege, as one of God's ministers, imparted to me as yet any fitness for the wonderful work of a preacher?

It must be supposed that such ideas do occur to young clergymen, and yet they overcome, apparently with ease, this difficulty which to us appears to be all but insurmountable. We have never been subjected in the way of ordination to the power of a bishop's hands. It may be that there is in them something that sustains the spirit and banishes the natural modesty of youth. But for ourselves we must own that the deep affection which Dominie Sampson felt for his young pupils has not more endeared him to us than the bashful spirit which sent him mute and inglorious from the pulpit when he rose there with the futile attempt to preach God's gospel.

There is a rule in our church which forbids the younger order of our clergymen to perform a certain portion of the service. The absolution must be read by a minister in priest's orders. If there be no such minister present, the congregation can have the benefit of no absolution but that which each may succeed in administering to himself. The rule may be a good one, though the necessity for it hardly comes home to the general understanding. But this forbearance on the part of youth would be much more appreciated if it were extended likewise to sermons. The only danger would be that congregations would be too anxious to prevent their young clergymen from advancing themselves in the ranks of the ministry. Clergymen who could not preach would be such blessings that they would be bribed to adhere to their incompetence.

Mr. Arabin, however, had not the modesty of youth to impede him, and he succeeded with his sermon even better than with the lessons. He took for his text two verses out of the second epistle of St. John, "Whosoever transgresseth, and abideth not in the doctrine of Christ, hath not God. He that abideth in the doctrine of Christ hath both the Father and Son. If there come any unto you and bring not this doctrine, receive him not into your house, neither bid him God speed." He told them that the house of theirs to which he alluded was this their church in which he now addressed them for the first time; that their most welcome and proper manner of bidding him God speed would be their patient obedience to his teaching of the gospel; but that he could put forward no claim to such conduct on their part unless he taught them the great Christian doctrine of works and faith combined. On this he enlarged, but not very amply, and after twenty minutes succeeded in sending his new friends home to their baked mutton and pudding well pleased with their new minister.

Then came the lunch at Ullathorne. As soon as they were in the hall Miss Thorne took Mr. Arabin's hand, and assured him that she received him into her house, into the temple, she said, in which she worshipped, and bade him God speed with all her heart. Mr. Arabin was touched, and squeezed the spinster's hand without uttering a word in reply. Then Mr. Thorne expressed a hope that Mr. Arabin found the church easy to fill, and Mr. Arabin having replied that he had no doubt he should do so as soon as he had learnt to pitch his voice to the building, they all sat down to the good things before them.

Miss Thorne took special care of Mrs. Bold. Eleanor still wore her widow's weeds, and therefore had about her that air of grave and sad maternity which is the lot of recent widows. This opened the soft heart of Miss Thorne, and made her look on her young guest as though too much could not be done for her. She heaped chicken and ham upon her plate, and poured out for her a full bumper of port wine. When Eleanor, who was not sorry to get it, had drunk a little of it,

Miss Thorne at once essayed to fill it again.   To this
Eleanor objected, but in vain.   Miss Thorne winked
and nodded and whispered, saying that it was the
proper thing and must be done, and that she knew all
about it; and so she desired Mrs. Bold to drink it up,
and not mind anybody.

"It is your duty, you know, to support yourself,"
she said into the ear of the young mother; "there's
more than yourself depending on it;" and thus she
coshered up Eleanor with cold fowl and port wine.
How it is that poor men's wives, who have no cold
fowl and port wine on which to be coshered up, nurse
their children without difficulty, whereas the wives of
rich men, who eat and drink everything that is good,
cannot do so, we will for the present leave to the
doctors and the mothers to settle between them,

And then Miss Thorne was great about teeth. Little
Johnny Bold had been troubled for the last few days
with his first incipient masticator, and with that free-
masonry which exists among ladies, Miss Thorne
became aware of the fact before Eleanor had half
finished her wing. The old lady prescribed at once a
receipt which had been much in vogue in the young
days of her grandmother, and warned Eleanor with
solemn voice against the fallacies of modern medicine.

"Take his coral, my dear," said she, "and rub it
well with carrot-juice; rub it till the juice dries on it,
and then give it him to play with—"

"But he hasn't got a coral," said Eleanor.

"Not got a coral!" said Miss Thorne, with almost
angry vehemence.   "Not got a coral—how can you
expect that he should cut his teeth? Have you got
Daffy's Elixir?"

Eleanor explained that she had not.   It had not been ordered by Mr. Rerechild, the Barchester doctor whom she employed; and then the young mother mentioned some shockingly modern succedaneum, which Mr. Rerechild's new lights had taught him to recommend.

Miss Thorne looked awfully severe.   "Take care, my dear," said she, "that the man knows what he's about; take care he doesn't destroy your little boy. But"—and she softened into sorrow as she said it, and spoke more in pity than in anger—"but I don't know who there is in Barchester now that you can trust.   Poor dear old Doctor Bumpwell, indeed—"

"Why, Miss Thorne, he died when I was a little girl."

"Yes, my dear, he did, and an unfortunate day it was for Barchester.   As to those young men that have come up since" (Mr. Rerechild, by the bye, was quite as old as Miss Thorne herself), "one doesn't know where they came from or who they are, or whether they know anything about their business or not."

"I think there are very clever men in Barchester," said Eleanor.

"Perhaps there may be; only I don't know them; and it's admitted on all sides that medical men arn't now what they used to be.   They used to be talented, observing, educated men.   But now any whipper-snapper out of an apothecary's shop can call himself a doctor.   I believe no kind of education is now thought necessary."

Eleanor was herself the widow of a medical man, and felt a little inclined to resent all these hard sayings.   But Miss Thorne was so essentially good-natured that it was impossible to resent anything she said. She therefore sipped her wine and finished her chicken.

"At any rate, my dear, don't forget the carrot-juice, and by all means get him a coral at once. My grandmother Thorne had the best teeth in the county, and carried them to the grave with her at eighty. I have heard her say it was all the carrot-juice. She couldn't bear the Barchester doctors. Even poor old Dr. Bumpwell didn't please her." It clearly never occurred to Miss Thorne that some fifty years ago Dr. Bumpwell was only a rising man, and therefore as much in need of character in the eyes of the then ladies of Ullathorne, as the present doctors were in her own.

The archdeacon made a very good lunch, and talked to his host about turnip-drillers and new machines for reaping; while the host, thinking it only polite to attend to a stranger, and fearing that perhaps he might not care about turnip crops on a Sunday, mooted all manner of ecclesiastical subjects.

"I never saw a heavier lot of wheat, Thorne, than you've got there in that field beyond the copse. I suppose that's guano," said the archdeacon.

"Yes, guano. I get it from Bristol myself. You'll find you often have a tolerable congregation of Barchester people out here, Mr. Arabin. They are very fond of St. Ewold's, particularly of an afternoon, when the weather is not too hot for the walk."

"I am under an obligation to them for staying away to-day, at any rate," said the vicar. "The congregation can never be too small for a maiden sermon."

"I got a ton and a half at Bradley's in High

Street," said the archdeacon, "and it was a complete take in. I don't believe there was five hundred-weight of guano in it."

"That Bradley never has anything good," said Miss Thorne, who had just caught the name during her whisperings with Eleanor. "And such a nice shop as there used to be in that very house before he came. Wilfred, don't you remember what good things old Ambleoff used to have?"

"There have been three men since Ambleoff's time," said the archdeacon, "and each as bad as the other. But who gets it for you at Bristol, Thorne?"

"I ran up myself this year and bought it out of the ship. I am afraid as the evenings get shorter, Mr. Arabin, you'll find the reading desk too dark. I must send a fellow with an axe and make him lop off some of those branches."

Mr. Arabin declared that the morning light at any rate was perfect, and deprecated any interference with the lime trees. And then they took a stroll out among the trim parterres, and Mr. Arabin explained to Mrs. Bold the difference between a naiad and a dryad, and dilated on vases and the shapes of urns. Miss Thorne busied herself among her pansies; and her brother, finding it quite impracticable to give anything of a peculiarly Sunday tone to the conversation, abandoned the attempt, and had it out with the archdeacon about the Bristol guano.

At three o'clock they again went into church; and now Mr. Arabin read the service and the archdeacon preached. Nearly the same congregation was present, with some adventurous pedestrians from the city, who had not thought the heat of the mid-day August sun

19*

too great to deter them. The archdeacon took his text from the Epistle to Philemon. "I beseech thee for my son Onesimus, whom I have begotten in my bonds." From such a text it may be imagined the kind of sermon which Dr. Grantly preached, and on the whole it was neither dull, nor bad, nor out of place.

He told them that it had become his duty to look about for a pastor for them, to supply the place of one who had been long among them; and that in this manner he regarded as a son him whom he had selected, as St. Paul had regarded the young disciple whom he sent forth. Then he took a little merit to himself for having studiously provided the best man he could without reference to patronage or favour; but he did not say that the best man according to his views was he who was best able to subdue Mr. Slope, and make that gentleman's situation in Barchester too hot to be comfortable. As to the bonds, they had consisted in the exceeding struggle which he had made to get a good clergyman for them. He deprecated any comparison between himself and St. Paul, but said that he was entitled to beseech them for their good will towards Mr. Arabin, in the same manner that the apostle had besought Philemon and his household with regard to Onesimus.

The archdeacon's sermon, text, blessing and all, was concluded within the half hour. Then they shook hands with their Ullathorne friends, and returned to Plumstead. 'Twas thus that Mr. Arabin read himself in at St. Ewold's.

CHAPTER XXIV.

MR. SLOPE MANAGES MATTERS VERY CLEVERLY AT PUDDINGDALE.

THE next two weeks passed pleasantly enough at Plumstead. The whole party there assembled seemed to get on well together. Eleanor made the house agreeable, and the archdeacon and Mrs. Grantly seemed to have forgotten her iniquity as regarded Mr. Slope. Mr. Harding had his violoncello, and played to them while his daughters accompanied him. Johnny Bold, by the help either of Mr. Rerechild or else by that of his coral and carrot-juice, got through his teething troubles. There had been gaieties too of all sorts. They had dined at Ullathorne, and the Thornes had dined at the Rectory. Eleanor had been duly put to stand on her box, and in that position had found herself quite unable to express her opinion on the merits of flounces, such having been the subject given to try her elocution. Mr. Arabin had of course been much in his own parish, looking to the doings at his vicarage, calling on his parishioners, and taking on himself the duties of his new calling. But still he had been every evening at Plumstead, and Mrs. Grantly was partly willing to agree with her husband that he was a pleasant inmate in a house.

They had also been at a dinner party at Dr. Stanhope's, of which Mr. Arabin had made one. He also, moth-like, burnt his wings in the flames of the signora's candle. Mrs. Bold, too, had been there, and had felt somewhat displeased with the taste, want of taste she called it, shown by Mr. Arabin in paying so much attention to Madame Neroni. It was as infallible that

Madeline should displease and irritate the women, as
that she should charm and captivate the men. The
one result followed naturally on the other. It was
quite true that Mr. Arabin had been charmed. He
thought her a very clever and a very handsome
woman; he thought also that her peculiar affliction
entitled her to the sympathy of all. He had never, he
said, met so much suffering joined to such perfect
beauty and so clear a mind. 'Twas thus he spoke of
the signora coming home in the archdeacon's carriage;
and Eleanor by no means liked to hear the praise. It
was, however, exceedingly unjust of her to be angry
with Mr. Arabin, as she had herself spent a very pleasant evening with Bertie Stanhope, who had taken her
down to dinner, and had not left her side for one moment after the gentlemen came out of the dining room.
It was unfair that she should amuse herself with Bertie
and yet begrudge her new friend his license of amusing
himself with Bertie's sister. And yet she did so. She was
half angry with him in the carriage, and said something
about meretricious manners. Mr. Arabin did not understand the ways of women very well, or else might have
flattered himself that Eleanor was in love with him.

But Eleanor was not in love with him. How many
shades there are between love and indifference, and
how little the graduated scale is understood! She had
now been nearly three weeks in the same house with
Mr. Arabin, and had received much of his attention,
and listened daily to his conversation. He had usually
devoted at least some portion of his evening to her
exclusively. At Dr. Stanhope's he had devoted himself exclusively to another. It does not require that a
woman should be in love to be irritated at this; it does

not require that she should even acknowledge to herself that it is unpleasant to her. Eleanor had no such self-knowledge. She thought in her own heart that it was only on Mr. Arabin's account that she regretted that he could condescend to be amused by the signora. "I thought he had more mind," she said to herself, as she sat watching her baby's cradle on her return from the party. "After all, I believe Mr. Stanhope is the pleasanter man of the two." Alas for the memory of poor John Bold! Eleanor was not in love with Bertie Stanhope, nor was she in love with Mr. Arabin. But her devotion to her late husband was fast fading, when she could revolve in her mind, over the cradle of his infant, the faults and failings of other aspirants to her favour.

Will any one blame my heroine for this? Let him or her rather thank God for all His goodness,—for His mercy endureth for ever.

Eleanor, in truth, was not in love; neither was Mr. Arabin. Neither indeed was Bertie Stanhope, though he had already found occasion to say nearly as much as that he was. The widow's cap had prevented him from making a positive declaration, when otherwise he would have considered himself entitled to do so on a third or fourth interview. It was, after all, but a small cap now, and had but little of the weeping-willow left in its construction. It is singular how these emblems of grief fade away by unseen gradations. Each pretends to be the counterpart of the forerunner, and yet the last little bit of crimped white crape that sits so jauntily on the back of the head, is as dissimilar to the first huge mountain of woe which disfigured the face of the weeper, as the state of the Hindoo is to the jointure of the English dowager.

But let it be clearly understood that Eleanor was in love with no one, and that no one was in love with Eleanor. Under these circumstances her anger against Mr. Arabin did not last long, and before two days were over they were both as good friends as ever. She could not but like him, for every hour spent in his company was spent pleasantly. And yet she could not quite like him, for there was always apparent in his conversation a certain feeling on his part that he hardly thought it worth his while to be in earnest. It was almost as though he were playing with a child. She knew well enough that he was in truth a sober thoughtful man, who in some matters and on some occasions could endure an agony of earnestness. And yet to her he was always gently playful. Could she have seen his brow once clouded she might have learnt to love him.

So things went on at Plumstead, and on the whole not unpleasantly, till a huge storm darkened the horizon, and came down upon the inhabitants of the rectory with all the fury of a waterspout. It was astonishing how in a few minutes the whole face of the heavens was changed. The party broke up from breakfast in perfect harmony; but fierce passions had arisen before the evening, which did not admit of their sitting at the same board for dinner. To explain this, it will be necessary to go back a little.

It will be remembered that the bishop expressed to Mr. Slope in his dressing-room, his determination that Mr. Quiverful should be confirmed in his appointment to the hospital, and that his lordship requested Mr. Slope to communicate this decision to the archdeacon. It will also be remembered that the archdeacon had indignantly declined seeing Mr. Slope, and had instead, written a strong letter to the bishop, in which he all but demanded the situation of warden for Mr. Harding. To this letter the archdeacon received an immediate formal reply from Mr. Slope, in which it was stated, that the bishop had received and would give his best consideration to the archdeacon's letter.

The archdeacon felt himself somewhat checkmated by this reply. What could he do with a man who would neither see him, nor argue with him by letter, and who had undoubtedly the power of appointing any clergyman he pleased? He had consulted with Mr. Arabin, who had suggested the propriety of calling in the aid of the master of Lazarus. "If," said he, "you and Dr. Gwynne formally declare your intention of waiting upon the bishop, the bishop will not dare to refuse to see you; and if two such men as you are see him together, you will probably not leave him without carrying your point."

The archdeacon did not quite like admitting the necessity of his being backed by the master of Lazarus before he could obtain admission into the episcopal palace of Barchester; but still he felt that the advice was good, and he resolved to take it. He wrote again to the bishop, expressing a hope that nothing further would be done in the matter of the hospital, till the consideration promised by his lordship had been given, and then sent off a warm appeal to his friend the master, imploring him to come to Plumstead and assist in driving the bishop into compliance. The master had rejoined, raising some difficulty, but not declining; and the archdeacon had again pressed his point, insisting on the necessity for immediate action. Dr. Gwynne unfortunately had the gout, and could therefore name no immediate day, but still agreed to come, if it should be finally found necessary. So the matter stood, as regarded the party at Plumstead.

But Mr. Harding had another friend fighting his battle for him, quite as powerful as the master of Lazarus, and this was Mr. Slope. Though the bishop had so pertinaciously insisted on giving way to his wife in the matter of the hospital, Mr. Slope did not think it necessary to abandon his object. He had, he thought, daily more and more reason to imagine that the widow would receive his overtures favourably, and he could not but feel that Mr. Harding at the hospital, and placed there by his means, would be more likely to receive him as a son-in-law, than Mr. Harding growling in opposition and disappointment under the archdeacon's wing at Plumstead. Moreover, to give Mr. Slope due credit, he was actuated by greater motives even than these. He wanted a wife, and he wanted money, but he wanted power more than either. He had fully realised the fact that he must come to blows with Mrs. Proudie. He had no desire to remain in Barchester as her chaplain. Sooner than do so, he would risk the loss of his whole connection with the diocese. What! was he to feel within him the possession of no ordinary talents; was he to know himself to be courageous, firm, and, in matters where his conscience did not interfere, unscrupulous; and yet be contented to be the working factotum of a woman-prelate? Mr. Slope had higher ideas of his own destiny. Either he or Mrs. Proudie must go to the wall; and now had come the time when he would try which it should be.

The bishop had declared that Mr. Quiverful should

be the new warden. As Mr. Slope went down stairs prepared to see the archdeacon if necessary, but fully satisfied that no such necessity would arise, he declared to himself that Mr. Harding should be warden. With the object of carrying this point, he rode over to Puddingdale, and had a further interview with the worthy expectant of clerical good things. Mr. Quiverful was on the whole a worthy man. The impossible task of bringing up as ladies and gentlemen fourteen children on an income which was insufficient to give them with decency the common necessaries of life, had had an effect upon him not beneficial either to his spirit, or his keen sense of honour. Who can boast that he would have supported such a burden with a different result? Mr. Quiverful was an honest, pains-taking, drudging man; anxious, indeed, for bread and meat, anxious for means to quiet his butcher and cover with returning smiles the now sour countenance of the baker's wife, but anxious also to be right with his own conscience. He was not careful, as another might be who sat on an easier worldly seat, to stand well with those around him, to shun a breath which might sully his name, or a rumour which might affect his honour. He could not afford such niceties of conduct, such moral luxuries. It must suffice for him to be ordinarily honest according to the ordinary honesty of the world's ways, and to let men's tongues wag as they would.

He had felt that his brother clergymen, men whom he had known for the last twenty years, looked coldly on him from the first moment that he had shown himself willing to sit at the feet of Mr. Slope; he had seen that their looks grew colder still, when it became bruited about that he was to be the bishop's new warden

at Hiram's hospital. This was painful enough; but it
was the cross which he was doomed to bear. He
thought of his wife, whose last new silk dress was six
years in wear. He thought of all his young flock,
whom he could hardly take to church with him on
Sundays, for there were not decent shoes and stockings
for them all to wear. He thought of the well-worn
sleeves of his own black coat, and of the stern face of
the draper from whom he would fain ask for cloth to
make another, did he not know that the credit would
be refused him. Then he thought of the comfortable
house in Barchester, of the comfortable income, of his
boys sent to school, of his girls with books in their
hands instead of darning needles, of his wife's face
again covered with smiles, and of his daily board
again covered with plenty. He thought of these things;
and do thou also, reader, think of them, and then
wonder, if thou canst, that Mr. Slope had appeared to
him to possess all those good gifts which could grace
a bishop's chaplain. "How beautiful upon the mountains are the feet of him that bringeth good tidings."

Why, moreover, should the Barchester clergy have
looked coldly on Mr. Quiverful? Had they not all
shown that they regarded with complacency the loaves
and fishes of their mother church? Had they not all,
by some hook or crook, done better for themselves
than he had done? They were not burdened as he
was burdened. Dr. Grantly had five children, and
nearly as many thousands a year on which to feed
them. It was very well for him to turn up his nose
at a new bishop who could do nothing for him, and a
chaplain who was beneath his notice; but it was cruel
in a man so circumstanced to set the world against

the father of fourteen children because he was anxious to obtain for them an honourable support! He, Mr. Quiverful, had not asked for the wardenship; he had not even accepted it till he had been assured that Mr. Harding had refused it. How hard then that he should be blamed for doing that which not to have done would have argued a most insane imprudence?

Thus in this matter of the hospital poor Mr. Quiverful had his trials; and he had also his consolations. On the whole the consolations were the more vivid of the two. The stern draper heard of the coming promotion, and the wealth of his warehouse was at Mr. Quiverful's disposal. Coming events cast their shadows before, and the coming event of Mr. Quiverful's transference to Barchester produced a delicious shadow in the shape of a new outfit for Mrs. Quiverful and her three elder daughters. Such consolations come home to the heart of a man, and quite home to the heart of a woman. Whatever the husband might feel, the wife cared nothing for frowns of dean, archdeacon, or prebendary. To her the outsides and insides of her husband and fourteen children were everything. In her bosom every other ambition had been swallowed up in the maternal ambition of seeing them and him and herself duly clad and properly fed. It had come to that with her that life had now no other purpose. She recked nothing of the imaginary rights of others. She had no patience with her husband when he declared to her that he could not accept the hospital unless he knew that Mr. Harding had refused it. Her husband had no right to be Quixotic at the expense of fourteen children. The narrow escape of throwing away his good fortune which her lord had had, almost paralysed

her.   Now, indeed, they had received the full promise
not only from Mr. Slope, but also from Mrs. Proudie.
Now, indeed, they might reckon with safety on their
good fortune.   But what if all had been lost?   What
if her fourteen bairns had been resteeped to the hips
in poverty by the morbid sentimentality of their father?
Mrs. Quiverful was just at present a happy woman, but
yet it nearly took her breath away when she thought
of the risk they had run.

"I don't know what your father means when he
talks so much of what is due to Mr. Harding," she
said to her eldest daughter.   "Does he think that Mr.
Harding would give him 450*l.* a year out of fine
feeling?   And what signifies it whom he offends, as
long as he gets the place?   He does not expect anything better.   It passes me to think how your father
can be so soft, while everybody around him is so
griping."

Thus, while the outer world was accusing Mr.
Quiverful of rapacity for promotion and of disregard
to his honour, the inner world of his own household
was falling foul of him, with equal vehemence, for his
willingness to sacrifice their interest to a false feeling
of sentimental pride.   It is astonishing how much difference the point of view makes in the aspect of all
that we look at!

Such were the feelings of the different members of
the family at Puddingdale on the occasion of Mr.
Slope's second visit.   Mrs. Quiverful, as soon as she
saw his horse coming up the avenue from the vicarage
gate, hastily packed up her huge basket of needlework,
and hurried herself and her daughter out of the room
in which she was sitting with her husband.   "It's Mr.

Slope," she said. "He's come to settle with you about the hospital. I do hope we shall now be able to move at once." And she hastened to bid the maid of all work go to the door, so that the welcome great man might not be kept waiting.

Mr. Slope thus found Mr. Quiverful alone. Mrs. Quiverful went off to her kitchen and back settlements with anxious beating heart, almost dreading that there might be some slip between the cup of her happiness and the lip of her fruition, but yet comforting herself with the reflection that after what had taken place, any such slip could hardly be possible.

Mr. Slope was all smiles as he shook his brother clergyman's hand, and said that he had ridden over because he thought it right at once to put Mr. Quiverful in possession of the facts of the matter regarding the wardenship of the hospital. As he spoke, the poor expectant husband and father saw at a glance that his brilliant hopes were to be dashed to the ground, and that his visitor was now there for the purpose of unsaying what on his former visit he had said. There was something in the tone of the voice, something in the glance of the eye, which told the tale. Mr. Quiverful knew it all at once. He maintained his selfpossession, however, smiled with a slight unmeaning smile, and merely said that he was obliged to Mr. Slope for the trouble he was taking.

"It has been a troublesome matter from first to last," said Mr. Slope; "and the bishop has hardly known how to act. Between ourselves—but mind this of course must go no further, Mr. Quiverful."

Mr. Quiverful said that of course it should not. "The truth is, that poor Mr. Harding has hardly known his own mind.   You remember our last conversation, no doubt."

Mr. Quiverful assured him that he remembered it very well indeed.

"You will remember that I told you that Mr. Harding had refused to return to the hospital."

Mr. Quiverful declared that nothing could be more distinct on his memory.

"And acting on this refusal, I suggested that you should take the hospital," continued Mr. Slope.

"I understood you to say that the bishop had authorised you to offer it to me."

"Did I? did I go so far as that? Well, perhaps it may be, that in my anxiety in your behalf I did commit myself further than I should have done. So far as my own memory serves me, I don't think I did go quite so far as that.   But I own I was very anxious that you should get it; and I may have said more than was quite prudent."

"But," said Mr. Quiverful, in his deep anxiety to prove his case, "my wife received as distinct a promise from Mrs. Proudie as one human being could give to another."

Mr. Slope smiled, and gently shook his head.   He meant that smile for a pleasant smile, but it was diabolical in the eyes of the man he was speaking to. "Mrs. Proudie!" he said.   "If we are to go to what passes between the ladies in these matters, we shall really be in a nest of troubles from which we shall never extricate ourselves.   Mrs. Proudie is a most excellent lady, kind-hearted, charitable, pious, and in every way estimable.   But, my dear Mr. Quiverful, the patronage of the diocese is not in her hands."

Mr. Quiverful for a moment sat panic-stricken and silent. "Am I to understand, then, that I have received no promise?" he said, as soon as he had sufficiently collected his thoughts.

"If you will allow me, I will tell you exactly how the matter rests. You certainly did receive a promise conditional on Mr. Harding's refusal. I am sure you will do me the justice to remember that you yourself declared that you could accept the appointment on no other condition than the knowledge that Mr. Harding had declined it."

"Yes," said Mr. Quiverful; "I did say that, certainly."

"Well; it now appears that he did not refuse it."

"But surely you told me, and repeated it more than once, that he had done so in your own hearing."

"So I understood him. But it seems I was in error. But don't for a moment, Mr. Quiverful, suppose that I mean to throw you over. No. Having held out my hand to a man in your position, with your large family and pressing claims, I am not now going to draw it back again. I only want you to act with me fairly and honestly."

"Whatever I do, I shall endeavour at any rate to act fairly," said the poor man, feeling that he had to fall back for support on the spirit of martyrdom within him.

"I am sure you will," said the other. "I am sure you have no wish to obtain possession of an income which belongs by all right to another. No man knows better than you do Mr. Harding's history, or can better appreciate his character. Mr. Harding is very desirous of returning to his old position, and the bishop feels that he is at the present moment somewhat hampered, though of course he is not bound, by the conversation which took place on the matter between you and me."

"Well," said Mr. Quiverful, dreadfully doubtful as to what his conduct under such circumstances should be, and fruitlessly striving to harden his nerves with some of that instinct of self-preservation which made his wife so bold.

"The wardenship of this little hospital is not the only thing in the bishop's gift, Mr. Quiverful, nor is it by many degrees the best. And his lordship is not the man to forget any one whom he has once marked with approval. If you would allow me to advise you as a friend—"

"Indeed I shall be most grateful to you," said the poor vicar of Puddingdale—

"I should advise you to withdraw from any opposition to Mr. Harding's claims. If you persist in your demand, I do not think you will ultimately succeed. Mr. Harding has all but a positive right to the place. But if you will allow me to inform the bishop that you decline to stand in Mr. Harding's way, I think I may promise you—though, by the bye, it must not be taken as a formal promise—that the bishop will not allow you to be a poorer man than you would have been had you become warden."

Mr. Quiverful sat in his arm chair silent, gazing at vacancy. What was he to say? All this that came from Mr. Slope was so true. Mr. Harding had a right to the hospital. The bishop had a great many good things to give away. Both the bishop and Mr. Slope would be excellent friends and terrible enemies to a man in his position. And then he had no proof of any promise; he could not force the bishop to appoint him.

"Well, Mr. Quiverful, what do you say about it?"

"Oh, of course, whatever you think fit, Mr. Slope. It's a great disappointment, a very great disappointment. I won't deny that I am a very poor man, Mr. Slope."

"In the end, Mr. Quiverful, you will find that it will have been better for you."

The interview ended in Mr. Slope receiving a full renunciation from Mr. Quiverful of any claim he might have to the appointment in question. It was only given verbally and without witnesses; but then the original promise was made in the same way.

Mr. Slope again assured him that he should not be forgotten, and then rode back to Barchester, satisfied that he would now be able to mould the bishop to his wishes.

CHAPTER XXV.

FOURTEEN ARGUMENTS IN FAVOUR OF MR. QUIVERFUL'S CLAIMS.

WE have most of us heard of the terrible anger of a lioness when, surrounded by her cubs, she guards her prey. Few of us wish to disturb the mother of a litter of puppies when mouthing a bone in the midst of her young family. Medea and her children are familiar to us, and so is the grief of Constance. Mrs. Quiverful, when she first heard from her husband the news which he had to impart, felt within her bosom all the rage of a lioness, the rapacity of the hound, the fury of the tragic queen, and the deep despair of the bereaved mother.

20*

Doubting, but yet hardly fearing, what might have been the tenor of Mr. Slope's discourse, she rushed back to her husband as soon as the front door was closed behind the visitor. It was well for Mr. Slope that he so escaped,—the anger of such a woman, at such a moment, would have cowed even him. As a general rule, it is highly desirable that ladies should keep their temper; a woman when she storms always makes herself ugly, and usually ridiculous also. There is nothing so odious to man as a virago. Though Theseus loved an Amazon, he showed his love but roughly; and from the time of Theseus downward, no man ever wished to have his wife remarkable rather for forward prowess than retiring gentleness. A low voice "is an excellent thing in woman."

Such may be laid down as a very general rule; and few women should allow themselves to deviate from it, and then only on rare occasions. But if there be a time when a woman may let her hair to the winds, when she may loose her arms, and scream out trumpet-tongued to the ears of men, it is when nature calls out within her not for her own wants, but for the wants of those whom her womb has borne, whom her breasts have suckled, for those who look to her for their daily bread as naturally as man looks to his Creator.

There was nothing poetic in the nature of Mrs. Quiverful. She was neither a Medea nor a Constance. When angry, she spoke out her anger in plain words, and in a tone which might have been modulated with advantage; but she did so, at any rate, without affectation. Now, without knowing it, she rose to a tragic vein.

"Well, my dear; we are not to have it." Such were the words with which her ears were greeted when she entered the parlour, still hot from the kitchen fire. And the face of her husband spoke even more plainly than his words:—

> "E'en such a man, so faint, so spiritless,
> So dull, so dead in look, so woe-begone,
> Drew Priam's curtain in the dead of night."

"What!" said she,—and Mrs. Siddons could not have put more passion into a single syllable,—"What! not have it? who says so?" And she sat opposite to her husband, with her elbows on the table, her hands clasped together, and her coarse, solid, but once handsome face stretched over it towards him.

She sat as silent as death while he told his story, and very dreadful to him her silence was. He told it very lamely and badly, but still in such a manner that she soon understood the whole of it.

"And so you have resigned it?" said she.

"I have had no opportunity of accepting it," he replied. "I had no witnesses to Mr. Slope's offer, even if that offer would bind the bishop. It was better for me, on the whole, to keep on good terms with such men than to fight for what I should never get!"

"Witnesses!" she screamed, rising quickly to her feet, and walking up and down the room. "Do clergymen require witnesses to their words? He made the promise in the bishop's name, and if it is to be broken, I'll know the reason why. Did he not positively say that the bishop had sent him to offer you the place?"

"He did, my dear. But that is now nothing to the purpose."

"It is everything to the purpose, Mr. Quiverful.

Witnesses indeed! and then to talk of *your* honour being questioned, because you wish to provide for fourteen children. It is everything to the purpose; and so they shall know, if I scream it into their ears from the town cross of Barchester."

"You forget, Letitia, that the bishop has so many things in his gift. We must wait a little longer. That is all."

"Wait! Shall we feed the children by waiting? Will waiting put George, and Tom, and Sam, out into the world? Will it enable my poor girls to give up some of their drudgery? Will waiting make Bessy and Jane fit even to be governesses? Will waiting pay for the things we got in Barchester last week?"

"It is all we can do, my dear. The disappointment is as much to me as to you; and yet, God knows, I feel it more for your sake than my own."

Mrs. Quiverful was looking full into her husband's face, and saw a small hot tear appear on each of those furrowed cheeks. This was too much for her woman's heart. He also had risen, and was standing with his back to the empty grate. She rushed towards him, and, seizing him in her arms, sobbed aloud upon his bosom.

"You are too good, too soft, too yielding," she said at last. "These men, when they want you, they use you like a cat's-paw; and when they want you no longer, they throw you aside like an old shoe. This is twice they have treated you so."

"In one way this will be all for the better," argued he. "It will make the bishop feel that he is bound to do something for me."

"At any rate, he shall hear of it," said the lady,

again reverting to her more angry mood. "At any rate he shall hear of it, and that loudly; and so shall she. She little knows Letitia Quiverful, if she thinks I will sit down quietly with the loss after all that passed between us at the palace. If there's any feeling within her, I'll make her ashamed of herself,"—and she paced the room again, stamping the floor as she went with her fat heavy foot. "Good heavens! what a heart she must have within her to treat in such a way as this the father of fourteen unprovided children!"

Mr. Quiverful proceeded to explain that he didn't think that Mrs. Proudie had had anything to do with it.

"Don't tell me," said Mrs. Quiverful; "I know more about it than that. Doesn't all the world know that Mrs. Proudie is bishop of Barchester, and that Mr. Slope is merely her creature? Wasn't it she that made me the promise, just as though the thing was in her own particular gift? I tell you, it was that woman who sent him over here to-day, because, for some reason of her own, she wants to go back from her word."

"My dear, you're wrong—"

"Now, Q., don't be so soft," she continued. "Take my word for it, the bishop knows no more about it than Jemima does." Jemima was the two-year-old. "And if you'll take my advice, you'll lose no time in going over and seeing him yourself."

Soft, however, as Mr. Quiverful might be, he would not allow himself to be talked out of his opinion on this occasion; and proceeded with much minuteness to explain to his wife the tone in which Mr. Slope had spoken of Mrs. Proudie's interference in diocesan matters. As he did so, a new idea gradually instilled

itself into the matron's head, and a new course of conduct presented itself to her judgment. What if, after
all, Mrs. Proudie knew nothing of this visit of Mr.
Slope's? In that case, might it not be possible that
that lady would still be staunch to her in this matter,
still stand her friend, and, perhaps, possibly carry her
through in opposition to Mr. Slope? Mrs. Quiverful
said nothing as this vague hope occurred to her, but
listened with more than ordinary patience to what her
husband had to say. While he was still explaining
that in all probability the world was wrong in its
estimation of Mrs. Proudie's power and authority, she
had fully made up her mind as to her course of action.
She did not, however, proclaim her intention. She
shook her head ominously as he continued his narra-
tion; and when he had completed she rose to go,
merely observing that it was cruel, cruel treatment.
She then asked him if he would mind waiting for a
late dinner instead of dining at their usual hour of
three, and, having received from him a concession on
this point, she proceeded to carry her purpose into
execution.

She determined that she would at once go to the
palace; that she would do so, if possible, before Mrs.
Proudie could have had an interview with Mr. Slope;
and that she would be either submissive piteous and
pathetic, or else indignant violent and exacting, according to the manner in which she was received.

She was quite confident in her own power. Strengthened as she was by the pressing wants of fourteen
children, she felt that she could make her way through
legions of episcopal servants, and force herself, if need
be, into the presence of the lady who had so wronged

her. She had no shame about it, no *mauvaise honte*, no dread of archdeacons. She would, as she declared to her husband, make her wail heard in the market-place if she did not get redress and justice. It might be very well for an unmarried young curate to be shamefaced in such matters; it might be all right that a snug rector, really in want of nothing, but still look-ing for better preferment, should carry on his affairs decently under the rose. But Mrs. Quiverful, with fourteen children, had given over being shamefaced, and, in some things, had given over being decent. If it were intended that she should be ill used in the manner proposed by Mr. Slope, it should not be done under the rose. All the world should know of it.

In her present mood, Mrs. Quiverful was not over careful about her attire. She tied her bonnet under her chin, threw her shawl over her shoulders, armed herself with the old family cotton umbrella, and started for Barchester. A journey to the palace was not quite so easy a thing for Mrs. Quiverful as for our friend at Plumstead. Plumstead is nine miles from Barchester, and Puddingdale is but four. But the archdeacon could order round his brougham, and his high-trotting fast bay gelding would take him into the city within the hour. There was no brougham in the coach-house of Puddingdale Vicarage, no bay horse in the stables. There was no method of locomotion for its inhabitants but that which nature has assigned to man.

Mrs. Quiverful was a broad heavy woman, not young, nor given to walking. In her kitchen, and in the family dormitories, she was active enough; but her pace and gait were not adapted for the road. A walk into Barchester and back in the middle of an August day would be to her a terrible task, if not altogether impracticable. There was living in the parish, about half a mile from the vicarage on the road to the city, a decent, kindly farmer, well to do as regards this world, and so far mindful of the next that he attended his parish church with decent regularity. To him Mrs. Quiverful had before now appealed in some of her more pressing family troubles, and had not appealed in vain. At his door she now presented herself, and, having explained to his wife that most urgent business required her to go at once to Barchester, begged that Farmer Subsoil would take her thither in his tax-cart. The farmer did not reject her plan; and, as soon as Prince could be got into his collar, they started on their journey.

Mrs. Quiverful did not mention the purpose of her business, nor did the farmer alloy his kindness by any unseemly questions. She merely begged to be put down at the bridge going into the city, and to be taken up again at the same place in the course of two hours. The farmer promised to be punctual to his appointment, and the lady, supported by her umbrella, took the short cut to the close, and in a few minutes was at the bishop's door.

Hitherto she had felt no dread with regard to the coming interview. She had felt nothing but an indignant longing to pour forth her claims, and declare her wrongs, if those claims were not fully admitted. But now the difficulty of her situation touched her a little. She had been at the palace once before, but then she went to give grateful thanks. Those who have thanks to return for favours received find easy admittance to the halls of the great. Such is not always the case with men, or even with women, who have favours to beg. Still less easy is access for those who demand the fulfilment of promises already made.

Mrs. Quiverful had not been slow to learn the ways of the world. She knew all this, and she knew also that her cotton umbrella and all but ragged shawl would not command respect in the eyes of the palatial servants. If she were too humble, she knew well that she would never succeed. To overcome by imperious overbearing with such a shawl as hers upon her shoulders, and such a bonnet on her head, would have required a personal bearing very superior to that with which nature had endowed her. Of this also Mrs. Quiverful was aware. She must make it known that she was the wife of a gentleman and a clergyman, and must yet condescend to conciliate.

The poor lady knew but one way to overcome these difficulties at the very threshold of her enterprise, and to this she resorted. Low as were the domestic funds at Puddingdale, she still retained possession of half-a-crown, and this she sacrificed to the avarice of Mrs. Proudie's metropolitan sesquipedalian serving-man. She was, she said, Mrs. Quiverful of Puddingdale, the wife of the Rev. Mr. Quiverful. She wished to see Mrs. Proudie. It was indeed quite indispensable that she should see Mrs. Proudie. James Fitzplush looked worse than dubious, did not know whether his lady were out, or engaged, or in her bed-room; thought it most probable she was subject to one of these or to some other cause that would make her invisible; but Mrs. Quiverful could sit down in the waiting-room while inquiry was being made of Mrs. Proudie's maid.

"Look here, my man," said Mrs. Quiverful; "I

must see her;" and she put her card and half-a-crown
—think of it, my reader, think of it; her last half-
crown—into the man's hand, and sat herself down on
a chair in the waiting-room.

Whether the bribe carried the day, or whether the
bishop's wife really chose to see the vicar's wife, it
boots not now to inquire. The man returned, and
begging Mrs. Quiverful to follow him, ushered her into
the presence of the mistress of the diocese.

Mrs. Quiverful at once saw that her patroness was
in a smiling humour. Triumph sat throned upon her
brow, and all the joys of dominion hovered about her
curls. Her lord had that morning contested with her a
great point. He had received an invitation to spend a
couple of days with the archbishop. His soul longed
for the gratification. Not a word, however, in his
grace's note alluded to the fact of his being a married
man; and, if he went at all, he must go alone. This
necessity would have presented no insurmountable bar
to the visit, or have militated much against the pleasure, had he been able to go without any reference to
Mrs. Proudie. But this he could not do. He could
not order his portmanteau to be packed, and start with
his own man, merely telling the lady of his heart that
he would probably be back on Saturday. There are
men—may we not rather say monsters?—who do
such things; and there are wives—may we not rather
say slaves?—who put up with such usage. But Doctor
and Mrs. Proudie were not among the number.

The bishop, with some beating about the bush,
made the lady understand that he very much wished
to go. The lady, without any beating about the bush,
made the bishop understand that she wouldn't hear of

it. It would be useless here to repeat the arguments that were used on each side, and needless to record the result. Those who are married will understand very well how the battle was lost and won; and those who are single will never understand it till they learn the lesson which experience alone can give. When Mrs. Quiverful was shown into Mrs. Proudie's room, that lady had only returned a few minutes from her lord. But before she left him she had seen the answer to the archbishop's note written and sealed. No wonder that her face was wreathed with smiles as she received Mrs. Quiverful.

She instantly spoke of the subject which was so near the heart of her visitor. "Well, Mrs. Quiverful," said she, "is it decided yet when you are to move into Barchester?"

"That woman," as she had an hour or two since been called, became instantly re-endowed with all the graces than can adorn a bishop's wife. Mrs. Quiverful immediately saw that her business was to be piteous, and that nothing was to be gained by indignation; nothing, indeed, unless she could be indignant in company with her patroness.

"Oh, Mrs. Proudie," she began, "I fear we are not to move to Barchester at all."

"Why not?" said that lady sharply, dropping at a moment's notice her smiles and condescension, and turning with her sharp quick way to business which she saw at a glance was important.

And then Mrs. Quiverful told her tale. As she progressed in the history of her wrongs she perceived that the heavier she leant upon Mr. Slope the blacker became Mrs. Proudie's brow, but that such blackness was

not injurious to her own cause.   When Mr. Slope was
at Puddingdale vicarage that morning she had regarded
him as the creature of the lady-bishop; now she perceived that they were enemies.   She admitted her mistake to herself without any pain or humiliation.   She
had but one feeling, and that was confined to her
family.   She cared little how she twisted and turned
among these new comers at the bishop's palace so long
as she could twist her husband into the warden's house.
She cared not which was her friend or which was her
enemy, if only she could get this preferment which she
so sorely wanted.

She told her tale, and Mrs. Proudie listened to it
almost in silence.   She told how Mr. Slope had cozened
her husband into resigning his claim, and had declared
that it was the bishop's will that none but Mr. Harding
should be warden.   Mrs. Proudie's brow became blacker.
At last she started from her chair, and begging Mrs.
Quiverful to sit and wait for her return, marched out
of the room.

"Oh, Mrs. Proudie, it's for fourteen children—for
fourteen children."   Such was the burden that fell on
her ear as she closed the door behind her.

CHAPTER XXVI.

MRS. PROUDIE WRESTLES AND GETS A FALL.

It was hardly an hour since Mrs. Proudie had left
her husband's apartment victorious, and yet so in-
domitable was her courage that she now returned thither
panting for another combat.   She was greatly angry
with what she thought was his duplicity.   He had so
clearly given her a promise on this matter of the

hospital. He had been already so absolutely vanquished on that point. Mrs. Proudie began to feel that if every affair was to be thus discussed and battled about twice and even thrice, the work of the diocese would be too much even for her.

Without knocking at the door she walked quickly into her husband's room, and found him seated at his office table, with Mr. Slope opposite to him. Between his fingers was the very note which he had written to the archbishop in her presence—and it was open! Yes, he had absolutely violated the seal which had been made sacred by her approval. They were sitting in deep conclave, and it was too clear that the purport of the archbishop's invitation had been absolutely canvassed again, after it had been already debated and decided on in obedience to her behests! Mr. Slope rose from his chair, and bowed slightly. The two opposing spirits looked each other fully in the face, and they knew that they were looking each at an enemy.

"What is this, bishop, about Mr. Quiverful?" said she, coming to the end of the table and standing there.

Mr. Slope did not allow the bishop to answer, but replied himself. "I have been out to Puddingdale this morning, ma'am, and have seen Mr. Quiverful. Mr. Quiverful has abandoned his claim to the hospital, because he is now aware that Mr. Harding is desirous to fill his old place. Under these circumstances I have strongly advised his lordship to nominate Mr. Harding."

"Mr. Quiverful has not abandoned anything," said the lady, with a very imperious voice. "His lordship's word has been pledged to him, and it must be respected."

The bishop still remained silent. He was anxiously

desirous of making his old enemy bite the dust beneath
his feet. His new ally had told him that nothing was
more easy for him than to do so. The ally was there
now at his elbow to help him, and yet his courage
failed him. It is so hard to conquer when the prestige
of former victories is all against one. It is so hard
for the cock who has once been beaten out of his
yard to resume his courage and again take a proud place
upon a dunghill.

"Perhaps I ought not to interfere," said Mr. Slope,
"but yet—"

"Certainly you ought not," said the infuriated
dame.

"But yet," continued Mr. Slope, not regarding this
interruption, "I have thought it my imperative duty
to recommend the bishop not to slight Mr. Harding's
claims."

"Mr. Harding should have known his own mind,"
said the lady.

"If Mr. Harding be not replaced at the hospital,
his lordship will have to encounter much ill will, not
only in the diocese, but in the world at large. Besides, taking a higher ground, his lordship, as I understand, feels it to be his duty to gratify, in this matter,
so very worthy a man and so good a clergyman as
Mr. Harding."

"And what is to become of the Sabbath-day school,
and of the Sunday services in the hospital?" said Mrs.
Proudie, with something very nearly approaching to a
sneer on her face.

"I understand that Mr. Harding makes no objection
to the Sabbath-day school," said Mr. Slope. "And as
to the hospital services, that matter will be best dis-

cussed after his appointment. If he has any permanent objection, then, I fear, the matter must rest."

"You have a very easy conscience in such matters, Mr. Slope," said she.

"I should not have an easy conscience," he rejoined, "but a conscience very far from being easy, if anything said or done by me should lead the bishop to act unadvisedly in this matter. It is clear that in the interview I had with Mr. Harding, I misunderstood him—"

"And it is equally clear that you have misunderstood Mr. Quiverful," said she, now at the top of her wrath. "What business have you at all with these interviews? Who desired you to go to Mr. Quiverful this morning? Who commissioned you to manage this affair? Will you answer me, sir?—who sent you to Mr. Quiverful this morning?"

There was a dead pause in the room. Mr. Slope had risen from his chair, and was standing with his hand on the back of it, looking at first very solemn and now very black. Mrs. Proudie was standing as she had at first placed herself, at the end of the table, and as she interrogated her foe she struck her hand upon it with almost more than feminine vigour. The bishop was sitting in his easy chair twiddling his thumbs, turning his eyes now to his wife, and now to his chaplain, as each took up the cudgels. How comfortable it would be if they could fight it out between them without the necessity of any interference on his part; fight it out so that one should kill the other utterly, as far as diocesan life was concerned, so that he, the bishop, might know clearly by whom it behoved him to be led. There would be the comfort of

quiet in either case; but if the bishop had a wish as
to which might prove the victor, that wish was certainly not antagonistic to Mr. Slope.

"Better the d——you know than the d——you don't
know," is an old saying, and perhaps a true one; but
the bishop had not yet realised the truth of it.

"Will you answer me, sir?" she repeated. "Who
instructed you to call on Mr. Quiverful this morning?"
There was another pause. "Do you intend to answer
me, sir?"

"I think, Mrs. Proudie, that under all the circumstances it will be better for me not to answer such a
question," said Mr. Slope. Mr. Slope had many tones
in his voice, all duly under his command; among them
was a sanctified low tone, and a sanctified loud tone;
and he now used the former.

"Did any one send you, sir?"

"Mrs. Proudie," said Mr. Slope, "I am quite aware
how much I owe to your kindness. I am aware also
what is due by courtesy from a gentleman to a lady.
But there are higher considerations than either of
those, and I hope I shall be forgiven if I now allow
myself to be actuated solely by them. My duty in
this matter is to his lordship, and I can admit of
no questioning but from him. He has approved of
what I have done, and you must excuse me if I say,
that having that approval and my own, I want none
other."

What horrid words were these which greeted the
ear of Mrs. Proudie? The matter was indeed too clear.
There was premeditated mutiny in the camp. Not
only had ill-conditioned minds become insubordinate
by the fruition of a little power, but sedition had been

overtly taught and preached. The bishop had not yet been twelve months in his chair, and rebellion had already reared her hideous head within the palace. Anarchy and misrule would quickly follow, unless she took immediate and strong measures to put down the conspiracy which she had detected.

"Mr. Slope," she said, with slow and dignified voice, differing much from that which she had hitherto used, "Mr. Slope, I will trouble you, if you please, to leave the apartment. I wish to speak to my lord alone."

Mr. Slope also felt that everything depended on the present interview. Should the bishop now be re-petticoated, his thraldom would be complete and for ever. The present moment was peculiarly propitious for rebellion. The bishop had clearly committed himself by breaking the seal of the answer to the archbishop; he had therefore fear to influence him. Mr. Slope had told him that no consideration ought to induce him to refuse the archbishop's invitation; he had therefore hope to influence him. He had accepted Mr. Quiverful's resignation, and therefore dreaded having to renew that matter with his wife. He had been screwed up to the pitch of asserting a will of his own, and might possibly be carried on till by an absolute success he should have been taught how possible it was to succeed. Now was the moment for victory or rout. It was now that Mr. Slope must make himself master of the diocese, or else resign his place and begin his search for fortune again. He saw all this plainly. After what had taken place any compromise between him and the lady was impossible. Let him once leave the room at her bidding, and leave the

21*

bishop in her hands, and he might at once pack up his portmanteau and bid adieu to episcopal honours, Mrs. Bold, and the Signora Neroni.

And yet it was not so easy to keep his ground when he was bidden by a lady to go; or to continue to make a third in a party between a husband and wife when the wife expressed a wish for a *tête-à-tête* with her husband.

"Mr. Slope," she repeated, "I wish to be alone with my lord."

"His lordship has summoned me on most important diocesan business," said Mr. Slope, glancing with uneasy eye at Dr. Proudie. He felt that he must trust something to the bishop, and yet that trust was so woefully ill-placed. "My leaving him at the present moment is, I fear, impossible."

"Do you bandy words with me, you ungrateful man?" said she. "My lord, will you do me the favour to beg Mr. Slope to leave the room?"

My lord scratched his head, but for the moment said nothing. This was as much as Mr. Slope expected from him, and was on the whole, for him, an active exercise of marital rights.

"My lord," said the lady, "is Mr. Slope to leave this room, or am I?"

Here Mrs. Proudie made a false step. She should not have alluded to the possibility of retreat on her part. She should not have expressed the idea that her order for Mr. Slope's expulsion could be treated otherwise than by immediate obedience. In answer to such a question the bishop naturally said in his own mind, that as it was necessary that one should leave the room, perhaps it might be as well that Mrs.

Proudie did so.   He did say so in his own mind, but externally he again scratched his head and again twiddled his thumbs.

Mrs. Proudie was boiling over with wrath.   Alas, alas! could she but have kept her temper as her enemy did, she would have conquered as she had ever conquered.   But divine anger got the better of her, as it has done of other heroines, and she fell.

"My lord," said she, "am I to be vouchsafed an answer or am I not?"

At last he broke his deep silence and proclaimed himself a Slopeite.   "Why, my dear," said he, "Mr. Slope and I are very busy."

That was all.   There was nothing more necessary. He had gone to the battle-field, stood the dust and heat of the day, encountered the fury of the foe, and won the victory.   How easy is success to those who will only be true to themselves!

Mr. Slope saw at once the full amount of his gain, and turned on the vanquished lady a look of triumph which she never forgot and never forgave.   Here he was wrong.   He should have looked humbly at her, and with meek entreating eye have deprecated her anger.   He should have said by his glance that he asked pardon for his success, and that he hoped for-giveness for the stand which he had been forced to make in the cause of duty.   So might he perchance have somewhat mollified that imperious bosom, and prepared the way for future terms.   But Mr. Slope meant to rule without terms.   Ah, forgetful, inex-perienced man!   Can you cause that little trembling victim to be divorced from the woman that possesses him?   Can you provide that they shall be separated

at bed and board? Is he not flesh of her flesh and
bone of her bone, and must he not so continue? It is
very well now for you to stand your ground, and
triumph as she is driven ignominiously from the room;
but can you be present when those curtains are drawn,
when that awful helmet of proof has been tied beneath
the chin, when the small remnants of the bishop's
prowess shall be cowed by the tassel above his head?
Can you then intrude yourself when the wife wishes
"to speak to my lord alone?"

But for the moment Mr. Slope's triumph was complete; for Mrs. Proudie without further parley left the
room, and did not forget to shut the door after her.
Then followed a close conference between the new
allies, in which was said much which it astonished
Mr. Slope to say and the bishop to hear. And yet
the one said it and the other heard it without ill will.
There was no mincing of matters now. The chaplain
plainly told the bishop that the world gave him credit
for being under the governance of his wife; that his
credit and character in the diocese were suffering; that
he would surely get himself into hot water if he
allowed Mrs. Proudie to interfere in matters which
were not suitable for a woman's powers; and in fact
that he would become contemptible if he did not throw
off the yoke under which he groaned. The bishop at
first hummed and hawed, and affected to deny the
truth of what was said. But his denial was not stout
and quickly broke down. He soon admitted by silence
his state of vassalage, and pledged himself, with Mr.
Slope's assistance, to change his courses. Mr. Slope
also did not make out a bad case for himself. He
explained how it grieved him to run counter to a lady

who had always been his patroness, who had be-
friended him in so many ways, who had, in fact,
recommended him to the bishop's notice; but, as he
stated, his duty was now imperative; he held a situation of peculiar confidence, and was immediately and
especially attached to the bishop's person. In such
a situation his conscience required that he should
regard solely the bishop's interests, and therefore he
had ventured to speak out.

The bishop took this for what it was worth, and
Mr. Slope only intended that he should do so. It
gilded the pill which Mr. Slope had to administer,
and which the bishop thought would be less bitter
than that other pill which he had so long been taking.

"My lord," had his immediate reward, like a good
child. He was instructed to write and at once did
write another note to the archbishop accepting his
grace's invitation. This note Mr. Slope, more prudent
than the lady, himself took away and posted with
his own hands. Thus he made sure that this act of
self-jurisdiction should be as nearly as possible a *fait
accompli.* He begged, and coaxed, and threatened the
bishop with a view of making him also write at once
to Mr. Harding; but the bishop, though temporarily
emancipated from his wife, was not yet enthralled to
Mr. Slope. He said, and probably said truly, that
such an offer must be made in some official form; that
he was not yet prepared to sign the form; and that
he should prefer seeing Mr. Harding before he did
so. Mr. Slope might, however, beg Mr. Harding to
call upon him. Not disappointed with his achievement
Mr. Slope went his way. He first posted the precious
note which he had in his pocket, and then pursued

other enterprises in which we must follow him in other chapters.

Mrs. Proudie, having received such satisfaction as was to be derived from slamming her husband's door, did not at once betake herself to Mrs. Quiverful. Indeed for the first few moments after her repulse she felt that she could not again see that lady. She would have to own that she had been beaten, to confess that the diadem had passed from her brow, and the sceptre from her hand! No, she would send a message to her with the promise of a letter on the next day or the day after. Thus resolving, she betook herself to her bed-room; but here she again changed her mind. The air of that sacred enclosure somewhat restored her courage, and gave her more heart. As Achilles warmed at the sight of his armour, as Don Quixote's heart grew strong when he grasped his lance, so did Mrs. Proudie look forward to fresh laurels, as her eye fell on her husband's pillow. She would not despair. Having so resolved, she descended with dignified mien and refreshed countenance to Mrs. Quiverful.

This scene in the bishop's study took longer in the acting than in the telling. We have not, perhaps, had the whole of the conversation. At any rate Mrs. Quiverful was beginning to be very impatient, and was thinking that farmer Subsoil would be tired of waiting for her, when Mrs. Proudie returned. Oh! who can tell the palpitations of that maternal heart, as the suppliant looked into the face of the great lady to see written there either a promise of house, income, comfort and future competence, or else the doom of continued and ever increasing poverty. Poor mother! poor wife! there was little there to comfort you!

"Mrs. Quiverful," thus spoke the lady with considerable austerity, and without sitting down herself, "I find that your husband has behaved in this matter in a very weak and foolish manner."

Mrs. Quiverful immediately rose upon her feet, thinking it disrespectful to remain sitting while the wife of the bishop stood.   But she was desired to sit down again, and made to do so, so that Mrs. Proudie might stand and preach over her.   It is generally considered an offensive thing for a gentleman to keep his seat while another is kept standing before him, and we presume the same law holds with regard to ladies.   It often is so felt; but we are inclined to say that it never produces half the discomfort or half the feeling of implied inferiority that is shown by a great man who desires his visitor to be seated while he himself speaks from his legs.   Such a solecism in good breeding, when construed into English, means this: "The accepted rules of courtesy in the world require that I should offer you a seat; if I did not do so, you would bring a charge against me in the world of being arrogant and ill-mannered; I will obey the world; but, nevertheless, I will not put myself on an equality with you.   You may sit down, but I won't sit with you.   Sit, therefore, at my bidding, and I'll stand and talk at you!"

This was just what Mrs. Proudie meant to say; and Mrs. Quiverful, though she was too anxious and too flurried thus to translate the full meaning of the manœuvre, did not fail to feel its effect.   She was cowed and uncomfortable, and a second time essayed to rise from her chair.

"Pray be seated, Mrs. Quiverful, pray keep your seat.   Your husband, I say, has been most weak and most foolish.   It is impossible, Mrs. Quiverful, to help people who will not help themselves.   I much fear that I can now do nothing for you in this matter."

"Oh! Mrs. Proudie,—don't say so," said the poor woman again jumping up.

"*Pray* be seated, Mrs. Quiverful.   I much fear that I can do nothing further for you in this matter.   Your husband has, in a most unaccountable manner, taken upon himself to resign that which I was empowered to offer him.   As a matter of course, the bishop expects that his clergy shall know their own minds.   What he may ultimately do—what we may finally decide on doing—I cannot now say.   Knowing the extent of your family—"

"Fourteen children, Mrs. Proudie, fourteen of them! and barely bread,—barely, bread!   It's hard for the children of a clergyman, it's hard for one who has always done his duty respectably!"   Not a word fell from her about herself; but the tears came streaming down her big coarse cheeks, on which the dust of the August road had left its traces.

Mrs. Proudie has not been portrayed in these pages as an agreeable or an amiable lady.   There has been no intention to impress the reader much in her favour. It is ordained that all novels should have a male and a female angel, and a male and a female devil.   If it be considered that this rule is obeyed in these pages, the latter character must be supposed to have fallen to the lot of Mrs. Proudie.   But she was not all devil. There was a heart inside that stiff-ribbed bodice, though not, perhaps, of large dimensions, and certainly not easily accessible.   Mrs. Quiverful, however, did gain access, and Mrs. Proudie proved herself a woman.

Whether it was the fourteen children with their probable bare bread and their possible bare backs, or the respectability of the father's work, or the mingled dust and tears on the mother's face, we will not pretend to say. But Mrs. Proudie was touched.

She did not show it as other women might have done. She did not give Mrs. Quiverful eau-de-Cologne, or order her a glass of wine. She did not take her to her toilet table, and offer her the use of brushes and combs, towels and water. She did not say soft little speeches and coax her kindly back to equanimity. Mrs. Quiverful, despite her rough appearance, would have been as amenable to such little tender cares as any lady in the land. But none such were forthcoming. Instead of this, Mrs. Proudie slapped one hand upon the other, and declared,—not with an oath; for as a lady and a Sabbatarian and a she-bishop, she could not swear,—but with an adjuration, that "she wouldn't have it done."

The meaning of this was that she wouldn't have Mr. Quiverful's promised appointment cozened away by the treachery of Mr. Slope and the weakness of her husband. This meaning she very soon explained to Mrs. Quiverful.

"Why was your husband such a fool," said she, now dismounted from her high horse and sitting confidentially down close to her visitor, "as to take the bait which that man threw to him? If he had not been so utterly foolish, nothing could have prevented your going to the hospital."

Poor Mrs. Quiverful was ready enough with her own tongue in accusing her husband to his face of being soft, and perhaps did not always speak of him to her children quite so respectfully as she might have done. But she did not at all like to hear him abused by others, and began to vindicate him, and to explain that of course he had taken Mr. Slope to be an emissary from Mrs. Proudie herself; that Mr. Slope was thought to be peculiarly her friend; and that, therefore, Mr. Quiverful would have been failing in respect to her had he assumed to doubt what Mr. Slope had said.

Thus mollified Mrs. Proudie again declared that "she would not have it done," and at last sent Mrs. Quiverful home with an assurance that, to the furthest stretch of her power and influence in the palace, the appointment of Mr. Quiverful should be insisted on. As she repeated the word "insisted," she thought of the bishop in his night-cap, and with compressed lips slightly shook her head. Oh! my aspiring pastors, divines to whose ears *nolo episcopari* are the sweetest of words, which of you would be a bishop on such terms as these?

Mrs. Quiverful got home in the farmer's cart, not indeed with a light heart, but satisfied that she had done right in making her visit.

CHAPTER XXVII.
A LOVE SCENE.

Mr. Slope, as we have said, left the palace with a feeling of considerable triumph. Not that he thought that his difficulties were all over; he did not so deceive himself; but he felt that he had played his first move well, as well as the pieces on the board would allow; and that he had nothing with which to reproach himself. He first of all posted the letter to the archbishop, and having made that sure he proceeded to push the advantage which he had gained. Had Mrs. Bold been at home, he would have called on her; but he knew that she was at Plumstead, so he wrote the following note. It was the beginning of what, he trusted, might be a long and tender series of epistles.

"My dear Mrs. Bold,—You will understand perfectly that I cannot at present correspond with your father. I heartily wish that I could, and hope the day may be not long distant when mists shall have cleared away, and we may know each other. But I cannot preclude myself from the pleasure of sending you these few lines to say that Mr. Q. has to-day, in my presence, resigned any title that he ever had to the wardenship of the hospital, and that the bishop has assured me that it is his intention to offer it to your esteemed father.

"Will you, with my respectful compliments, ask him, who I believe is now a fellow-visitor with you, to call on the bishop either on Wednesday or Thursday, between ten and one. *This is by the bishop's desire.* If you will so far oblige me as to let me have a line naming either day, and the hour which will suit Mr. Harding, I will take care that the servants shall have orders to show him in without delay. Perhaps I should say no more,—but still I wish you could make your father understand that no subject will be mooted between his lordship and him, which will refer at all to the method in which he may choose to perform his duty. I for one, am persuaded that no clergyman could perform it more satisfactorily than he did, or than he will do again.

"On a former occasion I was indiscreet and much too impatient, considering your father's age and my own. I hope he will not now refuse my apology. I still hope also that with your aid and sweet pious labours, we may live to attach such a Sabbath school to the old endowment, as may, by God's grace and furtherance, be a blessing to the poor of this city.

"You will see at once that this letter is confidential. The subject, of course, makes it so. But, equally of course, it is for your parent's eye as well as for your own, should you think proper to show it to him.

"I hope my darling little friend Johnny is as strong as ever,—dear little fellow. Does he still continue his rude assaults on those beautiful long silken tresses?

"I can assure you your friends miss you from Barchester sorely; but it would be cruel to begrudge you your sojourn among flowers and fields during this truly sultry weather.

"Pray believe me, my dear Mrs. Bold,
"Yours most sincerely,
"OBADIAH SLOPE.

"Barchester, Friday."

Now this letter, taken as a whole, and with the consideration that Mr. Slope wished to assume a great degree of intimacy with Eleanor, would not have been bad, but for the allusion to the tresses. Gentlemen do not write to ladies about their tresses, unless they are on very intimate terms indeed. But Mr. Slope could not be expected to be aware of this. He longed to put a little affection into his epistle, and yet he thought it injudicious, as the letter would, he knew, be shown to Mr. Harding. He would have insisted that the letter should be strictly private and seen by no eyes but Eleanor's own, had he not felt that such an injunction would have been disobeyed. He therefore restrained his passion, did not sign himself "yours affectionately," and contented himself instead with the compliment to the tresses.

Having finished his letter, he took it to Mrs. Bold's house, and learning there, from the servant, that things were to be sent out to Plumstead that afternoon, left it, with many injunctions, in her hands.

We will now follow Mr. Slope so as to complete the day with him, and then return to his letter and its momentous fate in the next chapter.

There is an old song which gives us some very good advice about courting:—

> "It's gude to be off with the auld luve
> Before ye be on wi' the new."

Of the wisdom of this maxim Mr. Slope was ignorant, and accordingly, having written his letter to Mrs. Bold, he proceeded to call upon the Signora Neroni. Indeed it was hard to say which was the old love and which the new, Mr. Slope having been smitten with both so nearly at the same time. Perhaps he thought it not amiss to have two strings to his bow. But two strings to Cupid's bow are always dangerous to him on whose behalf they are to be used. A man should remember that between two stools he may fall to the ground.

But in sooth Mr. Slope was pursuing Mrs. Bold in obedience to his better instincts, and the signora in obedience to his worser. Had he won the widow and worn her, no one could have blamed him. You, O reader, and I, and Eleanor's other friends would have received the story of such a winning with much disgust

and disappointment; but we should have been angry
with Eleanor, not with Mr. Slope. Bishop, male and
female, dean and chapter and diocesan clergy in full
congress, could have found nothing to disapprove of in
such an alliance. Convocation itself, that mysterious
and mighty synod, could in no wise have fallen foul of
it. The possession of 1000 *l.* a year and a beautiful
wife would not at all have hurt the voice of the pulpit
charmer, or lessened the grace and piety of the exemplary clergyman.

But not of such a nature were likely to be his
dealings with the Signora Neroni. In the first place
he knew that her husband was living, and therefore
he could not woo her honestly. Then again she had
nothing to recommend her to his honest wooing had
such been possible. She was not only portionless, but
also from misfortune unfitted to be chosen as the wife
of any man who wanted a useful mate. Mr. Slope
was aware that she was a helpless hopeless cripple.

But Mr. Slope could not help himself. He knew
that he was wrong in devoting his time to the back
drawing-room in Dr. Stanhope's house. He knew that
what took place there would if divulged utterly ruin
him with Mrs. Bold. He knew that scandal would soon
come upon his heels and spread abroad among the
black coats of Barchester some tidings, exaggerated
tidings, of the sighs which he poured into the lady's
ears. He knew that he was acting against the recognised
principles of his life, against those laws of conduct
by which he hoped to achieve much higher success.
But as we have said, he could not help himself.
Passion, for the first time in his life, passion was too
strong for him.

As for the signora, no such plea can be put forward for her, for in truth she cared no more for Mr. Slope than she did for twenty others who had been at her feet before him. She willingly, nay greedily, accepted his homage. He was the finest fly that Barchester had hitherto afforded to her web; and the signora was a powerful spider that made wondrous webs, and could in no way live without catching flies. Her taste in this respect was abominable, for she had no use for the victims when caught. She could not eat them matrimonially, as young lady-flies do whose webs are most frequently of their mothers' weaving. Nor could she devour them by any escapade of a less legitimate description. Her unfortunate affliction precluded her from all hope of levanting with a lover. It would be impossible to run away with a lady who required three servants to move her from a sofa.

The signora was subdued by no passion. Her time for love was gone. She had lived out her heart, such heart as she had ever had, in her early years, at an age when Mr. Slope was thinking of the second book of Euclid and his unpaid bill at the buttery hatch. In age the lady was younger than the gentleman; but in feelings, in knowledge of the affairs of love, in intrigue, he was immeasurably her junior. It was necessary to her to have some man at her feet. It was the one customary excitement of her life. She delighted in the exercise of power which this gave her; it was now nearly the only food for her ambition; she would boast to her sister that she could make a fool of any man, and the sister, as little imbued with feminine delicacy as herself, good naturedly thought it but fair that such amusement should be afforded to a poor invalid who was debarred from the ordinary pleasures of life.

Mr. Slope was madly in love, but hardly knew it. The signora spitted him, as a boy does a cockchafer on a cork, that she might enjoy the energetic agony of his gyrations. And she knew very well what she was doing.

Mr. Slope having added to his person all such adornments as are possible to a clergyman making a morning visit, such as a clean neck tie, clean hand-kerchief, new gloves, and a *soupçon* of not unnecessary scent, called about three o'clock at the doctor's door. At about this hour the signora was almost always alone in the back-drawing room. The mother had not come down. The doctor was out or in his own room. Bertie was out, and Charlotte at any rate left the room if any one called whose object was specially with her sister. Such was her idea of being charitable and sisterly.

Mr. Slope, as was his custom, asked for Mr. Stanhope, and was told, as was the servant's custom, that the signora was in the drawing-room. Upstairs he accordingly went. He found her, as he always did, lying on her sofa with a French volume before her, and a beautiful little inlaid writing case open on her table. At the moment of his entrance she was in the act of writing.

"Ah, my friend," said she, putting out her left hand to him across her desk, "I did not expect you to-day and was this very instant writing to you——"

Mr. Slope, taking the soft fair delicate hand in his, and very soft and fair and delicate it was, bowed over it his huge red head and kissed it. It was a sight to see, a deed to record if the author could fitly do it, a picture to put on canvass. Mr. Slope was big, awkward, cumbrous, and having his heart in his pursuit was ill at ease. The lady was fair, as we have said, and delicate; every thing about her was fine and refined; her hand in his looked like a rose lying among carrots, and when he kissed it he looked as a cow might do on finding such a flower among her food. She was graceful as a couchant goddess, and moreover, as self-possessed as Venus must have been when courting Adonis.

Oh, that such grace and such beauty should have condescended to waste itself on such a pursuit!

"I was in the act of writing to you," said she, "but now my scrawl may go into the basket;" and she raised the sheet of gilded note paper from off her desk as though to tear it.

"Indeed it shall not," said he, laying the embargo of half a stone weight of human flesh and blood upon the devoted paper. "Nothing that you write for my eyes, signora, shall be so desecrated," and he took up the letter, put that also among the carrots and fed on it, and then proceeded to read it.

"Gracious me! Mr. Slope," said she, "I hope you don't mean to say that you keep all the trash I write to you. Half my time I don't know what I write, and when I do, I know it is only fit for the back of the fire. I hope you have not that ugly trick of keeping letters."

"At any rate, I don't throw them into a waste-paper basket. If destruction is their doomed lot, they perish worthily, and are burnt on a pyre, as Dido was of old."

22*

"With a steel pen stuck through them, of course;" said she, "to make the simile more complete. Of all the ladies of my acquaintance I think Lady Dido was the most absurd. Why did she not do as Cleopatra did? Why did she not take out her ships and insist on going with him? She could not bear to lose the land she had got by a swindle; and then she could not bear the loss of her lover. So she fell between two stools. Mr. Slope, whatever you do, never mingle love and business."

Mr. Slope blushed up to his eyes, and over his mottled forehead to the very roots of his hair. He felt sure that the signora knew all about his intentions with reference to Mrs. Bold. His conscience told him that he was detected. His doom was to be spoken; he was to be punished for his duplicity, and rejected by the beautiful creature before him. Poor man. He little dreamt that had all his intentions with reference to Mrs. Bold been known to the signora, it would have added zest to that lady's amusement. It was all very well to have Mr. Slope at her feet, to show her power by making an utter fool of a clergyman, to gratify her own infidelity by thus proving the little strength which religion had in controlling the passions even of a religious man; but it would be an increased gratification if she could be made to understand that she was at the same time alluring her victim away from another, whose love if secured would be in every way beneficent and salutary.

The signora had indeed discovered with the keen instinct of such a woman, that Mr. Slope was bent on matrimony with Mrs. Bold, but in alluding to Dido she had not thought of it. She instantly perceived, however, from her lover's blushes, what was on his mind, and was not slow in taking advantage of it.

She looked him full in the face, not angrily, nor yet with a smile, but with an intense and overpowering gaze; and then holding up her forefinger, and slightly shaking her head she said:—

"Whatever you do, my friend, do not mingle love and business. Either stick to your treasure and your city of wealth, or else follow your love like a true man. But never attempt both. If you do, you'll have to die with a broken heart as did poor Dido. Which is it to be with you, Mr. Slope, love or money?"

Mr. Slope was not so ready with a pathetic answer as he usually was with touching episodes in his extempore sermons. He felt that he ought to say something pretty, something also that should remove the impression on the mind of his lady love. But he was rather put about how to do it.

"Love," said he, "true overpowering love, must be the strongest passion a man can feel; it must control every other wish, and put aside every other pursuit. But with me love will never act in that way unless it be returned;" and he threw upon the signora a look of tenderness which was intended to make up for all the deficiencies of his speech.

"Take my advice," said she. "Never mind love. After all, what is it? The dream of a few weeks. That is all its joy. The disappointment of a life is its Nemesis. Who was ever successful in true love? Success in love argues that the love is false. True love is always despondent or tragical. Juliet loved, Haidee loved, Dido loved, and what came of it? Troilus loved and ceased to be a man."

"Troilus loved and was fooled," said the more manly chaplain. "A man may love and yet not be a Troilus. All women are not Cressids."

"No; all women are not Cressids. The falsehood is not always on the woman's side. Imogen was true, but how was she rewarded? Her lord believed her to be the paramour of the first he who came near her in his absence. Desdemona was true and was smothered. Ophelia was true and went mad. There is no happiness in love, except at the end of an English novel. But in wealth, money, houses, lands, goods and chattels, in the good things of this world, yes, in them there is something tangible, something that can be retained and enjoyed."

"Oh, no," said Mr. Slope, feeling himself bound to enter some protest against so very unorthodox a doctrine, "this world's wealth will make no one happy."

"And what will make you happy—you—you?" said she, raising herself up, and speaking to him with energy across the table. "From what source do you look for happiness? Do not say that you look for none? I shall not believe you. It is a search in which every human being spends an existence."

"And the search is always in vain," said Mr. Slope. "We look for happiness on earth, while we ought to be content to hope for it in heaven."

"Pshaw! you preach a doctrine which you know you don't believe. It is the way with you all. If you know that there is no earthly happiness, why do you long to be a bishop or a dean? Why do you want lands and income?"

"I have the natural ambition of a man," said he.

"Of course you have, and the natural passions; and therefore I say that you don't believe the doctrine you preach. St. Paul was an enthusiast. He believed so that his ambition and passions did not war against his creed. So does the Eastern fanatic who passes half his life erect upon a pillar. As for me, I will believe in no belief that does not make itself manifest by outward signs. I will think no preaching sincere that is not recommended by the practice of the preacher."

Mr. Slope was startled and horrified, but he felt that he could not answer. How could he stand up and preach the lessons of his Master, being there as he was, on the devil's business? He was a true believer, otherwise this would have been nothing to him. He had audacity for most things, but he had not audacity to make a plaything of the Lord's word. All this the signora understood, and felt much interest as she saw her cockchafer whirl round upon her pin.

"Your wit delights in such arguments," said he, "but your heart and your reason do not go along with them."

"My heart!" said she; "you quite mistake the principles of my composition if you imagine that there is such a thing about me." After all, there was very little that was false in anything that the signora said. If Mr. Slope allowed himself to be deceived it was his own fault. Nothing could have been more open than her declarations about herself.

The little writing table with her desk was still standing before her, a barrier, as it were, against the enemy. She was sitting as nearly upright as she ever did, and he had brought a chair close to the sofa, so that there was only the corner of the table between

him and her.   It so happened that as she spoke her
hand lay upon the table, and as Mr. Slope answered
her he put his hand upon hers.

"No heart!" said he.   "That is a heavy charge
which you bring against yourself, and one of which I
cannot find you guilty—"

She withdrew her hand, not quickly and angrily,
as though insulted by his touch, but gently and slowly.

"You are in no condition to give a verdict on the
matter," said she, "as you have not tried me.   No;
don't say that you intend doing so, for you know
you have no intention of the kind; nor indeed have
I either.   As for you, you will take your vows
where they will result in something more substantial
than the pursuit of such a ghostlike, ghastly love as
mine—"

"Your love should be sufficient to satisfy the
dream of a monarch," said Mr. Slope, not quite clear
as to the meaning of his words.

"Say an archbishop, Mr. Slope," said she.   Poor
fellow! she was very cruel to him.   He went round
again upon his cork on this allusion to his profession.
He tried, however, to smile, and gently accused her of
joking on a matter, which was, he said, to him of such
vital moment.

"Why—what gulls do you men make of us," she
replied.   "How you fool us to the top of our bent;
and of all men you clergymen are the most fluent of
your honeyed caressing words.   Now look me in the
face, Mr. Slope, boldly and openly."

Mr. Slope did look at her with a languishing loving
eye, and as he did so, he again put forth his hand to
get hold of hers.

"I told you to look at me boldly, Mr. Slope; but confine your boldness to your eyes."

"Oh, Madeline!" he sighed.

"Well, my name is Madeline," said she, "but none except my own family usually call me so. Now look me in the face, Mr. Slope. Am I to understand that you say you love me?"

Mr. Slope never had said so. If he had come there with any formed plan at all, his intention was to make love to the lady without uttering any such declaration. It was, however, quite impossible that he should now deny his love. He had, therefore, nothing for it, but to go down on his knees distractedly against the sofa, and swear that he did love her with a love passing the love of man.

The signora received the assurance with very little palpitation or appearance of surprise. "And now answer me another question," said she; "when are you to be married to my dear friend Eleanor Bold?"

Poor Mr. Slope went round and round in mortal agony. In such a condition as his it was really very hard for him to know what answer to give. And yet no answer would be his surest condemnation. He might as well at once plead guilty to the charge brought against him.

"And why do you accuse me of such dissimulation?" said he.

"Dissimulation! I said nothing of dissimulation. I made no charge against you, and make none. Pray don't defend yourself to me. You swear that you are devoted to my beauty, and yet you are on the eve of matrimony with another. I feel this to be rather a compliment. It is to Mrs. Bold that you must defend yourself. That you may find difficult; unless, indeed, you can keep her in the dark. You clergymen are cleverer than other men."

"Signora, I have told you that I loved you, and now you rail at me?"

"Rail at you. God bless the man; what would he have? Come, answer me this at your leisure,—not without thinking now, but leisurely and with consideration,—Are you not going to be married to Mrs. Bold?"

"I am not," said he. And as he said it, he almost hated, with an exquisite hatred, the woman whom he could not help loving with an exquisite love.

"But surely you are a worshipper of hers?"

"I am not," said Mr. Slope, to whom the word worshipper was peculiarly distasteful. The signora had conceived that it would be so.

"I wonder at that," said she. "Do you not admire her? To my eye she is the perfection of English beauty. And then she is rich too. I should have thought she was just the person to attract you. Come, Mr. Slope, let me give you advice on this matter. Marry the charming widow; she will be a good mother to your children, and an excellent mistress of a clergyman's household."

"Oh, signora, how can you be so cruel."

"Cruel," said she, changing the voice of banter which she had been using for one which was expressively earnest in its tone; "is that cruelty?"

"How can I love another, while my heart is entirely your own?"

"If that were cruelty, Mr. Slope, what might you say of me if I were to declare that I returned your

passion? What would you think if I bound you even
by a lover's oath to do daily penance at this couch of
mine? What can I give in return for a man's love?
Ah, dear friend, you have not realised the conditions
of my fate."

Mr. Slope was not on his knees all this time. After
his declaration of love he had risen from them as
quickly as he thought consistent with the new position
which he now filled, and as he stood was leaning on
the back of his chair. This outburst of tenderness on
the Signora's part quite overcame him, and made him
feel for the moment that he would sacrifice everything
to be assured of the love of the beautiful creature
before him, maimed, lame, and already married as
she was.

"And can I not sympathise with your lot?" said
he, now seating himself on her sofa, and pushing away
the table with his foot.

"Sympathy is so near to pity!" said she. "If you
pity me, cripple as I am, I shall spurn you from me."

"Oh, Madeline, I will only love you," and again
he caught her hand and devoured it with kisses. Now
she did not draw it from him, but sat there as he
kissed it, looking at him with her great eyes, just as
a great spider would look at a great fly that was quite
securely caught.

"Suppose Signor Neroni were to come to Barchester," said she, "would you make his acquaintance?"

"Signor Neroni!" said he.

"Would you introduce him to the bishop, and Mrs.
Proudie, and the young ladies?" said she, again having
recourse to that horrid quizzing voice which Mr. Slope
so particularly hated.

"Why do you ask such a question?" said he.

"Because it is necessary that you should know that there is a Signor Neroni. I think you had forgotten it."

"If I thought that you retained for that wretch one particle of the love of which he was never worthy, I would die before I would distract you by telling you what I feel. No! were your husband the master of your heart, I might perhaps love you; but you should never know it."

"My heart again! how you talk. And you consider then, that if a husband be not master of his wife's heart, he has no right to her fealty; if a wife ceases to love, she may cease to be true. Is that your doctrine on this matter, as a minister of the Church of England?"

Mr. Slope tried hard within himself to cast off the pollution with which he felt that he was defiling his soul. He strove to tear himself away from the noxious siren that had bewitched him. But he could not do it. He could not be again heart free. He had looked for rapturous joy in loving this lovely creature, and he already found that he met with little but disappointment and self-rebuke. He had come across the fruit of the Dead Sea, so sweet and delicious to the eye, so bitter and nauseous to the taste. He had put the apple to his mouth, and it had turned to ashes between his teeth. Yet he could not tear himself away. He knew, he could not but know, that she jeered at him, ridiculed his love, and insulted the weakness of his religion. But she half permitted his adoration, and that half permission added such fuel to his fire that all the fountain of his piety could not quench it. He began to feel savage, irritated, and revengeful. He meditated some severity of speech, some taunt that should cut her, as her taunts cut him. He reflected as he stood there for a moment, silent before her, that if he desired to quell her proud spirit, he should do so by being prouder even than herself; that if he wished to have her at his feet suppliant for his love it behoved him to conquer her by indifference. All this passed through his mind. As far as dead knowledge went, he knew, or thought he knew, how a woman should be tamed. But when he essayed to bring his tactics to bear, he failed like a child. What chance has dead knowledge with experience in any of the transactions between man and man? What possible chance between man and woman? Mr. Slope loved furiously, insanely, and truly; but he had never played the game of love. The signora did not love at all, but she was up to every move of the board. It was Philidor pitted against a school-boy.

And so she continued to insult him, and he continued to bear it.

"Sacrifice the world for love!" said she, in answer to some renewed vapid declaration of his passion, "how has the same thing been said, and how invariably with the same falsehood!"

"Falsehood," said he. "Do you say that I am false to you? do you say that my love is not real?"

"False? of course it is false, false as the father of falsehood—if indeed falsehoods need a sire and are not self-begotten since the world began. You are ready to sacrifice the world for love? Come let us see what you will sacrifice. I care nothing for nuptial vows. The wretch, I think you were kind enough to call him so, whom I swore to love and obey, is so base that he can only be thought of with repulsive disgust.   In the council chamber of my heart I have divorced him.   To me that is as good as though aged lords had gloated for months over the details of his licentious life.   I care nothing for what the world can say.   Will you be as frank?   Will you take me to your home as your wife? Will you call me Mrs. Slope before bishop, dean, and prebendaries?"   The poor tortured wretch stood silent, not knowing what to say.   "What! you won't do that. Tell me, then, what part of the world is it that you will sacrifice for my charms?"

"Were you free to marry, I would take you to my house to-morrow and wish no higher privilege."

"I am free;" said she, almost starting up in her energy.   For though there was no truth in her pretended regard for her clerical admirer, there was a mixture of real feeling in the scorn and satire with which she spoke of love and marriage generally.   "I am free; free as the winds.   Come; will you take me as I am?   Have your wish; sacrifice the world, and prove yourself a true man."

Mr. Slope should have taken her at her word. She would have drawn back, and he would have had the full advantage of the offer.   But he did not.   Instead of doing so, he stood wrapt in astonishment, passing his fingers through his lank red hair, and thinking as he stared upon her animated countenance that her wondrous beauty grew more and more wonderful as he gazed on it.   "Ha! ha! ha!" she laughed out loud. "Come, Mr. Slope; don't talk of sacrificing the world again.   People beyond one-and-twenty should never dream of such a thing.   You and I, if we have the dregs of any love left in us, if we have the remnants

of a passion remaining in our hearts, should husband
our resources better. We are not in our *première
jeunesse.* The world is a very nice place. Your world,
at any rate, is so. You have all manner of fat rectories
to get, and possible bishoprics to enjoy. Come, confess; on second thoughts you would not sacrifice such
things for the smiles of a lame lady?"

It was impossible for him to answer this. In order
to be in any way dignified, he felt that he must be
silent.

"Come," said she—"don't boody with me: don't
be angry because I speak out some home truths. Alas,
the world, as I have found it, has taught me bitter
truths. Come, tell me that I am forgiven. Are we
not to be friends?" and she again put out her hand to
him.

He sat himself down in the chair beside her, and
took her proffered hand and leant over her.

"There," said she, with her sweetest softest smile
—a smile to withstand which a man should be cased
in triple steel, "there; seal your forgiveness on it,"
and she raised it towards his face. He kissed it again
and again, and stretched over her as though desirous
of extending the charity of his pardon beyond the
hand that was offered to him. She managed, however,
to check his ardour. For one so easily allured as this
poor chaplain, her hand was surely enough.

"Oh, Madeline!" said he, "tell me that you love
me—do you—do you love me?"

"Hush," said she. "There is my mother's step.
Our *tête-à-tête* has been of monstrous length. Now you
had better go. But we shall see you soon again, shall
we not?"

Mr. Slope promised that he would call again on the following day.

"And, Mr. Slope," she continued, "pray answer my note. You have it in your hand, though I declare during these two hours you have not been gracious enough to read it. It is about the Sabbath school and the children. You know how anxious I am to have them here. I have been learning the catechism myself, on purpose. You must manage it for me next week. I will teach them, at any rate, to submit themselves to their spiritual pastors and masters."

Mr. Slope said but little on the subject of Sabbath schools, but he made his adieu, and betook himself home with a sad heart, troubled mind, and uneasy conscience.

END OF VOL. I.

PRINTING OFFICE OF THE PUBLISHER.

Check Out More Titles From HardPress Classics Series In this collection we are offering thousands of classic and hard to find books. This series spans a vast array of subjects – so you are bound to find something of interest to enjoy reading and learning about.

Subjects:
Architecture
Art
Biography & Autobiography
Body, Mind &Spirit
Children & Young Adult
Dramas
Education
Fiction
History
Language Arts & Disciplines
Law
Literary Collections
Music
Poetry
Psychology
Science
…and many more.

Visit us at www.hardpress.net

CPSIA information can be obtained
at www.ICGtesting.com
Printed in the USA
BVHW081817220819
556561BV00020B/4535/P